CAIRNS
& Surrounds
A DISCOVERY GUIDE

Photography by Steve Parish
Text by Lynne Adcock

Steve Parish
PUBLISHING

www.steveparish.com.au

Contents

Introduction 4
How to Use this Book 6

The Big Picture 8–13

The Big Picture 8
Geology, Topography and Climate 10
Culture and Celebration 12

Cairns City 14–27

Cairns Heritage 16
Gateway City to Rainforest and Reef 18
City Arts and Entertainment 20
City Parks and Gardens 24
The Bayside 26

Cairns Surrounds 28–39

On the City's Doorstep 30
Northern Beaches 32
North-west Delights 34
Kuranda 36
Heading South 38

Reef and Islands 40–55

Green Island 42
Michaelmas Cay and Upolu Cay 44
Fitzroy Island National Park 46
Diving the Outer Reef 48

North of Cairns 56–81

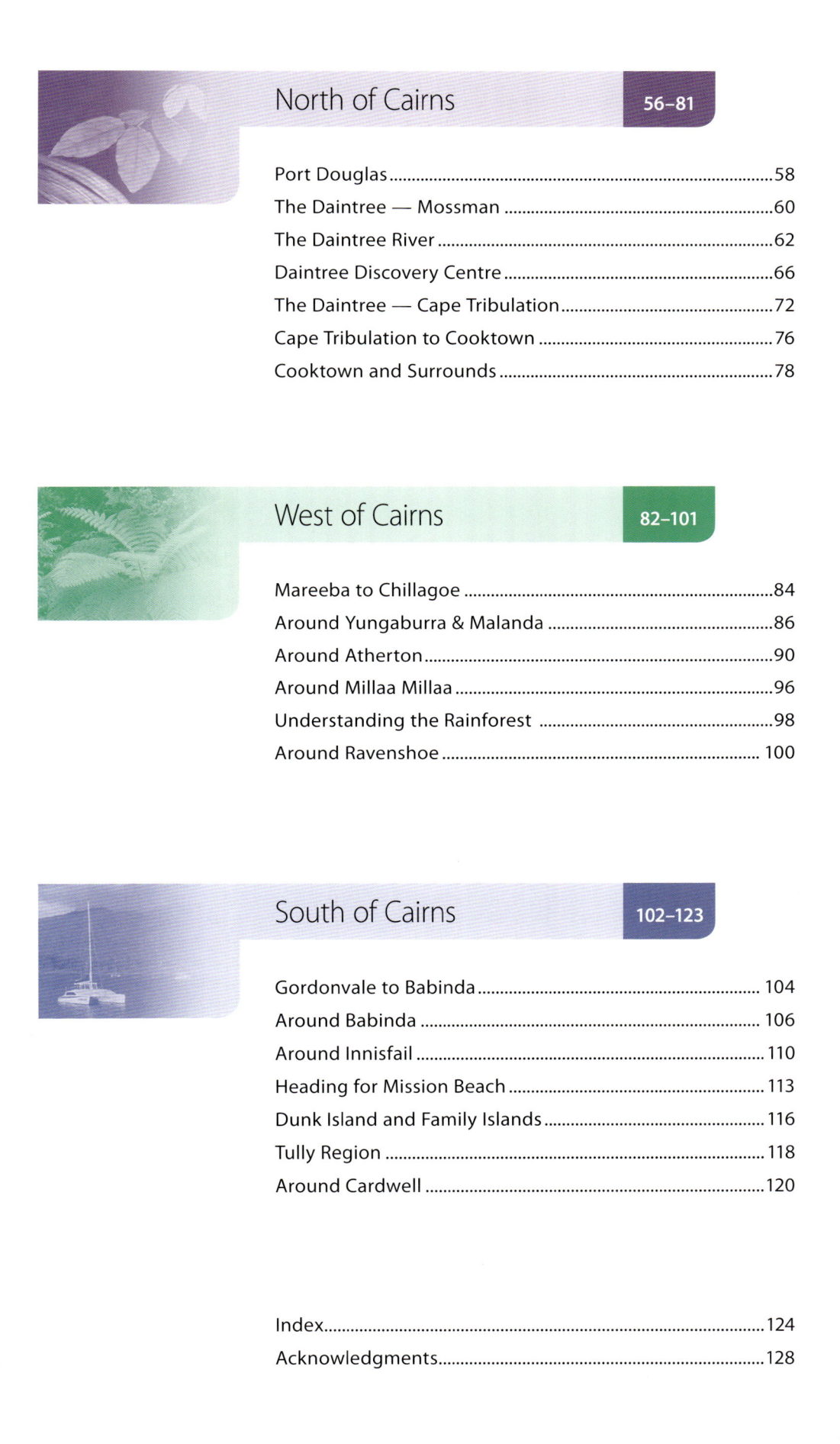

Port Douglas	58
The Daintree — Mossman	60
The Daintree River	62
Daintree Discovery Centre	66
The Daintree — Cape Tribulation	72
Cape Tribulation to Cooktown	76
Cooktown and Surrounds	78

West of Cairns 82–101

Mareeba to Chillagoe	84
Around Yungaburra & Malanda	86
Around Atherton	90
Around Millaa Millaa	96
Understanding the Rainforest	98
Around Ravenshoe	100

South of Cairns 102–123

Gordonvale to Babinda	104
Around Babinda	106
Around Innisfail	110
Heading for Mission Beach	113
Dunk Island and Family Islands	116
Tully Region	118
Around Cardwell	120

Index	124
Acknowledgments	128

Introduction

Tropical North Queensland is a region unlike any other in Australia. With both the Great Barrier Reef and the Wet Tropics World Heritage Areas converging at its doorstep, it is perhaps no exaggeration to suggest that Cairns and its surrounding areas offer an experience that is unique in this world. Every year three million visitors from all corners of the globe make this exotic area their preferred travel destination and it is easy to see why. Rainforests, reefs, beaches, rivers, lakes, waterfalls, caves and islands surround historic coastal and outback townships full of charismatic and colourful residents. The great range of festivals, markets, shopping and dining combine with the area's natural assets to make a tour of this region a truly unforgettable adventure.

I find Cairns and its surrounds one of the most visually stunning areas on Earth. From a purely photographic perspective, the region presents such an incredibly rich source of material. There is the deep, dark green of its nature — the forests of the Daintree and Cassowary Coast — which invoke a primal mood through their towering trees, plunging waterfalls and imposing gorges. There is the stoic beauty of the Gulf Savannah country — the harsh, honest hues of the outback and its vast tracts of dry, silent land. There is the endless blue of the Coral Sea and the almost impossible flourishes of colour that lie below its glittering surface. The sea and its inhabitants formed the original subjects for my photography and, having spent much of my early years honing my photographic skills underwater, the Great Barrier Reef holds a special place in my heart.

While the flora and fauna, both on land and offshore, make compelling subjects, the region's towns radiate with their own distinct spirit — Cairns, with its energetic backpacker buzz; Cooktown with its remote, frontier heritage; Atherton with its serene, rolling farmlands; Kuranda with its bohemian atmosphere; Port Douglas with its style and sophistication; Herberton with its rough and tumble mining origins... the list goes on. The relics of a hard-won history are evident in most places. From Mossman to Ingham the classic north Queensland architecture of breezy, wide verandahs, local wood and corrugated iron adds a charm and sense of tradition to towns' main streets. Also permeating the region is a rich Indigenous heritage, which survives in the Quinkan rock art and the thriving Aboriginal cultures — Indigenous art galleries, public artworks and performances abound.

Whenever I come to do a new book on Cairns and its surrounds I am always astonished at just how much this area has to offer. There is so much to discover, so many new adventures waiting around each corner, that I still feel enormous anticipation getting behind the wheel of my car whenever I am about to embark on a driving tour of this beautiful region. Whether you intend to use this guide to enliven your weekends, or whether you wish to embark on a longer driving tour of Tropical North Queensland, it is my hope that whenever you open this book and get a glimpse of what awaits, you will feel the same joyful anticipation that I feel on my frequent trips around the region — the knowledge that your exploration will reveal a truly unique part of Australia.

Steve Parish

Left, top to bottom: Native Rhododendron; Bolands Centre, Cairns; Cape Tribulation; Scuba diving on the Great Barrier Reef.
Opposite: Cairns and the Esplanade viewed from the air.

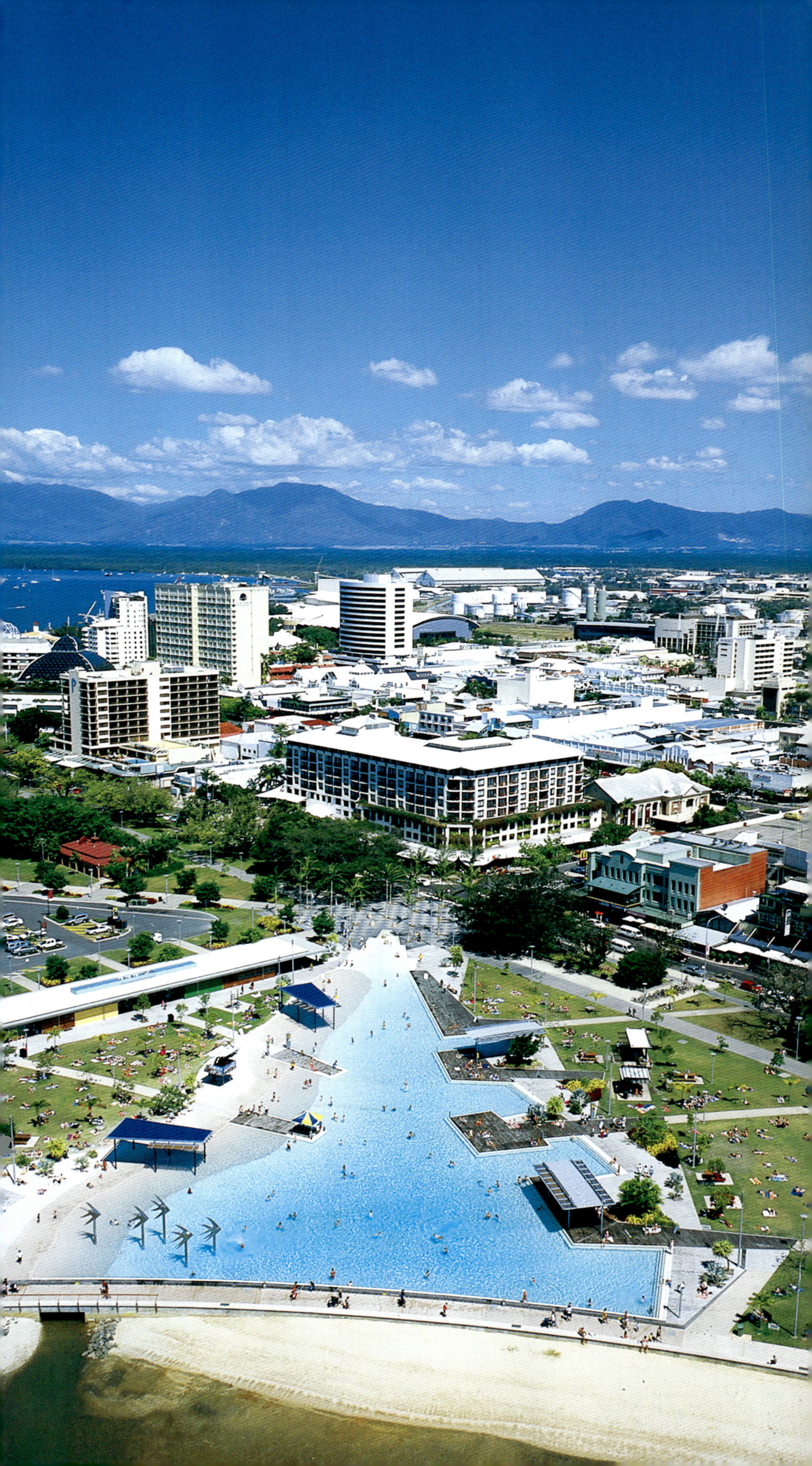

How to Use this Book

This book has been designed with all readers in mind, whether domestic travellers wanting to explore Cairns, or international adventurers planning a more extensive tour of the surrounding area. Whatever your objective, simple-to-follow maps, tried-and-tested driving tours, interesting snippets of natural history, as well as all of the "must see" attractions described in stand-out sidebars make this book one of the most straightforward guides to what you can expect to see on your travels throughout the Cairns region. Our local author has covered almost every kilometre of this vast area, so you can be sure that this guide recommends the very best that Cairns and its surrounds have to offer.

Region-by-Region Format

This guide is split into six sections with the pages throughout colour-coded by region. Each section contains a full page map, on which the major towns, attractions, national parks and driving tours along highways and byways are indicated. In each of the six regions — Cairns, Cairns Surrounds, Reef and Islands, West of Cairns, North of Cairns and South of Cairns — you'll be introduced to the area's history, geography and major industries. Also covered are national parks, flora and fauna, as well as the region's cultural and ecological significance.

This region-by-region format leads from Cairns, Tropical North Queensland's tourist nexus, to the surrounding towns, islands and countless natural attractions of the Wet Tropics and Great Barrier Reef World Heritage Areas. To the north of Cairns lie numerous beaches, the famous town of Port Douglas and the unparalleled magnificence of the Daintree rainforest. The "Cassowary Coast" stretches south and incorporates such popular destinations as Mission Beach and Hinchinbrook Island. To the west is the deep green of the Atherton Tableland with its sanctuary of surrounding waterfalls, walking trails and wilderness. Offshore, and always beckoning, is the allure of the Great Barrier Reef — one of our planet's greatest natural wonders.

Rather than being distinct entities, these regions overlap and merge, so wherever possible the tours and maps within this guide venture into the boundaries of adjoining regions to explain the easiest way to travel from one area to the next.

Natural History Breakout Boxes

The areas surrounding Cairns comprise some of the most diverse and ecologically significant habitats in the world. Reefs, rainforests, rivers, islands, lakes, coral cays, mountains and national parks teem with flora and fauna of all description, but even Cairns and the region's towns play host to a range of plant and animal species that keen-eyed visitors can hope to see. Eye-catching breakout boxes scattered throughout this guide explain the natural history of these areas — giving you a sneak preview of the wildlife and wild habitats you can expect to encounter journeying through this remarkable region.

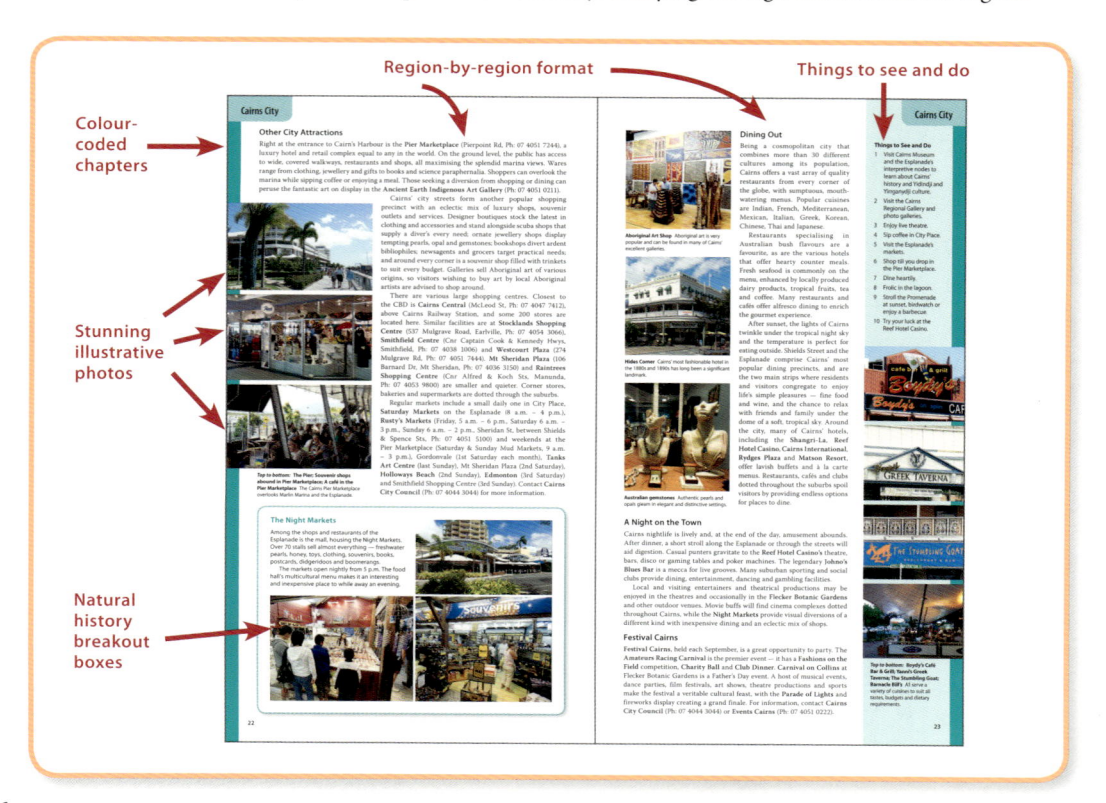

Location, Location, Location

For convenience, the location or contact details of rangers' stations, tourist attractions and advisory bodies are listed in the text in each chapter or in the **Things to See and Do** column on the relevant spread.

How to Use the Maps

Consistent, easy-to-read maps direct you to the major attractions and best tours for each section. Use the map in each chapter to locate the attractions, which are explained at length — giving address and contact details — in the text. Maps have been designed to show most of the major attractions mentioned.

Above: **Daintree Discovery Centre** The aerial walkway provides an easy, non-invasive way of exploring the rainforest. *Centre and bottom:* **Cape Tribulation; Driving through the Wet Tropics.**

Things to See and Do

Every area of Australia has its own unique character and offers a range of natural and artificial surprises. Listed in this section of all Steve Parish Travel Guides are the top activities for travellers wanting to make the most of their trips — be it a walking tour of heritage areas, a visit to bustling markets, a day of cultural events or annual festivals or the experience of camping in national parks. This section gives you the low-down on the area's not-to-be-missed activities, occasions and most memorable natural spectacles.

Dramatic Driving Tours

Scenic driving tours are a feature of north Queensland, with over 600 km of spectacularly panoramic roads intersecting the Wet Tropics World Heritage Area.

This guide takes you on a driving tour from Ingham to Cooktown, west to Chillagoe, following the best scenic routes. Use the instructive text, with the maps as back-up, to wind your way over the region's highways, stopping at the best lookouts, picnic areas, tourist sites, nature reserves and historic sites — all via the region's most charming towns.

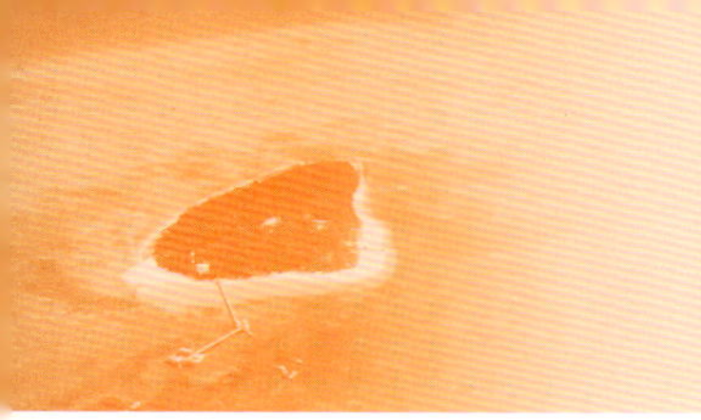

The Big Picture

Cairns and its surrounds lie at the centre of a thriving tourist industry driven by the phenomenal popularity of two significant natural wonders — the Great Barrier Reef and Wet Tropics World Heritage Areas. Cairns' intimate proximity to these attractions, together with its inviting climate, laid-back atmosphere and frontier sensibility, distinguishes it from all other Australian destinations. Cairns itself has a relatively small resident population of about 128,000. Even compared with Australia's lean standards, its surrounding areas are sparsely populated.

Despite a heavy tourist presence, visitors to Tropical North Queensland still revel in the region's sense of space, freedom and unbridled exotica. Cairns' popularity is not due to its natural beauty alone — its absorbing history is preserved in many historic sites, and its surrounding towns are coloured with down-to-earth characters and a welcoming spirit. Coupled with a range of novel tourist attractions and a strong Indigenous culture, it is easy to see why the area is one of Australia's most popular holiday destinations.

The tropical life North Queensland lends itself to a laid-back, outdoors existence.

Great Barrier Reef Numerous tourist vessels operate day trips from Cairns to the reef and islands.

Trains remain a great way to travel around the Cairns region.

The towns that cane built The sugar industry plays a major role in north Queensland.

Yellow-bellied Sunbird Over half of Australia's bird species are found in the Wet Tropics.

Colonisation to Settlement

James Cook first sighted the land on which Cairns would eventually be settled in 1770. His perception of the area as a place of impenetrable jungle and treacherous reef meant more than 100 years would pass before George Dalrymple led a government expedition to survey Trinity Inlet. Founded in 1876, and named after Sir William Wellington Cairns (then Governor of Queensland), Cairns first served as a seaport supporting gold exploration around the Palmer River.

Agriculture to Industry

By the late 19th century, the areas to the north and west of Cairns were already well established. Timber-getters were harvesting cedar at an unsustainable rate and gold deposits were exhausted. The rich agricultural lands opening up along the Cairns–Atherton railway line led to new enterprises and soon sugarcane farms came to dominate the landscape. With rail access to southern mills, sugar became the area's major industry.

Indigenous Heritage

Aboriginal tribes, who traditionally lived seasonal, hunter-gatherer lifestyles, have long experienced the bio-cultural virtues of the Wet Tropics and its surrounds — the rainforests and reefs are not just life-sustaining material resources, but together represent a complex cultural landscape that bears a range of totems and Dreamtime stories, which are traditionally passed onto younger generations.

Today, 18 different Indigenous groups maintain their connections to the Wet Tropics World Heritage Area.

The Big Picture

20th Century to Present

With the commercial viability of cane farming ensuring steady growth in north Queensland, Cairns officially became a town in 1903. However, by the start of the 20th century, fishing and pearling had attracted a new breed of entrepreneur.

As infrastructure and industry expanded, Cairns developed into a city (1923). After the outbreak of World War II, the region became an important supply centre and training base for the Allied Pacific fleet.

Life in the region returned to normal after WWII. Growth continued and, combined with Cairns' enviable tropical location, a new industry began to emerge — ecotourism. With the opening of the Cairns International Airport in 1984, and World Heritage status inscribed for both reef and rainforest, Cairns and its surrounds quickly developed into one of the country's premier tourist destinations.

Above: **The Cenotaph, Cairns** is dedicated to those who died in WWI.
Centre and bottom: **Australian Butterfly Sanctuary, Kuranda** gives visitors a close look at tropical invertebrates; **Kuranda Scenic Railway** takes in spectacular scenery.

A Brief History of Cairns

1770 – Lieutenant James Cook names Trinity Bay.

1872 – Gold discovered around the Palmer River.

1876 – Cairns founded. First street (Abbott St) surveyed.

1923 – Cairns proclaimed a city.

1942 – Allied forces establish training camps on the Atherton Tableland. Australia's biggest military hospital built at Rocky Creek.

1981 – Great Barrier Reef added to World Heritage list.

1984 – Cairns International Airport opens.

1988 – Wet Tropics added to World Heritage list.

2003 – Esplanade redevelopment completed.

Delights for the Visitor

The list of natural attractions around Cairns is truly impressive and the area has much to offer domestic and international visitors. The reef and rainforest, of course, are the ultimate enticement for visiting the region; however, a more thorough exploration will reveal an area blessed with an array of interesting diversions — limestone caves, outback walking trails, fine dining, art, cultural centres, festivals, scuba diving, sailing, game fishing and shopping.

The Big Picture

Geology, Topography and Climate

Cairns occupies a position on the long, narrow coastal strip between the Great Dividing Range and the Coral Sea. Cairns City Council administers over 1600 km² of land extending north to Ellis Beach and south to the Johnstone Shire boundary. The Wet Tropics World Heritage Area covers about 9000 km² and the entire Tropical North Queensland region (incorporating all of Cape York, except the south-west) is over 270,000 km². Including the Great Barrier Reef, this is, by any measure, a vast region.

Consequently, the terrain is diverse. Mountains (including Mt Bartle Frere, the State's highest at 1622 m), tablelands, coastal plains, upland and lowland rainforests, savannah, open eucalypt forests, swamps, tidal wetlands, mangroves, rivers, lakes, estuaries, mudflats and beaches make up this fascinating landscape. Offshore are inner-, mid- and outer-shelf reefs, continental islands and coral cays. Since the break up of the supercontinent Gondwana 100 million years ago, there has been little geological activity (such as mountain building) in north Queensland. The region's geology is considered ancient, extremely weathered and stable.

The region's tropical latitudes are conducive to hot, humid summers and mild winters. Cairns' mean daily temperatures in summer (Dec–Feb) are 31.2° C (max) and 23.5° C (min). Mean daily temperatures in winter (June–Aug) are 26° C (max) and 17.4° C (min). Being part of the monsoonal belt, the region is subject to distinct wet (Dec–Mar) and dry (Apr–Nov) seasons. Cairns' average rainfall during the Wet is 360 mm/month. Average rainfall during the Dry is 102.4 mm/month.

Extreme Weather

The tropical north experiences either one of two kinds of weather — hot and dry or hot and wet. Its location within the monsoonal strip means extreme weather conditions can occur along the coast of north Queensland. Monsoonal activity often results in major flooding of rivers and of catchment areas throughout north Queensland and Cape York. Tropical cyclones regularly form between November and May. Between 1997 and 2006 five notable cyclones affected the Cairns region. Tropical Cyclone Larry caused widespread devastation to buildings and land to the south and west of Cairns in 2006.

Millstream Falls is just one of many spectacular waterfalls in the Wet Tropics World Heritage Area. One of the most popular areas for viewing these impressive natural attractions is along the Atherton Tableland Waterfall Circuit, which also includes Zillie and Elinjaa Falls.

Walshs Pyramid Rising over 900 m above the coastal plain near Gordonvale, this hard, pointed granite protrusion (left standing after the erosion of softer surrounding rock) is part of the Bellenden Ker Range. The region includes a number of imposing mountains. Queensland's highest, Mt Bartle Frere, rises 1622 m.

Licuala, or the Fan Palm is the pin-up plant of the Wet Tropics, featuring in many a tourist brochure. The Daintree's "Valley of the Palms" is a great place to see this botanical celebrity in the wild.

Goldsborough Valley In the 1870s the creeks in this area were swarming with mineral prospectors eagerly seeking their fortunes. This pleasant area is now a State Forest.

The Big Picture

Contrasting Splendour — Mountains & Plains

The most distinctive geographical feature of Tropical North Queensland is the Great Dividing Range, which runs parallel to the coast and separates the region into two very different zones — the lush, fertile coastal strip to the east (including the Wet Tropics) and the harsh, dry outback area stretching to the west of the range — the Gulf Savannah (*below left*).

The coastal ranges inland from Cairns consist of numerous high plateaus (the Atherton, Evelyn and Hann Tablelands), which feature some astonishing national parks — areas of considerable ecological significance. Highland areas are characterised by cool air, lush farmlands, dense rainforests, volcanic crater lakes, rampaging rivers, steep gorges (*below right*) and plunging waterfalls.

On the other side of the Great Dividing Range is the Gulf Savannah. In contrast to the dark green altitudes of the Tablelands, this outback country is typically dry, flat and represents a genuine "big sky" experience. Areas around Chillagoe and Ravenshoe contain fascinating caves and geological formations.

Offshore Adventures

While plenty of attractions (both natural and artificial) keep visitors occupied on land, no trip to Tropical North Queensland is ever truly fulfilled without an expedition to the Great Barrier Reef.

Extending, in its entirety, from the top of Cape York to Bundaberg in the south of Queensland — a length of 2300 km — the Great Barrier Reef World Heritage Area encompasses over 345,000 km², with a virtually inexhaustible number of options available for its exploration. Cairns and Port Douglas are the most common departure points for the reef and both towns have a huge range of operators offering all kinds of offshore adventures — scuba diving, snorkelling, game fishing, reef fishing, sailing, power boating, semi-submersibles, helicopter tours, scenic flights, birdwatching, cay-hopping, daytrips, overnight trips and extended charters. There really is no end to the manner in which this thrilling natural phenomenon can be experienced.

Perhaps equally prominent on any itinerary is a trip to one of Tropical North Queensland's many famous tropical islands. From north to south, some of the more popular destinations are Lizard, Green, Fitzroy, Bedarra, Dunk and stunning Hinchinbrook. Whatever your inclination, there is an island to suit everyone — some are serviced by luxury resorts, others offer an untamed wilderness experience.

Fitzroy Island Continental islands are coastal mountain ranges that have been cut off from the mainland, with their cargo of plant and animal life intact, by a rise in sea levels. Fitzroy Island, and the nearby Frankland Islands, traditionally used by specific Aboriginal groups, are superb examples of this type of island. Together with their fringing reefs, these islands comprise part of the Great Barrier Reef World Heritage Area.

Lizard Island North of Cooktown, this tropical paradise attracts thousands of tourists to its resort each year. Its research station is a crucial base for marine researchers studying the Great Barrier Reef.

The Big Picture

Watch the Indigenous art of basket weaving at Cairns Markets.

Innisfail Many of Innisfail's buildings date back to the 1920s and 1930s.

Colour and culture enliven the Kuranda Markets.

Mission Beach annually celebrates the Aquatic Festival, paying tribute to sun, sea and surf.

Culture and Celebration

Tropical North Queensland's reputation as a leisure mecca is thoroughly justified. The great range of outdoor pursuits — sailing, diving, snorkelling, fishing and hiking, among others — still allows enough time for an eclectic calendar of celebrations and cultural comings-together. Of course any day in Cairns is reason enough to party (or so the endless throngs of young international backpackers would have you believe), but a select number of days are officially reserved for fervent festivity every year — in Cairns itself and also throughout the surrounding region. From the tropical outback to towns up and down the coast, local residents have found many reasons to revel in their chosen lifestyles and locations. These occasions range from the relatively mainstream to the thoroughly madcap, and together invoke north Queensland's fantastic spirit.

Celebrations in the Centres

Cairns and it surrounds present the perfect locale for outdoor celebration. While the region toes the traditional line of national celebration (Australia Day, Anzac day etc.), there are a number of occasions that are unique to the area. **Festival Cairns** (Aug–Sep) is the region's showcase event — a three-week extravaganza of creative, cultural and sporting challenges. In May, Ingham hosts **Aussitaliano Carnivale** — a colourful tribute to Hinchinbrook Shire's Italian heritage, which attracts 25,000 people annually. Innisfail celebrates its heritage during **Chinese New Year** (Jan/Feb), **Feast of the Senses** (Mar), a gourmet extravaganza of tropical produce, and the **Innisfail Festival** (Nov) — a four-day event, which celebrates the region's harvest time. Also held in Innisfail is **Kulture Karnivale** (Aug), which celebrates the Johnstone Shire's multicultural heritage. The tropical outback's gala occasion is the **Torimba Festival** (Oct), held in Ravenshoe and featuring the famous **Festival of the Forest** (a competitive exhibition of timber craft) and the **Torimba Market & Mardi Gras**. Cooktown's premier event is its **Discovery Festival** (Queen's Birthday weekend), which includes a hugely popular re-enactment of James Cook's landing in 1770.

Revelry around the Region

Not to be outdone by the region's larger towns, many smaller centres host their own range of exuberant annual events. The **Mission Beach Aquatic Festival** (Oct), a joyous family occasion, celebrates sun, sand and seaside in the heart of the Cassowary Coast. Similarly, the Port Douglas **Reef & Rainforest Festival** (May) pays homage to life and culture in the tropics with ten days of lively street performances, gourmet indulgence, sporting competitions and artistic exhibitions.

Indigenous Festivals

Right: Indigenous culture on display at Tjapukai Aboriginal Culture Park.

North Queensland's Indigenous communities celebrate their traditions and customs throughout the year. NAIDOC Week (first week in July) recognises the country's Indigenous cultures and their contribution to Australian society. National Reconciliation Week (27 May – 3 June) is a great chance for people to pay respect to Indigenous cultures. The Laura Dance Festival (every 2nd June) attracts Indigenous and non-Indigenous peoples from across northern Australia for a celebration of traditional song and dance. Torres Strait Islanders annually commemorate the "Coming of the Light" (1 July), celebrating the arrival of Christianity in the Torres Strait.

The Big Picture

For over 25 years the **Yungaburra Folk Festival** (Oct) has enthralled punters with its range of dancers, artists, comedians and musicians, all delivering energetic performances in classic folk tradition. The **Kuranda Spring Fair** (Oct) puts on show the various talents of its locals, including the spirited circus skills of "Blackrobats" — a resident troupe of Indigenous performers. Atherton's annual **Maize Festival** (Sep) features street parades (resplendent with decorated floats), wood chopping competitions and a gala ball. Nearby, the **Tinaroo Barra Bash** (Nov) attracts anglers from all over the world keen to lock horns with Australia's most iconic sportfish. Further west, the Undara Lava Tubes form a magnificent backdrop for a weekend of camping and music during **Opera in the Outback** (Oct).

Above: **Festival Cairns** Revellers anticipate a sensory and gourmet feast on opening night.

Below: **Street Parade, Festival Cairns** Every September Cairns takes centre stage in one of Tropical North Queensland's largest celebrations. Featuring local and international acts and innovative cultural and tourist attractions, this event is enjoyed by all.

Bottom right: Regional rodeos form an exciting arena for brushing shoulders with some of the region's true characters.

Further Information

Cairns Visitor Information Centre
Cnr Esplanade & Shields St, Cairns
(Ph: 07 4031 0784)

Daintree Discovery Centre
Cnr Cape Tribulation & Tulip Oak Rds, Cow Bay
(Ph: 07 4098 9171)

Mission Beach Tourism
Porter Promenade, Mission Beach
(Ph: 07 4068 7099)

Nature's PowerHouse
Cooktown Botanic Gardens, Cooktown
(Ph: 07 4069 6004)

Atherton Tableland Information Centre
95–97 Main St, Atherton
(Ph: 07 4091 4222)

Sports of Kings and Clowns

The north's frontier traditions survive in a number of regional horse racing and rodeo events. The **Cooktown Cup** (July), **Cairns Amateurs** (Sep), **Einasleigh Races** (Apr), and **Mt Garnet Races** (Apr) are just a few of the many colourful equine events in the area. A hugely popular institution is the local rodeo. The **Big Weekend Chillagoe Rodeo** (May) and the legendary **Mareeba Rodeo** (July) are two of the region's biggest wrangle-fests.

Cairns City

Australian pelican

Cairns, Australia's premier tropical destination, hosts more than 3 million visitors a year. Situated on the narrow coastal strip between the Coral Sea and the Great Dividing Range, Cairns is set among some of the prettiest marine and terrestrial scenery in Australia. Built around the picturesque Trinity Inlet, the city stretches some 30 km along the northern beaches and 60 km into agricultural land to the south. The multicultural population blends Aboriginal, European, Asian and Pacific people, all of whom played an important role in the city's history. Voted Australia's most liveable regional city, Cairns' 128,000 residents enjoy a leisurely, outdoor life based around the city's gardens, parks, beaches, waterways and the two surrounding World Heritage areas.

History

Cairns encompasses the traditional country of the Djabugay, Yidindji and Yirrganydji people, with the Kunggandji people nearby. Their lives changed dramatically with European exploration. **Trinity Bay**, named by Captain James Cook on Trinity Sunday in June 1770, was used by pearlers and bêche-de-mer fishermen for shelter, water and firewood from the mid-1800s. On 7 October 1876, William Wellington Cairns, then Governor of Queensland, proclaimed it a port for the **Hodgkinson goldfields** to the north-west and the timber-getting industry of the hinterland and **Barron River**. Cairns grew steadily, always centred on the modern CBD. By the 1920s it had become a prosperous sugar milling and port city, and was an important military base during the Pacific War in World War II. The international airport, built in 1984, presented Cairns to the world.

Cairns Today

Modern Cairns is a vibrant port and major business centre for Tropical North Queensland. The balmy climate and location by the sea lend it a languid, natural ambience. With its lively nightlife, alfresco dining, shopping, cultural events and close proximity to the **Great Barrier Reef** and stunning tropical rainforest, Cairns is a tourist haven. Safe, easy to explore and populated with friendly, helpful locals, this green city is much loved by its millions of visitors.

Top to bottom: **The Esplanade; Cairns Reef Hotel Casino; Grafton Street; Esplanade Lagoon** Residents and visitors enjoy Cairns' parks, gardens and outdoor meeting places.

Famous for Birdwatching

Once a long sandy beach, apparently turned into a mudflat by the continued dredging of Trinity Inlet's shipping channel, the waterfront by the Esplanade is famous for its birdlife. Home to flocks of pelicans, ibises, spoonbills, egrets, terns, gulls and other species, the area is also visited by numerous species of migratory waders during spring and summer. White-bellied Sea-Eagles, Brahminy Kites, Ospreys and Peregrine Falcons soar overhead. Along the mudflats, birds feed, hover, wheel and preen for the cameras, all within convenient focal reach. Tourists, birdwatchers and locals all enjoy the spectacle.

Top, left to right: A Royal Spoonbill and Australian White Ibis scour the mudflats; A photographer takes aim on the Esplanade.

Cairns City

Getting Around

Cairns is easily navigated by bus, car, motorbike, bicycle or on foot. Inexpensive bus services that run to all parts of Cairns and the northern beaches regularly depart from **City Place Transit Mall** in Lake Street. A network of bikeways and walking trails intersect the city, linking many of its tourist attractions. Most tour operators have courtesy coaches to major hotels and accommodation, thus simplifying sightseeing logistics. The city is well serviced by taxis. Car, motorcycle and bicycle hire is simple and straightforward with any of the city's rental companies.

Sun Palm Transport (Ph: 07 4084 2626), **BTS Tours** (Ph: 07 4099 5665) and **Coral Reef Coaches** (Ph: 07 4098 2800) run to **Port Douglas**, the **Daintree** and **Cape Tribulation**. **Cairns Explorer** continuous city sights bus tours leave from City Place Transit Mall on Lake St (Ph: 1800 221 607), as do **Sunbus** (Ph: 07 4057 7411), which provide a service from the Marlin Coast to northern beaches.

Further Information
Tourism Tropical NQ
Gateway Discovery Centre,
Level 2, 51 the Esplanade
(Ph: 07 4051 3588)

QPWS
5B Sheridan St
(Ph: 07 4046 6600)

Wet Tropics Management Authority
Level 1, 15 Lake St
(Ph: 07 4052 0555)

Black and White Taxis
City Place Taxi Rank
(Ph: 131 008)

Cairns' city skyline after a tropical storm Cairns is a city of shifting moods. On winter days, the sun shines gloriously warm under a clear blue sky, but on hot and humid summer days, tropical storms roll in across the sea and monsoonal showers frequently drench the city.

Cairns viewed from the sea, showing its mountainous backdrop Behind the Esplanade, with its parks, shops and motels, the inner city gives way to suburbs that sprawl into the fringing hills. Few of the world's cities can boast such breathtaking scenery.

Historic Cairns

Cairns was officially founded in 1876. The initial site on Trinity Bay, an area of dense mangrove and forest, was developed as a seaport to service the Hodgkinson goldfields. The city's business centre was first built around the wharf end of Abbott St (*left*) — named after Henry Abbott, the first Land Commissioner and Surveyor. The opening of the coastal railway in 1924 saw a surge in business and building activity and residential expansion.

Cairns City

City of Contrasts

Much of the city's charm derives from its blend of architecture. Graceful, colonial shops and grand public and commercial buildings survive from the city's early days and stand side-by-side with rambling country pubs and trendy hotels. Deep verandahs and roof space help to cool the buildings. Cairns' wide streets are lined with awnings and broad, covered walkways designed for outdoor living in the tropics. Numerous cafés and restaurants, in buildings both old and new, provide alfresco dining. At the end of each sun-drenched day, the city's streets resonate with the murmur of content, relaxed banter.

Top to bottom: Barrier Reef Hotel; Esplanade Architecture from the 1920s stands alongside contemporary buildings.

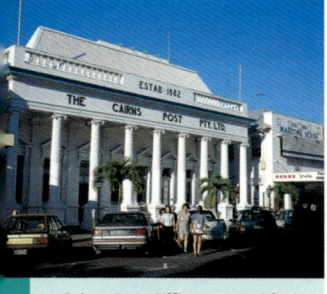

Cairns Post Office is a modified inter-war Academic Classical–styled building.

The Boland Centre Erected in 1912–13, this was one of the city's first concrete buildings.

Cairns Heritage

Cairns' colourful history is evident in the layout and design of the city and its buildings. The first survey peg was staked in 1876 near the wharves at the corner of Abbott Street. With much clearing and landfilling, the town grew around Abbott, Spence, Aplin and Lake Streets, and the Esplanade.

Originally built in timber, the town was devastated by a cyclone in 1920. Many early buildings were destroyed. Subsequent buildings of brick and reinforced concrete could better survive tropical storms, but, sadly, during extensive redevelopment through the 1970s and 1980s, many of Cairns' historic landmarks and heritage links were lost catering to growing tourism and population demands. Despite this, Cairns still has enough of its older buildings to demonstrate the charm of 19th- and early 20th-century tropical architecture.

Historic Buildings

The oldest surviving buildings in Cairns include **Bolands on Spence** (1902), the **School of Arts** (1907), which houses the **Cairns Historical Society** and **Cairns Museum**, the original **Cairns Post** building (1908), **Central Hotel** (1909), and **Bolands Corner** (1913) — for many years the tallest structure in Cairns and now a local landmark.

The **Old Telegraph Office** and former **Post Office**, **Court House** and **City Council Chambers**, dating to the 1920s and 1930s, reflect the style of that era. Other heritage attractions include wharf buildings, several hotels, shops, houses of worship, the **Pioneer Cemetery** and the **Cairns War Memorial** situated on the Esplanade.

Cutting cane the traditional way The sugar industry has played a key role in the history of Cairns city.

Cairns Heritage City Walk

Walk through the streets and visit the older buildings to gain an insight of Cairns' history — these are where pioneering residents lived, worked and played. The changing architectural styles are evident. A walking tour map, produced by the **Cairns City Council**, **Cairns Historical Society** and **National Trust of Queensland**, is available from **Cairns City Council** (119–145 Spence St, Ph: 07 4044 3044). The **Cairns Heritage City Walk** begins at the **Cairns Museum** (City Place, Cnr Lake & Shields St, Ph: 07 4051 5582), from which the Cairns Historical Society provides further information about Cairns and the surrounding area.

World War II

In 1942, when the Pacific War escalated, over half of Cairns' population was evacuated and buildings were used by the military. Cairns became the regional HQ, operations base and supply port for the Allied air force and navy. Air, road and rail infrastructure was improved and training facilities sprang up on the Atherton Tableland.

War memorials on the Esplanade include The Cenotaph *(left)*, the RAAF Catalina Squadron's Memorial and the RSL Hall of Memories (115 the Esplanade, Ph: 07 4051 5804), which has a collection of photos and memorabilia from World War II.

Cairns City

LEGEND
- Residential Area
- Parkland
- Highway
- Major Road
- Other road
- Railway, Railway station

TRINITY BAY

CAIRNS NORTH

CAIRNS

Cairns Harbour

Trinity Inlet

N

Streets (Cairns North area)
JAMES ST, SMITH ST, DIGGER ST, ESPLANADE, McLEOD ST, SHERIDAN ST, LAKE ST, CHARLES ST, GROVE ST, DUNN ST, GATTON ST, KERWIN ST, (CAPTAIN COOK HWY), UPWARD ST, McLEOD, GRAFTON ST, ABBOTT ST, WATER ST, MINNIE ST, FLORENCE ST, APLIN ST, SHIELDS ST, SPENCE ST, BUNDA ST, NORTH COAST RAILWAY, HARTLEY ST, DUTTON ST, WHARF ST, MARLIN PDE, DRAPER ST, KENNY ST

Labeled Locations
- Pioneer Cemetery
- Cairns Base Hospital
- Wet Tropics Management Authority
- Esplanade Tennis Courts
- Calvary Hospital
- Muddy's Playground
- Australian Federal Police
- Munro Martin Park
- Cairns RSL Club Hall of Memories
- Centre of Contemporary Arts
- Table Tennis Stadium
- Cairns Civic Theatre
- Employment National
- Former Council Chambers & Park
- Cairns City Council Library
- Cairns Night Market
- Promenade
- Lagoon
- The Pier Marketplace
- The Pier
- Cairns Central
- Museum
- School of Arts
- Transit Mall
- City Place
- Cairns Regional Art Gallery
- Shield Street Plaza
- TTNQ Discovery Centre
- Shangri-La Hotel
- Hides Corner
- Old Court House
- Cairns Post
- Fogarty Park
- Global Palace
- Bolands on Spence
- Sound Shell
- Reef Fleet Terminal
- Marlin Marina
- Central Hotel
- Old Telegraph Office
- Cairns Seaport
- Cinemas
- Reef Plaza
- Rusty's Market
- The Boland Centre
- Cairns Reef Hotel Casino
- Volunteer Coastguard Headquarters
- Court House
- Yacht Club
- Cairns Port Authority
- Barrier Reef Hotel
- Cairns Wildlife Dome
- QLD Parks & Wildlife Service
- Cairns Convention Centre
- Trinity Wharf

Trinity Inlet

Lily Creek

Cairns City

Gateway City to Rainforest and Reef

Cairns is the gateway to two World Heritage areas — the **Wet Tropics** rainforest and the **Great Barrier Reef**. The growth of ecotourism has seen Cairns evolve into the tourist "capital" of north Queensland. Its airport is the fifth busiest in Australia. Each day, more than 25 scheduled services travel to the Great Barrier Reef and islands from the commercial seaport, making it Queensland's busiest. It is also the country's busiest cruise port, with over 200 visits a year by international and domestic cruise ships.

Cairns easily accommodates its tourist demand. The **Reef Hotel Casino** and **Shangri-La Hotel** offer five-star opulence right in the heart of town. Luxury motels are dotted along the Esplanade and provide memorable Coral Sea views. Backpacker hostels, lodges and caravan parks are also plentiful. Cairns has a fine variety of restaurants that cater to all budgets and tastes. The city also hosts national and international conventions at the **Cairns Convention Centre** (voted among the top 10 venues of its kind in the world), and stages a full calendar of cultural events. Shopping facilities are superb.

The Waterfront

The relaxed atmosphere belies the city's rampant tourist activity. The waterfront bustles with energy from early in the morning till late at night. Morning sees masses heading out from Trinity Inlet on reef and island tours. The **Pier Marketplace** soon comes to life as bargains and souvenirs are hunted. On the Esplanade, walkers, runners and cyclists weave past each other. Tour boats return in the afternoon and, after watching the sun set, residents and visitors mingle to dine and stroll around the marina.

Cairns and Trinity Inlet Originally founded as a seaport, Cairns has fully utilised its coastal position beside Trinity Inlet in the years since. Each year the seaport handles huge cargo, exporting to communities as far north as the Torres Strait Islands. Cairns is recognised as the pre-eminent gateway to the Great Barrier Reef and is also the country's busiest cruise port.

Planning a Visit to the Reef

Right, top to bottom: Snorkelling from a pontoon on the reef; Green Island, a popular day trip, is the closest island to Cairns.

Cairns has island and reef adventures to suit everyone. Each day, powered catamarans and yachts carry visitors to the nearby continental islands, coral cays and pontoons on the outer reef to marvel at the marine life, soak up the sun or dive in the water. Travel time is minimal and visitors can spend up to five hours on the reef. Helicopter and float plane flights are available for those on tighter schedules.

Tour operators offer various activities — supervised snorkelling and scuba diving, glass-bottomed boat tours and visits to underwater observatories where interpretive commentaries enhance the experience. Many tours include tropical island walks and chances to explore life along the island beaches. Extended visits are possible at Green and Fitzroy Islands, both within 30 km of Cairns and with accommodation choices. Camping is permitted on selected islands (QPWS, 5B Sheridan St, Ph: 07 4046 6600).

Daily tours depart the Reef Fleet Terminal (1 Spence St, Ph: 07 4052 3888), except on Christmas Day and in rough weather (wind speeds of 35+ knots). Temperatures are most comfortable from April to September. Naturally, boating is more fun in fine weather and visibility is best on sunny days. Reef trips in good weather yield better sightseeing, but be sure to take hats, sunscreen and water. Medical certificates are a prerequisite for diving.

Cairns City

Visiting the Rainforest

Clockwise from top: Suspension bridge, Rex Creek, Mossman Gorge; Interpretive signs at Mossman Gorge; Daintree Discovery Centre.

The World-Heritage-listed tropical forests are close to Cairns — the Daintree (north), the Tablelands (west) and the Great Green Way (south) are accessible year round, although roads may become flooded and unsafe during the Wet. There are bus tours, 4WD safaris, helicopter and small aircraft flights, or motorcycle tours and self-drive trips.

Coral Reef Coaches (Ph: 07 4098 2800) or Sun Palm Transport (Ph: 07 4084 2626), Mission Beach–Dunk Island Connections (Ph: 07 4059 2709) and Whitecar Coaches (Ph: 07 4091 1855) go to the Daintree, towns south of Cairns, and Kuranda and the Tablelands, respectively. Wet Tropics Visitor Centres (Wet Tropics Management Authority, Ph: 07 4052 0555), such as the Daintree Discovery Centre (Tulip Oak Rd, Cow Bay, 07 4098 9171), explain the forests and their inhabitants. Walking tracks of varying lengths and grades span the parks. Wildlife parks showcase the region's unique fauna. Birdwatching peaks in November when seasonal migrants arrive.

During the Wet, leeches and mosquitoes are rife, while mid-year there are more ticks. Protection from stinging and biting critters is a must, so wear long pants, socks, leather boots, a hat and insect repellent. Be wary of snakes, stinging trees, "wait-a-while" vines and cassowaries!

Rainforest roads Visitors soon get a feeling for these ancient forests, sometimes meeting cassowaries and other wildlife along Cape Tribulation Road (heed the signs and be sure to drive carefully). Other roads that pass through rainforests include the Kuranda Range Road, the Palmerston Highway and the roads into Mission Beach.

Sailing on the reef is a special experience Boat and skippered yacht charters are great ways to explore the reef at a leisurely pace.

Outdoor Adventures

Ecotourism has been a bourgeoning industry in the Cairns region for many years. These days there is a veritable smorgasboard of outdoor and adventure tours on offer. From horse-riding and hot-air ballooning to kayaking and canoeing, fishing charters and trips in all-terrain-vehicles, an amazing number of tour operators provide easy access to the region's natural jewels and unforgettable experiences. For those wanting to explore the region themselves, there are many places to hire cars and campers, boats and canoes, and regional maps are readily available. A network of accredited information centres offer maps and brochures that make self-guided exploration easy and eventful. Visitors can follow a number of trails, including the **Queensland Heritage Trail Network** (www.heritagetrails.qld.gov.au) and the **Taste of the Tropics Food Trail** (Australian Tropical Foods, Ph: 07 4040 4415). Information and assistance with route planning and bookings can be obtained in Cairns through the staff of the **Tourism Tropical North Queensland** (Gateway Discovery Centre, Ph: 07 4051 3588).

Cairns City

Life Stories
The traditional custodians of the Cairns' area incorporate arts and entertainment in daily and ceremonial life. In such oral cultures, stories are told in music, drama, dance, painting and weaving. In this way, important information and cultural practices are passed from generation to generation. Traditional Aboriginal culture encompasses didgeridoos, boomerangs, and dance performances, as seen along the Esplanade or at Rusty's Markets (Sheridan St, between Shields & Spence Sts, Ph: 07 4051 5100).

Top to bottom: Cairns City Council Library; Inside Cairns Convention Centre.

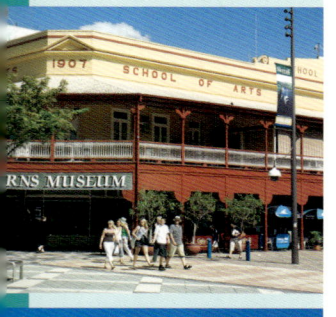

Top to bottom: Cairns Museum; Cairns Regional Art Gallery.

City Arts and Entertainment

Early Cairns was a rough frontier town with a hotel on almost every corner. These establishments were the focus of social life, be it luxury dining at Hides Hotel or drinking and carousing at pubs by the wharves. As the town prospered, entertainment multiplied. Ballroom dancing, watching movies, picnicking and promenading along the Esplanade, enjoying sing-alongs or rousing band recitals at the Esplanade rotunda, or welcoming or farewelling visitors on cruise boats at the wharf were popular activities. Nightlife buzzed during WWII when Allied troops and residents came together in regular celebration.

Today, a lively arts scene is inspired by the colours of the tropics. A regional centre for the arts, Cairns is fuelled by the energy and expertise of artists who have relocated to rediscover their muses. The city has first-class arts and entertainment facilities, both indoor and outdoor. Artistic media are everywhere, from colourful designs in shop windows to landscaped gardens and parks, to public sculptures and tropical architecture. Designs echo the city's tropical position between the reef and the rainforest. During September, **Festival Cairns** (contact Cairns City Council, Ph: 07 4044 3044 or Events Cairns, Ph: 07 4033 7454), with its enviable program of parades, plays, concerts and more, attracts visitors from near and far.

Outdoor Entertainment

Open-air entertainment suits the tropics. **Fogarty Park** (Esplanade) and **City Place Soundshell** (Lake St) are popular venues for Australia Day, Chinese New Year, Christmas Carols, Festival Cairns, and free concerts and community events throughout the year (Cairns City Council, Ph: 07 4044 3044). **Flecker Botanic Gardens** (Collins Ave, Edge Hill, Ph: 07 4044 3398) hosts Starry Night Cinema evenings and theatre productions among its leafy surrounds.

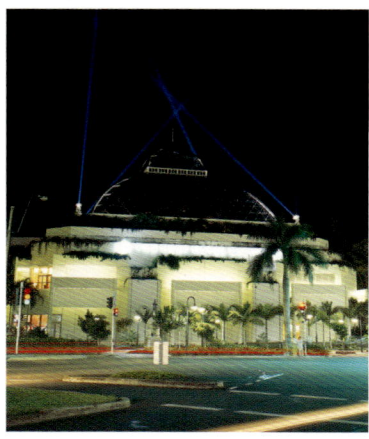

Top to bottom: **The Adventure Duck** This 44-seat amphibious vehicle is a novel way to explore Cairns' city streets and waterways; Cairns Reef Hotel Casino by night.

Performances and Galleries

A host of talented actors, musicians and dancers fill the calendar at the **Centre of Contemporary Arts** (96 Abbott St, Ph: 07 4050 9401), **Tanks Art Centre** (46 Collins Ave, Edge Hill, Ph: 07 4032 2349), **Rondo Theatre** (Greenslopes St, Edge Hill, Ph: 07 4053 5350) and **Cairns Civic Theatre** (Cnr Florence & Sheridan Sts, Ph: 07 4031 9933, bookings at ticketLiNK, Ph: 07 4031 9555).

Touring national and international musicians and theatre companies generally perform at Cairns Civic Theatre or **Cairns Convention Centre** (Cnr Sheridan & Wharf Sts, Ph: 07 4042 4200). The **Cairns Regional Gallery** (Cnr Abbott & Shields Sts, Ph: 07 4046 4800), Centre of Contemporary Arts and the Tanks Art Centre showcase regional and visiting artists and exhibitions. Photographic galleries display the work of several professional photographers based in the region and numerous gallery–shops scattered through the city offer a range of fine arts and Aboriginal artwork. Fascinating history can be unearthed by reading the displays or talking to members of the **Historical Society of Cairns** at the **Cairns Museum** (City Place, Cnr Lake & Shields Sts, Ph: 07 4051 5582). A trip to the **Royal Flying Doctor Service Visitors Centre** (1 Junction St, Edge Hill, Ph: 07 4053 5687) imparts an appreciation for the remoteness of Tropical North Queensland's outlying communities.

Cairns City

The Place to Be

City Place (Cnr Lake & Shields Sts), with its transit mall, is a hive of activity from daybreak to dark. Outdoor cafés line the footpaths, market stalls sell inexpensive jewellery, clothing and souvenirs, live music and entertainment are often staged, and backpacker hostels — with their internet cafés and travel booking services — add colour and atmosphere.

This is the heart of old Cairns and a charming place to sit, relax, chat and enjoy the lively atmosphere while sipping coffee or enjoying a meal. Movies are shown at the **Cairns City Cinema** (108 Grafton St, Ph: 07 4031 1077) and at **Cairns Central** (Ph: 07 4052 1166) and **Stocklands** (Ph: 07 4057 0000) centres.

City tours can be booked through **Cairns Explorer** (Ph: 1800 221 607), the **Adventure Duck** (Ground Floor, Pier Marketplace, Pierpoint Rd, Ph: 1300 765 022) and **Cairns Discovery Tours** (24 Mazlin St, Edge Hill, Ph: 07 4053 5259). For an uplifting reef or rainforest experience, **GBR Helicopter Group** (General Aviation, Cairns Airport, Ph: 07 4035 9400) has thrilling tours around Cairns.

Top to bottom: **The Central Hotel; Palace Backpackers** Initially Cairns developed around Abbott Street and the wharves. In the early 1900s, Lake and Spence Streets were developed and became the new heart of Cairns.

Rainforest Dome

Clockwise, from top right: Female Eclectus Parrot; Female Red-tailed Black-Cockatoo; This interactive zoo in the city is sure to enthral all visitors.

A diverse collection of Australian flora and fauna can be seen up-close-and-personal right in the heart of the city. Situated in the atrium atop The Reef Hotel Casino, Cairns Wildlife Dome houses over 60 species of magnificent animals.

An elevated boardwalk passes through tall palms and clinging vines under the 20 m high glass dome, providing a wonderful vantage for viewing the Dome's resident wildlife. Famous Australians include the Koala, Laughing Kookaburra and Estuarine Crocodile, while lesser-known species include the Papuan Frogmouth, a rare night bird. Cairns Rainforest Dome offers visitors a rare opportunity to observe and marvel at these animals' behaviour. Tours and presentations uncover the secrets of the region's amazing Wet Tropics rainforests.

Cairns City

Other City Attractions

Right at the entrance to Cairn's Harbour is the **Pier Marketplace** (Pierpoint Rd, Ph: 07 4051 7244), a luxury hotel and retail complex equal to any in the world. On the ground level, the public has access to wide, covered walkways, restaurants and shops, all maximising the splendid marina views. Wares range from clothing, jewellery and gifts to books and science paraphernalia. Shoppers can overlook the marina while sipping coffee or enjoying a meal. Those seeking a diversion from shopping or dining can peruse the fantastic art on display in the **Ancient Earth Indigenous Art Gallery** (Ph: 07 4051 0211).

Cairns' city streets form another popular shopping precinct with an eclectic mix of luxury shops, souvenir outlets and services. Designer boutiques stock the latest in clothing and accessories and stand alongside scuba shops that supply a diver's every need; ornate jewellery shops display tempting pearls, opal and gemstones; bookshops divert ardent bibliophiles; newsagents and grocers target practical needs; and around every corner is a souvenir shop filled with trinkets to suit every budget. Galleries sell Aboriginal art of various origins, so visitors wishing to buy art by local Aboriginal artists are advised to shop around.

There are various large shopping centres. Closest to the CBD is **Cairns Central** (McLeod St, Ph: 07 4047 7412), above Cairns Railway Station, and some 200 stores are located here. Similar facilities are at **Stocklands Shopping Centre** (537 Mulgrave Road, Earlville, Ph: 07 4054 3066), **Smithfield Centre** (Cnr Captain Cook & Kennedy Hwys, Smithfield, Ph: 07 4038 1006) and **Westcourt Plaza** (274 Mulgrave Rd, Ph: 07 4051 7444). **Mt Sheridan Plaza** (106 Barnard Dr, Mt Sheridan, Ph: 07 4036 3150) and **Raintrees Shopping Centre** (Cnr Alfred & Koch Sts, Manunda, Ph: 07 4053 9800) are smaller and quieter. Corner stores, bakeries and supermarkets are dotted through the suburbs.

Regular markets include a small daily one in City Place, **Saturday Markets** on the Esplanade (8 a.m. – 4 p.m.), **Rusty's Markets** (Friday, 5 a.m. – 6 p.m., Saturday 6 a.m. – 3 p.m., Sunday 6 a.m. – 2 p.m., Sheridan St, between Shields & Spence Sts, Ph: 07 4051 5100) and weekends at the Pier Marketplace (Saturday & Sunday Mud Markets, 9 a.m. – 3 p.m.), Gordonvale (1st Saturday each month), **Tanks Art Centre** (last Sunday), Mt Sheridan Plaza (2nd Saturday), **Holloways Beach** (2nd Sunday), **Edmonton** (3rd Saturday) and Smithfield Shopping Centre (3rd Sunday). Contact **Cairns City Council** (Ph: 07 4044 3044) for more information.

Top to bottom: **The Pier; Souvenir shops abound in Pier Marketplace; A café in the Pier Marketplace** The Cairns Pier Marketplace overlooks Marlin Marina and the Esplanade.

The Night Markets

Among the shops and restaurants of the Esplanade is the mall, housing the Night Markets. Over 70 stalls sell almost everything — freshwater pearls, honey, toys, clothing, souvenirs, books, postcards, didgeridoos and boomerangs.

The markets open nightly from 5 p.m. The food hall's multicultural menu makes it an interesting and inexpensive place to while away an evening.

Cairns City

Aboriginal Art Shop Aboriginal art is very popular and can be found in many of Cairns' excellent galleries.

Hides Corner Cairns' most fashionable hotel in the 1880s and 1890s has long been a significant landmark.

Australian gemstones Authentic pearls and opals gleam in elegant and distinctive settings.

Dining Out

Being a cosmopolitan city that combines more than 30 different cultures among its population, Cairns offers a vast array of quality restaurants from every corner of the globe, with sumptuous, mouth-watering menus. Popular cuisines are Indian, French, Mediterranean, Mexican, Italian, Greek, Korean, Chinese, Thai and Japanese.

Restaurants specialising in Australian bush flavours are a favourite, as are the various hotels that offer hearty counter meals. Fresh seafood is commonly on the menu, enhanced by locally produced dairy products, tropical fruits, tea and coffee. Many restaurants and cafés offer alfresco dining to enrich the gourmet experience.

After sunset, the lights of Cairns twinkle under the tropical night sky and the temperature is perfect for eating outside. Shields Street and the Esplanade comprise Cairns' most popular dining precincts, and are the two main strips where residents and visitors congregate to enjoy life's simple pleasures — fine food and wine, and the chance to relax with friends and family under the dome of a soft, tropical sky. Around the city, many of Cairns' hotels, including the **Shangri-La**, **Reef Hotel Casino**, **Cairns International**, **Rydges Plaza** and **Matson Resort**, offer lavish buffets and à la carte menus. Restaurants, cafés and clubs dotted throughout the suburbs spoil visitors by providing endless options for places to dine.

A Night on the Town

Cairns nightlife is lively and, at the end of the day, amusement abounds. After dinner, a short stroll along the Esplanade or through the streets will aid digestion. Casual punters gravitate to the **Reef Hotel Casino's** theatre, bars, disco or gaming tables and poker machines. The legendary **Johno's Blues Bar** is a mecca for live grooves. Many suburban sporting and social clubs provide dining, entertainment, dancing and gambling facilities.

Local and visiting entertainers and theatrical productions may be enjoyed in the theatres and occasionally in the **Flecker Botanic Gardens** and other outdoor venues. Movie buffs will find cinema complexes dotted throughout Cairns, while the **Night Markets** provide visual diversions of a different kind with inexpensive dining and an eclectic mix of shops.

Festival Cairns

Festival Cairns, held each September, is a great opportunity to party. The **Amateurs Racing Carnival** is the premier event — it has a **Fashions on the Field** competition, **Charity Ball** and **Club Dinner**. **Carnival on Collins** at Flecker Botanic Gardens is a Father's Day event. A host of musical events, dance parties, film festivals, art shows, theatre productions and sports make the festival a veritable cultural feast, with the **Parade of Lights** and fireworks display creating a grand finale. For information, contact **Cairns City Council** (Ph: 07 4044 3044) or **Events Cairns** (Ph: 07 4051 0222).

Things to See and Do

1. Visit Cairns Museum and the Esplanade's interpretive nodes to learn about Cairns' history and Yidindji and Yirrganydji culture.
2. Visit the Cairns Regional Gallery and photo galleries.
3. Enjoy live theatre.
4. Sip coffee in City Place.
5. Visit the Esplanade's markets.
6. Shop till you drop in the Pier Marketplace.
7. Dine heartily.
8. Frolic in the lagoon.
9. Stroll the Promenade at sunset, birdwatch or enjoy a barbecue.
10. Try your luck at the Reef Hotel Casino.

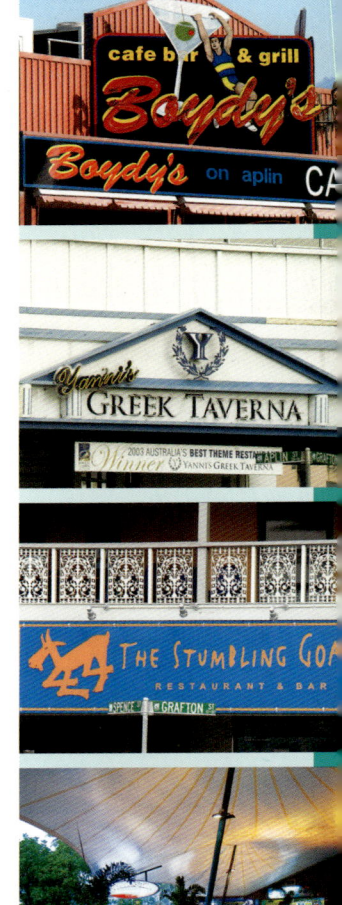

Top to bottom: **Boydy's Café Bar & Grill; Yanni's Greek Taverna; The Stumbling Goat; Barnacle Bill's** All serve a variety of cuisines to suit all tastes, budgets and dietary requirements.

23

Cairns City

City Parks and Gardens

Seen from above, Cairns is a green paradise with roofs barely visible among the trees. Foliage and flowers in the parks and gardens burst with tropical vitality. The climate lures most people outdoors to appreciate these splendid green spaces.

The **Esplanade** is undeniably Cairns' most popular park. Early morning fitness fanatics cruise the boulevard or work out at the exercise stations, while more laid-back residents enjoy breakfast and coffee. As the day warms up, tourists and locals enjoy the parkland's free facilities — water fountains, barbecues, children's playgrounds, the skate park, public artworks and tennis courts — as they gather with friends or relax in solitude. An excellent place to people-watch, the Esplanade is particularly busy at sunset, with residents relaxing after work and visitors enjoying the tropical evening weather before dining.

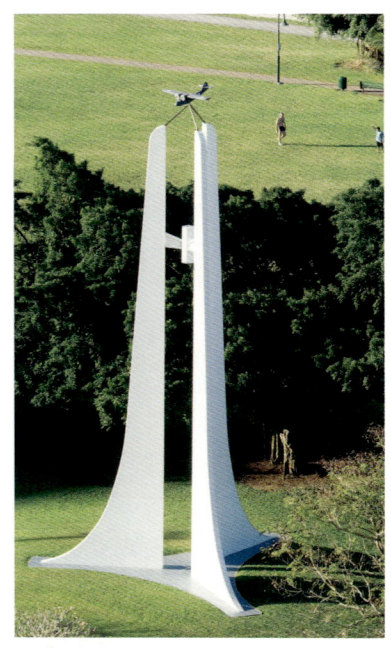

Open-air Venues

At **Fogarty Park** on the southern end of the Esplanade, the sound shell is a popular venue for open-air concerts and events (Ph: 07 4044 3044) throughout the year, as is the **City Place Soundshell** (Ph: 07 4044 3044). Open-air cinema and theatre productions are staged periodically at **Flecker Botanic Gardens** (Collins Ave, Edge Hill, Ph: 07 4044 3398).

RAAF Catalina Squadron's World War II Memorial commemorates the role played by Catalina flying-boat pilots during the War in the Pacific.

Two particularly popular children's playgrounds are **Muddy's Playground**, with its totem poles, water features, café and specially designed toddler's playground, and the **Endeavour Fun Ship** playground. Both are situated in the northern section of the Esplanade, and admission is free. Numerous smaller parks and reserves with toilets, picnic and barbecue facilities, playgrounds and swimming spots are scattered around the city and suburbs. They are linked by a network of walking and cycling paths. For a copy of the **Cairns Cycling and Walking Guide**, contact Cairns City Council (Ph: 07 4044 3044).

Sporting Facilities

The people of Cairns enjoy a lively and varied sporting scene. Both indoor and outdoor facilities are found throughout the suburbs. Behind the city at **Parramatta Park** is the **Cairns Showgrounds**, venue for the annual **Cairns Show** held in July (Cairns Show Association, Ph: 07 4051 6699), and the **Cannon Park Racecourse** (Bruce Highway, Woree, Ph: 07 4054 1036), where regular race meetings and the September **Amateurs Racing Carnival** are held (for more information, contact Cairns Amateurs, Ph: 07 4041 4911).

Cairns City Council (Ph: 07 4044 3044) maintains public facilities, including swimming pools, sports grounds and recreation centres. Numerous privately owned and operated indoor and outdoor centres provide facilities for all manner of racquet and ball sports, roller-blading, ice-skating, cycling, as well as gymnasiums and swimming pools.

Memorials

War memorials and monuments are a feature of the Esplanade, particularly opposite the **Cairns RSL Club** (115 the Esplanade, Ph: 07 4051 5804). Within the club is a **Hall of Memories** that displays military memorabilia and photographs. The **RAAF Catalina Squadron's WWII Memorial** lies further north, almost opposite Cairns Base Hospital.

All of these memorials serve as a sober reminder to the courage and sacrifice of those who gave their lives for others in wartime and in peace.

Cairns Esplanade park and activities The Esplanade is designed for maximum outdoor living. All day people can be seen walking their dogs, enjoying a leisurely cycle, chatting with friends, reading, birdwatching, meditating, skating, or playing tennis or volleyball.

Cairns City

Clockwise from top left: **Scenes from Flecker Botanic Gardens** Main garden; Rainforest Boardwalk to Centenary Lakes; Hybrid orchid; Botanic Gardens Licensed Café; Palms and heliconias line the pathways; Pleomele and Brazilian Cloak.

Flecker Botanic Gardens

With a collection featuring hundreds of species of native tropical plants and exotics from as far afield as South-East Asia and South America, **Flecker Botanic Gardens** (Collins Ave, Edge Hill, Ph: 07 4044 3398) are the only botanic gardens in Queensland's Wet Tropics and a magical place to relax. Extending over 300 ha, the gardens feature a simulated tropical rainforest, which comes complete with palms and tall trees laced in vines, orchids and bromeliads, a fernery, an orchid house, and a comprehensive collection of heliconias, gingers, bamboos and tropical fruits. In a similar vein to other botanic gardens around the world, Flecker Botanic Gardens serves to protect rare and threatened plant species, to provide research facilities, and to assist the local community in tropical plant identification.

Two interesting features within the gardens are the **Gondwana Garden** and **Aboriginal Plant Use Garden**. The Gondwana Garden displays many plants believed to be relics from the ancient Gondwanan rainforests and traces the evolution of flowering plants. The Aboriginal Plant Use Garden highlights some of the local plants traditionally used by rainforest Aboriginal groups as a source of food and medicine, and as materials to craft shelter, clothing, tools, weapons and utensils. Interestingly, many of the tropical rainforest fruits are toxic and need to undergo very specific and complex treatments to be rendered edible.

The gardens are open every day of the week (weekdays 7.30 a.m. – 5.30 p.m., weekends and public holidays 8.30 a.m. – 5.30 p.m.). Admission is free, although donations that will support the work of the gardens are gratefully received. The information centre, with books and gifts, is open from 8.30 a.m. – 4.30 p.m. (weekdays only), and the **Botanic Gardens Licensed Café** is open seven days a week from 8.30 a.m.– 4.30 p.m. (Ph: 07 4053 7087).

Things to See and Do

1. Take guided tours on weekdays (except public holidays) for $11 per person.
2. Enjoy plant displays, bimonthly talk and walk sessions ($5 pp).
3. See Starry Nights Cinema (mid-monthly, May to November) and occasional concerts and plays.
4. Explore the rich plant and animal life of Saltwater and Freshwater Lakes, part of the gardens' Centenary Lakes.

Centenary Lakes are adjacent to Flecker Botanic Gardens and are linked via a boardwalk through rainforest and melaleuca swamp (Collins Ave, Edge Hill, Ph: 07 4044 3398).

Cairns City

The Bayside

Founded as a port, **Cairns Harbour** and bayside have long been the focus of the city's commercial and social life, with shipping playing an essential role in trade, commerce and employment.

From the beginning, large passenger and cargo ships on **Trinity Bay** have been a familiar sight. During the city's early years, large ships dropped anchor offshore and passengers and cargo were ferried to and from the wharf area. Later, with the dredging of the channel and the development of shipping facilities in **Trinity Inlet**, the port prospered, at one time employing close to 1000 wharfies. Although the days may be long gone of Cairns' residents dutifully making their pilgrimage to the wharf to farewell guests with brass bands and streamers, Cairns is still the country's busiest cruise port with over 200 visits each year by international and domestic cruise ships.

Trinity Bay Named by Lieutenant James Cook of HM Bark *Endeavour*, on Trinity Sunday in June 1770, the bay encompasses the traditional country of several Aboriginal groups, particularly the Kunggandji, Yidindji and Yirrganydji people, who fished and traded along the coastline. Pearlers and bêche-de-mer fishermen used its resources for shelter, water and firewood from the mid-1800s. It served as a port from 1876.

Trinity Inlet

This is the focus of Cairns' commerce and tourism. At the entrance are the **Pier Marketplace** (Pierpoint Rd, Ph: 07 4051 7244) and **Marlin Marina**, providing safe mooring for luxury cruisers, yachts and game fishing boats. Nearby is the **Reef Fleet Terminal** (1 Spence St, Ph: 07 4052 3888) — main departure point to the **Great Barrier Reef**, **Green** and **Fitzroy Islands**.

Ocean liners dock at **Trinity Wharf** or **Cairns Cruise Port**. Along the waterfront are **Cairns Seaport's** consolidation and redistribution facilities. The port handles a huge annual cargo of sugar and molasses, petroleum, fertiliser and LPG, and offers extensive ship-building and maintenance services. Historic wharf buildings, yacht clubs, small yachts and other craft moored along the inlet add interest. Absorb the scenery on a walk along the waterfront or an evening harbour cruise on the harbour (**Ocean Spirit Cruises**, Cnr Shields St & the Esplanade, Ph: 1800 644 227), or **Gondola Classique** (C Finger, Marlin Marina, in front of Pier Marketplace, Pierpoint Road, Ph: 0417 790 628 or 07 4055 6279).

Sailing on the bay Trinity Bay is the perfect yachting playground. From the inlet's safe harbour, travel to nearby Green and Fitzroy Islands, race around the bay, or cruise north to Port Douglas or south to Innisfail via the Frankland Islands.

Commercial fishing trawlers at the wharf The Cairns Seaport houses one of Australia's largest fishing fleets. Over 800 vessels fish regional waters, returning to the port with reef and freshwater fish, prawns, lobsters, bugs and crabs for export and local consumption.

Cairns City

Wetlands, Mangroves and Mudflats

Right, top to bottom: Overlooking the Esplanade mudflats at high tide; Jack Barnes Bicentennial Mangrove Walk.

Development dramatically changed the face of Trinity Bay, once a place of sand dunes, swamps and mangroves. Vast volumes of landfill were used to reclaim the low-lying areas and provide level foundations for Cairns. More recent reclamations include the International Airport and the redeveloped Esplanade and foreshore. Fortunately, pockets of original lowland rainforest and swamp habitat are preserved at Centenary Lakes (Flecker Botanic Gardens, Collins Ave, Edge Hill, Ph: 07 4044 3398) and remnants of Cairns Central Swamp are scattered through the suburbs. The Jack Barnes Bicentennial Mangrove Walk (Airport Ave, Aeroglen, Ph: 07 4044 3044 for more information) leads through tropical mangrove forest vital to biodiversity. Forming important bird habitats, fish and shellfish nurseries, water purifiers and flood mitigators, these tidal wetlands are a crucial buffer between urban-agricultural lands and the Great Barrier Reef. Two wheelchair-accessible walks (830 m circuit, 600 m one way) traverse the reserve.

The Esplanade

Hugging the shores of the harbour north of **Trinity Inlet** is the Esplanade, an extensive tropical park. Everyone loves its long boulevards, fresh sea breezes and magnificent harbour views. Overlooking the channel and linking the CBD to Trinity Inlet, it has always been the hub of social life in Cairns and the place to meet people, walk, enjoy lazy picnics, swim and be seen.

The focus of the redeveloped Esplanade is **Esplanade Lagoon** and its surrounding lawns and barbecue areas. Wheelchair-accessible paths link the lagoon and surrounds to the nearby **Pier Marketplace** and **Marlin Marina** on **Trinity Inlet**. To the north, the Esplanade continues with the **Foreshore Promenade**, exercise stations, interpretive nodes, memorials, children's playgrounds and barbecue facilities. Across the road, the Esplanade is lined with restaurants, shops, the **Night Markets** and many motels.

Esplanade Lagoon Finding somewhere safe to swim on a humid summer's day in the tropics can be difficult. The region's two major swimming hazards, marine stingers and crocodiles, make many inviting waterways unsafe. Free of these dangers, the Esplanade Lagoon is a safe and pleasant place to cool off. The award-winning pool blends in well with Trinity Bay's natural environs. The facilities around the lagoon are a huge hit with locals and visitors alike.

Saturday markets on the Esplanade These lively markets, open from 8 a.m. – 4 p.m., showcase quality, handmade arts and crafts, jewellery, clothing, Aboriginal and Torres Strait Islander artworks, toys, food and knick-knacks. Buskers and street entertainers add to the ambience. From the striped market tents to the wild outfits of the performers, this colourful occasion brings Cairns together and promotes a positive weekend vibe.

Cairns Surrounds

Cairns sits amid scenery of great beauty and wonder — so many natural diversions are close to the city. For more than a century, cruise boats have brought eager travellers face to face with the miracle of the tropics. Kuranda, the lush rainforests and the mighty Barron Falls became popular when the Kuranda Range Railway opened in 1891. While the days of coastal steamers are long gone, and Cairns is no longer the distant frontier it once was, its tropical surrounds still possess the same timeless magnetism.

Orange-eyed Tree-frog

Nature at its Best

Set in the Wet Tropics World Heritage Area, **Kuranda** attracts millions of visitors who reach the town in different ways — by car, bus, train or cable car. The forested hills to the south and west are the source of crystal-clear streams that cascade and wind their way to the swamps and mangroves surrounding Cairns then flow into Trinity Bay. North of Cairns lie long, palm-lined beaches — their golden sands and turquoise waters an irresistible invitation to visitors from the south during cooler months. Even the interspersed patches of green agricultural land have a special appeal. Few other cities in Australia, or indeed the world, can boast such wondrously diverse scenery and such a suitable climate for exploration.

Sightseeing and Adventures

As well as having this wealth of natural attractions on its doorstep, Cairns also has the means to explore it all — from **Skyrail Rainforest Cableway** and **Kuranda Scenic Railway** to lagoon cruises at **Hartley's Crocodile Adventures,** and scenic drives, walking tracks and lookouts scattered throughout the Wet Tropics World Heritage Area.

Numerous outdoor adventure activities are on offer, as well as the chance to experience something of the culture of the Aboriginal groups who traditionally live in and care for this rainforest area. Art, history and simple outdoor experiences, such as walking along a sandy beach, swimming in a refreshing pool beneath a cascade and discovering the fascination of Australian animals in a wildlife park, are just a few of the many different experiences that cater to all tastes and interests.

Top to bottom: Palm Cove; Skyrail Rainforest Cableway; Barron Falls; Lagoon at Hartley's Crocodile Adventures.

Half Moon Bay Marina, Yorkeys Knob Yorkeys Knob, an understated and delightful northern beaches destination, is only 15 minutes drive north of Cairns.

Cairns Surrounds

LEGEND
- Major road
- Main road
- Minor road
- Railway
- Aboriginal Trust Area
- Urban area
- National park
- Wet Tropics World Heritage Area

Kilometres 0 5 10 15

Places and features

Port Douglas
Craiglie
Douglas Beach
MOWBRAY NP
Mowbray River
4WD Vehicles Only
Black Mountain (Harris Peak)
Rifle Creek
Scrubby Creek
Cassowary Creek
Packers Creek
Pebbly Beach
White Cliffs
Mount Garioch
Oak Beach
Little Reef Beach
Turtle Creek Beach
Hartleys Creek
White Cliff Point
Hartley's Crocodile Adventures
Wangetti Beach
Red Cliff Point
4WD Vehicles Only
Mt Formartine
Flaggy Creek
Simpson Point
Buchan Point
Double Island
Haycock Island (Scouts Hat)
Palm Cove
Cliffton Beach
Kewarra Beach
Koah
Barron River
Cairns Railway
Myola
Australian Butterfly Sanctuary
KURANDA
Barron Falls
Wrights Lookout
BARRON GORGE NP
Kuranda Scenic Railway
Lake Placid
Smithfield
Skyrail Rainforest Cableway
Trinity Beach
Yorkeys Knob
Holloways Beach
Machans Beach
Barron River
Redlynch
Freshwater
Casuarina Point
Ellie Point
Mt Whitfield Conservation Park
Mt Williams (Tokim Peak)
Brinsmead
Cairns Harbour
Koombal
False Cape
Cape Grafton
Chujeba Peak
Manunda
Mission Bay
Rocky Island
Jigol Peak
Freshwater Ck
CAIRNS
Giangurra
Yarrabah
Turtle Bay
Bare Hill
DAVIES CREEK NP
Copperlode Dam
Crystal Cascades
Earlville
Admiralty Island
White Rock
Mt Murray Prior
Grant Hill
Little Turtle Bay
Davies Creek Falls
Lake Morris
Kahlpahlim Rock
Glen Boughton
Mt Gorton
Wide Bay
Little Fitzroy Island
Bridle Creek
Bindle Creek
Groves Creek
Clohesy Creek
Davies Creek
Blackwater Creek
KENNEDY HIGHWAY
Edmonton
May Peaks
Deception Point
Fitzroy Island NP
Mt Tiptree
Mulgrave River
Little Mulgrave
Aboriginal
Mt Haig
GREY PEAKS NP
Grey Peaks
Gordonvale
Aloomba
Trust
Lamb Range
Little Mulgrave
Walshs Pyramid
Bell Peak North
Bell Peak South
Area
Lake Tinaroo
Mackey Creek
BRUCE HWY
Mt Sophia
Mt Harold
Kearneys Falls
Bellenden Ker (North Peak)
Deeral
CRATER LAKES NP
Lake Barrine
Lake Eacham
Goldsborough Valley State Forest
Toohey Creek
Butcher Creek
Behana Creek
WOOROONOORAN NP
Bellenden Ker (Central Peak)
RUSSELL RIVER NP
Palmer Point
High Island
Flirt Point
Russell Heads
FRANKLAND GROUP NP
Normanby Island
Mabel Island
Round Island

Batt Reef
Trinity Opening
Pixie Reef
TRINITY BAY
Great Barrier Reef Marine Park Cairns Section
Oyster Reef
Upolu Cay NP
Green Island NP
Frankland Islands

Cairns Surrounds

Natural Refreshments

Situated on the narrow coastal plain between the Great Dividing Range and the Coral Sea, Cairns is not only surrounded by spectacular scenery but has a wealth of aquatic playgrounds right on its doorstep. Residents and visitors have been enjoying the freshwater spoils of the Wet Tropics for years. To the south-west of Cairns are Crystal Cascades (something of a local secret) and Lake Morris — both of which are within 25 km of the city.

Above: **Crystal Cascades** is a popular haunt for locals seeking a refreshing swim on a hot summer's day.

Below: **Lake Morris** has picnic and barbecue facilities, a kiosk, and stunning views over the 45,000 megalitre dam and its 44 km² forested catchment.

On the City's Doorstep

The large waterways on **Trinity Bay** between **Trinity Inlet** and the **Barron River** are fundamental to Cairns' history and social life. Just as significant is **Freshwater Creek**, rising in the **Lamb Range** to the south-west and flowing north-east through **Redlynch**, **Brinsmead** and **Freshwater** to the Barron River.

This creek was Cairns' original water supply, later augmented by **Behana Creek** south of **Gordonvale**. **Copperlode Falls** was chosen as the site for an earth and rock-fill dam to cater for the increased population. Construction of **Copperlode Dam** (end of Lake Morris Road, Ph: 07 4055 7414) and Freshwater Creek Water Treatment Plant was not completed until March 1976.

At the dam, a short walk along the edge overlooks the infrastructure and a series of longer walks head to the **Atherton Tableland** (information available at **Lake Morris Kiosk**, Ph: 07 4055 7414). Cook a barbecue while enjoying dam and forest views or grab a bite at Lake Morris Kiosk. Facilities are open from 8 a.m. – 6 p.m. daily. Vehicle size limits apply on Lake Morris Road (coaches or caravans are not permitted).

Freshwater Creek State Forest

At **Crystal Cascades** (Intake Road, Redlynch, contact Cairns City Council on Ph: 07 4044 3044) just downstream from **Lake Morris**, water tumbles over falls and cascades down a sheer, rainforested valley.

A walking track from the car park (toilet and picnic facilities) provides swimming access. For cabins or caravan and camping facilities, visitors can base themselves at the nearby **Crystal Cascades Holiday Park** (Rocks Road, Redlynch, Ph: 07 4039 1036). For daytrippers, **Genoma Park** and **Goomboora Park** have picnic and barbecue facilities (Cairns City Council, Ph: 07 4044 3044, for the Cairns Walking Guide).

Left to right: **Freshwater Connection with Kuranda Scenic Railway; Red Lynch's cottage at Freshwater Connection** With its restaurant arranged in 85-year-old rail carriages and its museum full of information about the Kuranda Range Railway (1887–91), Freshwater Connection is a tribute to the railway's pioneers. Hundreds of men toiled on this first section of the Cairns–Herberton line, the 320 m climb up the range negotiated by 15 tunnels, 93 curves and a multitude of bridges over ravines and waterfalls. The Kuranda Scenic Railway has been popular since 1891. Freshwater Connection (1984) celebrates this heritage. It incorporates a cottage, reputedly that of Red Lynch, the foreman on the first section of the line. Museum and cottage are open daily, admission is included with the Kuranda Scenic Railway ticket (Ph: 07 4036 9333).

Cairns Surrounds

Trinity Inlet Situated right on the city's doorstep, and a popular aquatic playground for anglers, jet skiers and sailers alike, this huge tidal basin has over 90 km of winding, mangrove-lined waterways available for exploration. The estuary once formed the mouth of the Mulgrave River, which over time forged a new course further south when sediment (carried from the mountains) built up, choked, then eventually diverted its flow. Trinity Inlet is home to a multitude of animal species and Cairns Habitat Cruises (Reef Fleet Terminal, 1 Spence St, Ph: 07 4031 4007) is a great way to observe life in this habitat. Forest and wading birds such as the Black-necked Stork, White-breasted Sea-Eagle and Rainbow Bee-eaters may be seen along the inlet. For information on fishing charters contact Fishing Cairns (Ph: 07 4938 1144).

Mt Whitfield Conservation Park

The walking track near **Flecker Botanic Gardens** (Collins Ave, Edge Hill, Ph: 07 4044 3398), just 4.3 km north of Cairns' post office, enters **Mt Whitfield Conservation Park**. This isolated patch of mixed rainforest, eucalypt forest and grassland covers the slopes of **Mt Whitfield** (365 m) and **Mt Lumley** (325 m) within the traditional country of the Yirrganydji people. The **Red Arrow Circuit** (1.3 km, 1 hr) passes through lowland rainforest. It has some steep sections but is fine for most people, being used daily by hikers and joggers. Self-guiding, interpretive materials (available from Flecker Botanic Gardens) highlight the Yirrganydji use of plants, identify features of the landscape and discuss aspects of Cairns' history. The **Blue Arrow Circuit** (5.4 km, 4–5 hr) is a rugged (and potentially perilous) bush track up Mt Whitfield and Mt Lumley and should be undertaken only by fit and experienced bushwalkers.

The park's diverse vegetation and wildlife is revealed on the walks. Australian Brush-turkeys scratch in the forest leaf litter, while the reclusive Orange-footed Scrubfowl is more often heard than seen. Buff-breasted Paradise Kingfishers nest in the park over summer. Small holes in terrestrial termite mounds form the entrances to their nesting chambers. In open grassland, Agile Wallabies are seen feeding in small family groups in the early morning and late afternoon. Further information is available from **Queensland Parks and Wildlife Service** (5B Sheridan St, Ph: 07 4046 6600).

Sugarworld

Southern suburbs of Cairns were, for many years, used for sugar production. The first sugarcane farm in Cairns was **Hop Wah Plantation** and its **Pioneer Mill**. It was established in 1881 and operated by a syndicate of Chinese men on the site of **Stocklands Shopping Centre** in present-day **Earlville**. Further south (now **Edmonton**) was **Hambledon Estate**, which also grew tropical fruits.

In recent years, economic factors have made cane growing difficult and the expansion of the city of Cairns along the southern access corridor has seen many cane farms converted to suburbs. Today Hambledon Estate is open to the public as **Hambledon House Community Centre** (177 Bruce Hwy, Edmonton, Ph: 07 4045 0222). There is also **Sugarworld Gardens** (Hambledon Dr, Edmonton, Ph: 07 4040 8813) and the adjacent **Sugarworld Waterslides** (Ph: 07 4055 5477), which, with their picnic and barbecue facilities set among established tropical gardens and a tropical fruit orchard, are particularly popular for social gatherings.

Above, left to right: Sugarcane is grown on the plains around Edmonton; Cane harvesters are still a familiar sight in Cairns' outer southern suburbs.

Cairns Surrounds

Bountiful Beaches

With glorious golden sands, expansive palm-fringed beaches, turquoise waters, islands at arms' reach and tropical temperatures, Cairns' northern beaches have all the hallmarks of an ideal paradise.

Various leisure and adventure activities make these beaches a popular destination for sun-worshippers looking to breathe the salt air and unwind.

Holloways Beach has an atmosphere far removed from the pace of busy city life.

Trinity Beach is a popular place to swim, enjoy water sports and soak up the sunshine.

Clifton Beach Looking north along quiet Clifton Beach to Palm Cove and Double Island.

Palm Cove Palm Cove's famous long, curved beach with Macalister Range beyond.

Northern Beaches

A beautiful coastline of beaches, offshore islands and reefs stretches for almost 30 km north of Cairns. For thousands of years it was the traditional land and sea country of the Djabugay and Yirrganydji people. Now popular swimming spots for locals, the northern beaches once formed camps and training grounds for Allied troops during World War II. **Machans Beach**, **Holloways Beach**, **Yorkeys Knob**, **Trinity Beach**, **Kewarra Beach**, **Clifton Beach**, **Palm Cove** and **Ellis Beach** are located just off the Captain Cook Highway. All are well serviced with beach patrols, toilets, barbecue facilities, accommodation, shops, medical centres, restaurants and cafés.

Nearby **Smithfield** services the beaches and gives access to **Kuranda**. Attractions include **The Opal Factory** (Cnr Cook Hwy & Sharon St, Smithfield, Ph: 07 4038 2366); bungy jumping (**AJ Hackett Bungy Cairns**, McGregor Rd, Smithfield, Ph: 07 4057 7188); cable water-skiing (**Cable Ski Cairns**, Lot 5 Captain Cook Hwy, Smithfield, Ph: 07 4038 1304); go-kart racing (**Cairns Go Kart Hire Track**, Cnr Captain Cook Hwy & Walkers Rd, Ph: 07 4055 0355); and cable hang-gliding (**Flying Leap Cairns**, Aeroglen Dr, Aeroglen, Ph: 07 4036 2127).

Closest to Cairns are the (primarily) residential Machans and Holloways Beaches, but Holloways has varied accommodation, a boat ramp, cafés, restaurants and shops. Yorkeys Knob has a playground, golf course, marina and good fishing around the groyne. Super liners sometimes anchor offshore. There are a number of accommodation options, including hotels and holiday rentals.

Trinity Beach

Trinity Beach is a long-time local favourite for evening picnics, dining and barbecues. Activities include squash and tennis, a football club, gymnasium, lawn bowling greens, windsurfing, beach volleyball, sailing, wave-skiing and boogie boarding (equipment can be hired at the beach), fishing charters and fishing from the beach and headland. Camp at **Cairns Trinity Beach Holiday Park** (116 Trinity Beach Rd, Ph: 07 4055 6306).

Top to bottom: Anglers wet a line a Palm Cove; Catamarans for hire at Palm Cove.

Kewarra & Clifton Beaches

Kewarra and **Clifton Beaches** are quiet, dreamy settlements. The spacious beachfront parks are perfect for playing, reading, meditating, walking, jogging and cycling. Kewarra Beach has a golf club and small luxury resort. At the **Outback Opal Mine** (24 Alexandra St, Clifton Beach, Ph: 07 4055 3492), visitors can walk through a replica opal mine and admire cut stones and jewellery. Clifton Beach has a variety of accommodation options.

Palm Cove

Famous as a playground for the rich, **Palm Cove** nonetheless caters to all. Attractions include a public swimming enclosure, boat ramp and fishing jetty near **Palm Cove Campground** (1149 Williams Esplanade, Ph: 07 4055 3824). **Cairns Tropical Zoo** and **Cairns Night Zoo** (Captain Cook Hwy, Ph: 07 4055 3669) are popular, so too is kayaking and sailing. Contact **Beach Fun Co** (Cnr Harpa St & Williams Esplanade, Ph: 0411 848 580) and **Palm Cove Watersports** (Cnr Cedar St & Williams Esplanade, Ph: 0402 861 011). Exclusive **Double Island** is nearby.

Cairns Surrounds

Ellis Beach

North of **Buchan Point**, the Captain Cook Highway skirts the Coral Sea and leads to **Ellis Beach**. Mango trees line the highway, which runs parallel to the beach and provides easy access to this idyllic haven. The trees were planted by Dick Ellis, caretaker of the work camp during construction of the highway in the 1930s.

Ellis Beach Surf Life Saving Club (Ph: 07 4055 3695) and a kiosk and store (**Ellis Beach Bar & Grill**, Ph: 07 4055 3534) provide everything necessary for a relaxed afternoon at the beach. The beach itself is steepish with small surf, but is safe for walking, swimming in the patrolled enclosure, and fishing. Longer-term visitors often stay at **Ellis Beach Oceanfront Bungalows and Leisure Park** (Ph: 1800 637 036).

Relaxing in the shade of paperbarks at Palm Cove With wonderful views over the nearby islands, this is the perfect place to laze and dream.

Further north, the highway passes attractive smaller beaches good for walking, swimming and fishing. Practically everywhere is a photographer's dream. **Simpson Point** and **Red Cliff Point** are worth a visit. **Wangetti Beach**, one of Australia's most photographed, yet least visited beaches, is accessible from either end. **Hartley's Creek** forms a lagoon behind the northern section of the beach, not far from **Hartley's Crocodile Adventures** (Captain Cook Hwy, Palm Cove, Ph: 07 4055 3576). At White Cliff Point, **Rex Lookout** offers extensive views over the Coral Sea and coastline. In favourable conditions, hang-gliders rise on thermals and hover over the cliff. Further north, the Captain Cook Highway passes **Turtle Beach** (occupied by a private resort), **Little Reef Beach** (with its small onshore reef), **Oak Beach**, **White Cliffs**, **Pebbly Beach** and **Douglas Beach**, before continuing on to **Port Douglas**.

Things to See and Do
1. Enjoy the beaches.
2. Try an adventure activity or go fishing.
3. Visit wildlife parks to learn about the region's unique fauna.
4. Be water safe! Swim at patrolled beaches, and in enclosures in stinger season (May–Nov).
5. Spoil yourself with a luxury spa or some fine dining.
6. Admire the Coral Sea from nearby lookouts.
7. For more info contact: Palm Cove Promotion Association (Ph: 07 4055 3901).

Haycock Island, otherwise known as the Scout's Hat, at sunset.

Hartley's Crocodile Farm

For the thrill of seeing crocodiles in a natural setting, Hartley's Crocodile Adventures (open 9 a.m. – 5 p.m. daily) is hard to beat. This sanctuary displays Estuarine (*bottom right*) and Freshwater Crocodiles and fauna that share their forest and wetland habitat — Southern Cassowaries (*top left*), Merten's Water Monitors (*bottom left*), Koalas, turtles, snakes, frogs and all manner of waterbirds. Allow time for the crocodile farm tour, lagoon cruise, wildlife walks on the boardwalks, presentations about crocodile lifestyles, restaurant overlooking the lily-covered lagoon (*top right*) and gift shop.

33

Cairns Surrounds

North-west Delights

Kuranda, settled in the cool hinterland a mere 25 km from Cairns, is affectionately known as the "village in the rainforest". It sits 380 m above sea level atop a steep escarpment often cloaked in mist. Getting there is a remarkable adventure in itself. The **Kuranda Scenic Railway** (trains depart Cairns Railway Station, Bunda St, or Freshwater Railway Station, Kamerunga Road, Freshwater, Ph: 07 4036 9333) offers breathtaking views and thrills as it winds its way up the range along the historic railway line — an engineering marvel of its day.

A trip on the **Skyrail Rainforest Cableway** (Cnr Kamerunga Rd & Cook Hwy, Smithfield, Ph: 07 4038 1555), its modern counterpart, is equally exhilarating. Visitors enjoy breathtaking views over the World Heritage rainforests via cable car as it glides 7.5 km over the **Kuranda Range**.

Clockwise from top left: Kuranda Scenic Railway historic carriage; Tjapukai Aboriginal Cultural Park; Skyrail's cable cars offer a birds' eye view of Barron Gorge National Park and the Cairns Highlands as well as the Coral Sea with its islands and reefs; the Kuranda Scenic Railway's iron and lattice bridge at Stoney Creek Falls was completed in the mid-1890s.

Boardwalks, lookouts and an interpretive centre at mid-stations allow rainforest exploration. Another option is to drive up the Kuranda Range Road through the forest, stopping at the **Henry Ross Lookout** to oversee the coastal plain and Coral Sea. **Kuranda Bus** (Ph: 0418 772 953) and **Whitecar Coaches** (Ph: 07 4091 1855) offer trips. Energetic visitors can hike along traditional Aboriginal or pioneer trails.

Beside the Smithfield **Skyrail** terminal is a famous cultural attraction, **Tjapukai Aboriginal Cultural Park** (Cnr Kamerunga Rd & Cook Hwy, Smithfield, Ph: 07 4042 9999). Here, theatrical presentations and interactive tours introduce visitors to aspects of Djabugay Aboriginal culture. The Djabugay people have lived in the **Barron Gorge** and its surrounds for many thousands of years. Many of the gorge's natural formations feature in their cultural stories. Nearby, **Barron Gorge Hydro Power Station** provides renewable energy to 36,000 houses. The station's visitor centre (Barron Gorge Rd, Kamerunga, Ph: 07 4035 0255) provides information about the power station and the surrounding **Barron Gorge National Park**.

Barron Gorge, Barron Gorge National Park Barron Gorge formed when the Barron River "captured" some of the headwaters of the Mitchell River (strengthening its flow and cleaving a steep, narrow gorge into the valley). The national park contains a network of historic mining tracks and traditional Aboriginal trails.

Lake Placid (Lake Placid Road, Kamerunga, Ph: 07 4039 2661) is a popular freshwater playground. Cairns residents and visitors enjoy swimming, canoeing and picnicking around the clear waters. The kiosk serves meals and snacks and has paddle boats for hire.

Cairns Surrounds

Barron Gorge National Park

Barron Gorge National Park, established 1940, was included in the Wet Tropics World Heritage Area in 1988. The 2820 ha park extends from the coastal lowlands behind Cairns up the **Kuranda Range** to the eastern edge of the **Atherton Tableland**. It is rugged terrain, with peaks, valleys and ravines covered in verdant eucalypt forest and tropical rainforest. Its vertiginous cliff-faces, waterfalls and mountain scenery make it stunningly picturesque. Particularly spectacular is **Barron Falls**, the largest waterfall in the World Heritage Area. When in flood during the Wet, so much water flows over the 250 m cliff-face that visitors to the **Barron Falls Lookout** are commonly enveloped in a cloud of mist.

Left to right: **Barron Falls; The walk to the falls** Barron Falls has always inspired awe. Known to the Djabugay people as *Din Din*, it is the place to celebrate the birth of *Bulurru*, the Creator Spirit and Rainbow Serpent. The Lookout is visited by thousands of people each year. The walk to the falls along the spectacular elevated boardwalk is wheelchair-accessible.

The area is easy to explore. From Kuranda it is 6 km to the falls lookout boardwalk (570 m, 20 min one way) and then a kilometre to **Wrights Lookout** (1 km, 30 min one way, with views to Cairns). Bushwalkers can take day hikes across the park. The tracks follow Djabugay pathways between lowlands and uplands, although some were adapted by European pioneers in the late 1800s. They are accessed from **Speewah** camp ground, 15 km west of Kuranda, Wrights Lookout and **Kamerunga**.

For whitewater rafting in the Barron Gorge, contact **Raging Thunder Pty Ltd** (52–54 Fearnley St, Ph: 07 4030 7900) or **R'n'R Rafting** (278 Hartley St, Ph: 07 4041 9444).

Things to See and Do

1. Visit Kuranda Visitor Information Centre, Centenary Park, Coondoo St, Kuranda (Ph: 07 4093 9311).
2. Enjoy the gardens and teahouses at Kuranda Railway Station, Arara St, Kuranda (Ph: 07 4036 9333).
3. Glimpse the country through Aboriginal eyes by joining Djabugay Country Tours, Rob Veivers Dr, Kuranda (Ph: 07 4093 9111 or 0408 746 054).
4. Enjoy bushwalking through Barron Gorge National Park.
5. Experience the adrenalin rush of a whitewater rafting adventure down Barron Gorge.
6. Relax in the tranquil surroundings of Lake Placid Recreation Area, (at the end of Lake Placid Rd).
7. Pick out a peaceful nook and enjoy some wildlife spotting.
8. For more information contact Queensland Parks & Wildlife Service, 5B Sheridan St, Cairns (Ph: 07 4046 6600) or Djabugay Ranger Agency (Ph: 07 4093 9296).

Wildlife of Barron Gorge National Park

The altitude and topographical range of Barron Gorge National Park supports diverse vegetation communities — open woodland, grassland, upland heath and misty tropical rainforest. Not surprisingly, profuse native animal species make their homes here. By day, Musky Rat-kangaroos, Emerald Doves, Brush-turkeys and Orange-footed Scrubfowl forage on the forest floor. In the trees, Rainbow and Scaly-breasted Lorikeets screech and Wompoo Pigeons call loudly. Southern Cassowaries are rare. Consider yourself lucky if you spy one of these magnificent birds. Ulysses and Cairns Birdwing Butterflies light up the forest. Echidnas, Lace Monitors, pythons and other snakes are sometimes met. In the river are Platypus, Barramundi, Jungle Perch, catfish, eels, freshwater turtles, Freshwater Crocodiles and (downstream from Lake Placid) Estuarine Crocodiles. Nocturnal mammals seen by spotlight include Striped Possums (*above right*), Long-tailed Pygmy Possums, Lumholtz's Tree-kangaroos, Spectacled Flying-foxes and insectivorous bats. Many frog species, such as the Orange-eyed Tree-frog (*below right*) live here.

Cairns Surrounds

Arts and Crafts Nexus

Kuranda Village is a sensory extravaganza. Its shaded streets buzz with art shows, live music and street entertainment. Kuranda is home to many eclectic artists and craft workers, who, having escaped city life, draw inspiration from the beauty of their natural surroundings. For this small multicultural community, art and music are a unifying force that creates a powerful ambience.

Kuranda's main drag is the perfect place to pick up something special.

Kuranda Railway Station is renowned for its prize-winning gardens.

Tall trees add a deep, verdant shade to the town's peaceful streetscapes.

Doongal Aboriginal Art features art and artefacts crafted by Aboriginal artists.

Kuranda

Kuranda is known by the Djabugay people, the traditional custodians of **Barron Gorge** and its surrounds, as *Ngoonbi*, the place of the Platypus. An important crossing on the **Barron River** for gold prospectors, timber-getters and farmers in the late 1870s, the village was known as "Middle Crossing". Once the **Cairns Range Railway** was opened in 1891, it became popular with Cairns residents seeking to escape the coastal humidity. It was, nevertheless, a sleepy village during the 1920s and 1930s. Tourism was eclipsed with a military presence in the 1940s. The Kuranda Range Road, completed in 1942, opened the path for more settlers. A steady influx of people looking for an alternative lifestyle arrived during the 1960s and 1970s. They converted the village into an arts and crafts hub. Kuranda now has a vibrant, close-knit, multicultural community, that enjoys a leisurely tropical lifestyle. It continues to attract and delight tourists.

Markets, Shops and Galleries

Kuranda's market scene thrived during the 1970s and the village still revolves around its markets. They operate every day, but really come to life on Wednesday, Thursday, Friday and Sunday.

The original markets, **Kuranda Markets Pty Ltd** (Cnr Therwine & Thoree Sts, Ph: 07 4093 7261) are in the rainforest behind the **New Kuranda Markets** (23 Coondoo St, Ph: 0418 848 616). **Kuranda Heritage Markets** (Rob Veivers Dr, Ph: 07 4093 8060) are across the street. Shops and art galleries, including the **Kuranda Arts Co-op** (Shop 6, 12 Rob Veivers Drive, Kuranda, Ph: 07 4093 9026) line the main street. The Indigenous community proudly showcases its culture through traditional artefacts, engaging visual arts and tribal dance. Itinerant musicians and street entertainers add colour to the mix.

Kuranda Markets The range of expertly handcrafted goods includes leather wares, wood and jewellery items, pottery, paintings, photographs, clothing and toys. Most is the work of local artisans and craft workers. Souvenirs from opals to T-shirts are also sold.

Cafés and Restaurants

A few historic buildings house fine restaurants and cafés filled with tasty treats to be enjoyed while sipping locally grown tea and coffee. Snack bars, take-away shops and a hotel cater for other tastes, time schedules and budgets. Alfresco dining, of which Kuranda has its share, is one of the joys of tropical living. What better place to eat, meet the locals and watch the world go by?

Wildlife and Cultural Heritage

A variety of wildlife can be observed in and around the village. Parrots, figbirds and butterflies are often seen in the sprawling branches of fig trees that line the main street. A stroll through Kuranda's small parks or along the river bank can be rewarded with the sight of a lizard or Freshwater Crocodile basking in the sun, a bandicoot or Southern Cassowary foraging for food, giant Ulysses Butterflies or beautiful kingfishers gracing the air, or even a Platypus, python, flying-fox or Common Green Tree-frog.

To glimpse rainforest life, gain an insight into Djabugay culture and discover the history of Kuranda from an Aboriginal perspective, **Djabugay Country Tours** (Rob Veivers Dr, Kuranda, Ph: 07 4093 9111 or 0408 746 054) offers an intimate experience of the local area.

Cairns Surrounds

Nature Tours

A choice of tours explore the natural environs. **Kuranda Riverboat and Rainforest Tours** (24 Coondoo St, Ph: 07 4093 7476 or 0412 159 212) takes wildlife cruises along the **Barron River**. Hire canoes from **Smiley's Adventure Hire** (River Esp, Ph: 0412 775 184). Specialist naturalist guides lead walks and safaris with **Wild Watch Australia** (Ph: 4097 7408 or 0429 438 064), **NatureTour Australia** (Kuranda, Ph: 07 4093 7287), **Mountain Night Wildlife Safari** (Black Mountain Rd, Ph: 07 4093 7287). Hummer and helicopter trips are available through **Kangaventure** (Ph: 07 4093 7418). Take a horse ride on the historic **Douglas Track (Carioca Lodge Equestrian Centre**, Ph: 07 4093 0314) or try **Australian ATV Tours** (131 Lake St, Ph: 0412 674 569) for "mild or wild" bush tours.

Kuranda walks A number of short walks, collectively known as the "Kuranda Rainforest Story", explore the Aboriginal and European history of the area. From the railway station, the River Walk, Jungle Walk and Jumrun Creek Walk form a circuit.

Things to See and Do

1. Soak up Kuranda's ambience while enjoying the market and café scene.
2. See Kuranda's natural environs on the Kuranda Rainforest Story walk.
3. Visit a wildlife park to see native animals. Enjoy Australian bird species at The Aviary (8 Thongon St, Ph: 07 4093 7411).
4. Learn about wildlife care at BATReach Wildlife Rescue and Rehab Centre (start of Jungle Walk, Ph: 07 4093 8858).
5. Explore the forest and lakes at Rainforestation Nature Park (Kennedy Hwy, Ph: 07 4085 5008).

Australian Butterfly Sanctuary

The flowering plants of the Wet Tropics World Heritage Area are home to 60% of Australia's 382 butterfly species. Thousands of other colourful insects light up the forest as they dance from flower to flower, pollinating and perpetuating these botanical arks.

The Australian Butterfly Sanctuary (8 Rob Veivers Dr, Ph: 07 4093 7575), the largest butterfly farm in Australia, houses over 1500 butterflies in a 3666 m, all-weather, free-flight aviary that simulates their natural habitat. Guided tours (30 min) are included in the entry price. Open daily, except Christmas Day, 9.45 a.m. – 4.00 p.m.

Clockwise from above: A tour guide explains the lives of these intriguing invertebrates; Female Cairns Birdwing; Female Cruiser.

Natural Worlds

Australia's largest collection of free-flying birds is found at **Birdworld Kuranda** (Rob Veivers Drive, Ph: 07 4093 9188), including the Pied Imperial Pigeon (*right*), and various exotics like the South American Macaw. Go to **Kuranda Koala Gardens** (Rob Veivers Dr, Ph: 07 4093 9953), to see Koalas (*far right*), Freshwater Crocodiles, wallabies, wombats and visit a walk-through snake-house. The **Australian Venom Zoo** (8 Coondoo St, Ph: 07 4093 8905), displays an amazing collection of spiders, centipedes and other Australian venomous creatures.

Cairns Surrounds

Heading South

Cairns extends south along the Bruce Highway to **Gordonvale** and **Babinda**. South of **Edmonton**, suburbs melt into cane fields. About 5 km south of Edmonton is the turn-off to the **Cairns Crocodile Farm** (only accessible via **Cairns Habitat Cruises**, Ph: 07 4031 4001), and **Yarrabah Aboriginal Community**, for many years only accessible by boat.

On the eastern side of **Trinity Inlet**, the **Murray Prior Range** forms a scenic backdrop to Cairns and Trinity Inlet. Partly national park and Aboriginal reserve, this is the traditional country of the Kunggandji people. Their traditional country also encompasses offshore reefs and islands (including **Green**, **Fitzroy** and part of the **Frankland Islands**). Founded as a mission by Rev Ernest Gribble on 17 June 1892, Yarrabah Aboriginal Community is now governed by its own Shire Council. **Menmuny Museum** (Back Beach Road, Yarrabah, Ph: 07 4056 9154) houses photographs of Yarrabah's early mission days and illustrates traditional Aboriginal lifestyle through displays of tools and weapons and dance performances. Visitors can walk along a boardwalk and identify plant species used for food, medicines, tools and implements, or study pottery, didgeridoos, baskets and other items crafted by local Aboriginal people using traditional techniques. The museum is open to the public (for opening times, costs and group bookings, Ph: 07 4056 9154). For further information about Yarrabah Aboriginal Community, contact the **Yarrabah Aboriginal Shire Council** (Ph: 07 4056 9120).

Above, top to bottom: **Gordonvale's main street; Ye Olde Gordonvale Pub** The historic buildings along Gordonvale's streets resonate with character and reflect the prosperous early years of this old sugar mill town. Gordonvale became a military base for US parachute units during World War II.

Gordonvale

A mere 23 km south of Cairns is **Gordonvale**, governed by the Mulgrave Shire Council until its amalgamation with Cairns City Council in 1995. Founded as a timber/gold/sugar town in the late 1890s, Gordonvale is a small country town set in a tropical location. Sitting at the base of the **Atherton Tableland**, within the traditional country of the Yidindji Aboriginal people, the surrounding area was the scene of "red gold" fever from 1878–80 ("red gold" being the area's highly prized cedar). Some 30 men cut over 1 million feet of cedar logs from the nearby **Mulgrave Valley** and **George Alley**, much of it finding its way to England from Cairns. The discovery of gold in 1879 in the Mulgrave Valley ensured an influx of prospectors, and the early teamsters forged tracks from Trinity Inlet through the rainforest to the **Tinaroo** tin fields. Early farmers tried various crops with mixed success until sugarcane farms were established. Replacing the earlier **Pyramid Mill**, the **Mulgrave Central Mill** (1896) has survived cyclones and fluctuating sugar prices, standing as testimony to the endurance of the cane industry in the region. In the crushing season, cane trains rumble and creak their way to the mill.

The town prospered during the 1910s and 1920s, and many commercial buildings, houses and community facilities date from this period,

Cane Toad World

The Cane Toad, introduced into Queensland in June 1935 in an attempt to control the scourge of Cane Beetles, is infamous for the ecological havoc it has wrought all over northern and eastern Australia.

A native of Central and South America, it has few natural predators in Australia as its fast-acting poison renders it deadly to all but the hardiest native snakes, birds and mammals. This, combined with its prolific breeding, has let it spread across Queensland, northern New South Wales and the Northern Territory, causing the extinction or near extinction of many species of frog-eating natives. Gordonvale has the dubious honour of being the town where the Cane Toad was first released. In Norman Park a curious mural and sculpture-cum-playground commemorates this infamous amphibian.

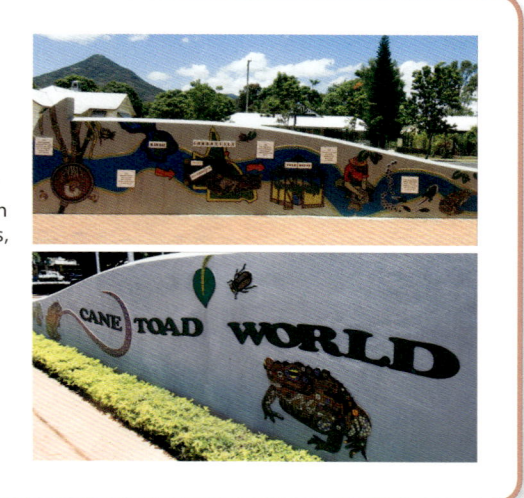

Cairns Surrounds

exemplifying "Old Queenslander" architecture. Some line Norman Street, also the site of the **Heritage Walk Way** — colourful pavement mosaics that portray the town's history and way of life. **St Michael's Catholic Church** (Mill Street), built in the 1930s in Romanesque style, replaced the 1922 original.

Norman Park has large shady trees, a playground, tennis court, sculptures, monuments and memorials. Previously used as the Native Mounted Police's horse paddock, the park was then the site of parachute-packing sheds in World War II. Prominent at the Norman Street entrance to the park is the **Cane Farmer Statue and Drinking Fountain** and the **Sugar Industry Mosaic**, memorials to those who have toiled in the cane fields. The **Mulgrave Settlers Museum** (Gordon St, Ph: 07 4056 1810 for entry fee), established in 1992, traces the area's history and displays a collection of artefacts. The museum is open from 10 a.m. – 2 p.m., Monday to Saturday (after hours by appointment). The public picnic ground at the **Mulgrave River** is popular for swimming and picnicking, but facilities are limited.

Walshs Pyramid

At 922 m, **Walshs Pyramid**, affectionately dubbed "The Pyramid" by locals, is the highest free-standing peak in the world. Part of Yidindji country, its traditional name is *Bunda Djarragun*, meaning the nest of *Djarruga* — the scrubfowl. This conical granite hill is believed to be a volcanic core. Covered with dry eucalypt forest, it is part of the Wet Tropics World Heritage Area. Accessed via a sign-posted track on the Bruce Highway 800 m south of the Mulgrave River crossing, The Pyramid has no facilities except a walking track suitable only for fit and experienced bushwalkers. The steep and arduous trail (1 km one way) leads to the summit and a 360° view of the surrounding rainforest, hills, agricultural plains and settlements. The best time to climb it is from April to June — it is cooler and there is no smoke from cane-burning to obscure the outstanding views.

Each August **Gordonvale** hosts the **Great Pyramid Race and Country Fair**. According to local legend, the race began as a challenge between two cane farmers who wanted to settle a dispute; it generated so much interest that bets were taken by the local bookmaker. The first official race was held in 1959 as part of Queensland's Centenary Celebrations. Since then it has become nationally and internationally recognised. It now attracts some of the world's finest athletes and hundreds of visitors and locals. The record for the 12 km run from Gordonvale and back is 76 minutes. The fair accompanying the race is an extravaganza — featuring the **Magical Mystical Pyramid Ball**, live music, cultural performances, street entertainment, demonstrations and fireworks. For further information, contact the **Great Pyramid Race and Country Fair Association Inc** (Ph: 0438 710 954 or 07 4056 6106).

Walshs Pyramid from Gordonvale Only a few kilometres from Gordonvale, The Pyramid dominates the landscape. Each August or September the township hosts "The Great Pyramid Race", a 12 km run from Gordonvale to the summit and back. The event attracts many of the world's best runners, as well as local runners and walkers.

Goldsborough Valley

Approximately 6 km west of Gordonvale, along the Gillies Highway, a partially sealed 15 km road (unsuitable for caravans) leads to the **Goldsborough Valley**. Traditional Aboriginal life was interrupted by gold and cedar fever in the 1870s and 1880s. The valley's forest is punctuated with allotments and a small residential development. The swimming hole at **Ross and Locke Reserve** in the **Mulgrave River** is a popular destination. At the road's end is the **Goldsborough Valley State Forest** (QPWS, 5B Sheridan St, Cairns, Ph: 07 4046 6600, or QPWS on site management, Ph: 07 4056 2597). Swimming in the Mulgrave River, canoeing and bushwalking are popular activities. The **Goldfield Trail** crosses 19 km of rainforest to link the valley camping ground with the **Babinda Boulders**. Formed by 1930s prospectors, the track crosses the saddle between Queensland's highest peaks, **Mt Bartle Frere** (1622 m) and **Mt Bellenden Ker** (1592 m). Signs on **Kearneys Falls Track** (870 m) explain the traditional lifestyle of the valley's Yidindji custodians. Camping permits ($4 pp) are available from a self-registration booth or by advance booking (Ph: 131 304).

Above, top and bottom: Goldsborough Valley Expansive camping, picnicking and barbecue facilities in the shade on the banks of the Mulgrave River make Goldsborough Valley State Forest a truly beautiful place for a sojourn into the tropical rainforest.

Reef and Islands

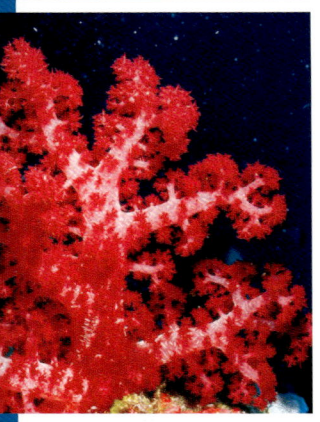

Visible from the moon with the naked eye, the Great Barrier Reef is the largest collection of coral reefs in the world. Stretching more than 2000 km along Queensland's coast, from Fraser Island to the tip of Cape York Peninsula, and covering 35 million ha, the Great Barrier Reef comprises almost 3000 individual reefs and 1000 islands. With more than 1500 species of fish, 4000 species of mollusc, 400 species of sponge and 350 species of hard coral, and new species still being discovered, this World Heritage Area is the most biodiverse ecosystem on the planet.

Masked Bannerfish

Unsurpassed Beauty

Each reef is really a thin layer of tiny coral polyps living in colonies atop fortresses of coralline limestone exoskeletons that are cemented together with sponges and other organisms. Zooxanthellae, microscopic plants living inside the polyps' tissues, convert energy from the sun into food for the polyps, augmenting their capacity to form limestone. These hard corals grow in a stunning variety of shapes reminiscent of baskets, brains, mushrooms, plates, staghorns and tables. Growing among them are dramatically coloured soft corals, which do not secrete limestone exoskeletons. Soft corals also form oddly shaped colonies — some cup-like, others tree-like, yet others lobed and leathery.

The resulting reefs are complex coral wonderlands where many other organisms find food, hide from predators and reproduce — the reef literally teems with life. Many reef creatures are brightly coloured and have bizarre body shapes, lifestyles and habits, making the Great Barrier Reef a fascinating expression of the creativity of life.

Reef Bounty

Above the reef waters soar waterbirds that nest on islands, cays and atolls. The reef also supports six species of sea turtle and approximately 30 species of marine mammal, including dolphins, Dugongs and whales. Aboriginal and Torres Strait Islander people have harvested the bounty of the reef and its islands for many thousands of years and many of its islands and surrounding seas are culturally significant sites.

Underwater World

The Great Barrier Reef inspires awe and wonder. This is a place to return to time and time again — a place to forget everyday life by plunging into the depths of a different world.

Cairns, the main northern gateway to the reef, offers a range of island and reef adventures, from sailing trips to helicopter and float-plane flights. Visitors can watch this watery wonderland from an underwater observatory, snorkel in tranquil lagoons or dive in its clear depths.

Trained tour operators help interpret the experience, yet the fullest introduction to reef dynamics is given by Reef Teach (14 Spence St, Ph: 07 4031 7794). For those seeking a deeper understanding of the reef, these seminars are a must.

Top to bottom: **Longfin Bannerfish; Soft coral; Sea star; Longnosed Butterflyfish.**

Reef and Islands

Reef and Islands

Island Paradise

On Green Island, the closest island to Cairns, visitors do as little or as much as they please, focusing on relaxing, soaking up the sun and absorbing the wonder of the Great Barrier Reef. The beaches and resort facilities are perfect for relaxing, while Green Island's dense tropical vegetation, extensive coral reef platform and surrounding lagoon give active visitors plenty to explore.

Golden sand, clear water, tropical forest and blue skies define idyllic Green Island.

Guided reef walks reveal the island's coral ecosystems.

Within easy reach of Cairns, Green Island is a popular offshore playground.

Enjoying the crystalline water of Green Island's beaches.

Green Island

Green Island is a small, forested coral cay, approximately 12 ha in area and sitting on a 710 ha platform reef. The island is made of sand and coral debris that has broken from the nearby reef and been deposited where water slowed as it swirled over the reef crest. The teardrop-shaped cay emerged above the high-tide level sometime in the last 6000 years and was colonised by plant life as seeds and nutrients were deposited by birds, wind and waves slowly over time. Initially covered in grasses and shrubs, the vegetation developed into a closed vine forest, complete with a 25 m high canopy, which has regrown since being cleared in the late 1800s.

Some 35 species of sea bird and 28 species of woodland bird reside around the island. Ospreys, sea eagles, egrets and terns fly over the reef and lagoon, while Emerald Doves, Rose-crowned Fruit-Doves, White-breasted Woodswallows, Silvereyes and Pheasant Coucals feed in the forest. In summer, Pied Imperial-Pigeons roost on the island, which is also visited by Beach Stone-curlews. Skinks and geckoes occupy the undergrowth, butterflies flit from flower to flower and a colony of Spectacled Flying-foxes roosts in the canopy.

Reef life is rich and diverse in the sheltered lagoon, with hard corals (such as staghorn and plate corals) interspersed among soft corals and giant clams in magnificent coral gardens. A myriad of colourful fish and invertebrates inhabit this coral wonderland, forming a complex web of life. Sea cucumbers, sea urchins and sea stars feed along the sea floor, anemonefish seek shelter in between the stinging tentacles of sea anemones, triggerfish use their strong jaws to munch on algae and invertebrates on the sea bed, and brightly coloured parrotfish, named for their strong, beak-like, fused teeth (used to graze on corals), drift past. Giant Trevally are often seen under the jetty preying on smaller fish, while Manta Rays, gentle behemoths of the marine world, feed on small fish and plankton, using their huge fins to "fly" gracefully through the water. Sea turtles and Dugongs graze on seagrass meadows on the island's north-east.

Both the coral cay and its surrounding reef are part of the sea country of the Kunggandji Aboriginal people, and mark places of special cultural significance.

Green Island, a mere 27 km north-east of Cairns, is an emerald jewel set in the turquoise Coral Sea.

Green Island The beach overlooking the jetty and boats is a popular place to laze in the sun.

Reef and Islands

Snorkelling on Green Island

The wonders of the Great Barrier Reef's amazing underwater world are easily accessible to snorkellers in Green Island's lagoon. Fascinating sea creatures of differing shapes, sizes, colours and lifestyles, carry on their normal lives right before visitors' eyes.

Although they can be viewed from a glass-bottomed or semi-submersible boat, or from the underwater observatory, it is more enthralling to be part of these creatures' marine environment by snorkelling *(below)*. Be warned that snorkelling can become addictive! In the sheltered lagoon, Oblique-banded Sweetlips *(right)* and many smaller fish can be seen flitting among the corals.

Exploring the Island

Departing from the **Reef Fleet Terminal** (1 Spence St), commercial operators offer half- and full-day trips to the island with snorkelling, scuba and helmet diving, glass-bottom boat and semi-submersible boat tours (**Big Cat Green Island Reef Cruises**, Ph: 07 4051 0444; **Great Adventures**, Ph: 07 4044 9944). Alternatively, visitors can fly to Green Island (**Cairns Heli-Scenic**, City Heliport, Pier Marketplace, Ph: 07 4031 5999; **Helitours**, Ph: 1300 733 274).

Around the island, there is much to explore, from the lagoon to the shores. The **Island Circuit Walk** (2 km) circumnavigates the island through closed vine forest, then moves onto the southern shores near the reef flats. **Green Island Resort** (Ph: 07 4031 3300) promotes guided walks with naturalists.

For day visitors, the resort has the **Underwater Observatory** and watersports equipment for hire. At **Marineland Melanesia Crocodile Habitat**, there are a collection of artefacts from the Coral Sea, reef-life exhibits and crocodile presentations. Parasailing, scenic seaplane and helicopter flights are available at the resort along with luxury accommodation and dining facilities.

Green Island's forests and reefs are protected within the national park, part of the **Great Barrier Reef World Heritage Area**, so its natural cycles of season and tide remain intact.

A tourist history Named by Lieutenant James Cook in 1770, after HM Bark *Endeavour's* astronomer, Charles Green, Green Island was used as a base by bêche-de-mer fishermen in the mid 1800s. During the 1920s, tour operators began regular services to Green Island and it has been a popular destination for daytrippers ever since. A hotel was built in the 1940s to cater for overnight visitors. Development continued with the world's first underwater observatory (installed in 1954), the Marineland Melanesia (built in 1972) and Green Island's current resort (built during the 1990s). Each year, Green Island receives many thousands of visitors who come to explore the wonders of its environment.

Reef and Islands

Vital Rookeries

Michaelmas Cay is the most important sea bird breeding site in the Cairns region, and one of the Great Barrier Reef's seven most important rookeries. Thousands of birds (of sixteen different species) visit the island every year, with up to nine species breeding there. In order to protect the colonies, access to the island is strictly limited, making a visit to this area a very special privilege.

The Masked Booby feeds over the deep ocean, beyond the continental shelf.

A Roseate Tern hovers over its nest of coral and rubble.

The Brown Booby often flies low over the waves, alone or in flocks.

Pied Oystercatchers scamper along the tideline in search of marine invertebrates.

Michaelmas Cay and Upolu Cay

Beyond **Green Island**, some 40 km north-east of Cairns, lies **Michaelmas Cay** on **Michaelmas Reef**. This sand island is a national park within the **Great Barrier Reef Marine Park**. Covered in grass and low vegetation, it makes an ideal habitat for ground-nesting sea birds. More than 20,000 Sooty Terns and 8000 Common Noddies nest here each year. Crested and Lesser Crested Terns also nest in large numbers — this is the only rookery in Queensland where Sooty and Crested Terns breed side by side in large numbers.

Humans walking through the rookery will panic the birds into flight, exposing eggs and chicks to predators such as Silver Gulls and Ruddy Turnpikes; access, therefore, is restricted. During breeding season, up to 50 visitors at a time may go on the beach between 9 a.m. and 3 p.m. Alternatively, activity in the rookeries can easily be observed via boat with binoculars.

Visiting the Cays

The waters of **Michaelmas Reef** are rich with corals, fish and giant clams. Nearby **Upolu Cay** is also popular with nature lovers. Upolu is named after a schooner that struck the reef on Easter Sunday, 25 April 1886, prompting its crew to seek safety in their lifeboat.

Upolu Cay Reef has important fish-spawning aggregation sites and is monitored by the Australian Institute of Marine Science every three years. Both the reefs and cays lie within the traditional sea country of the Kunggandji people.

Several Cairns-based tour operators visit these national parks. **Ocean Spirit Cruises** (140 Mulgrave Rd, Ph: 07 4031 2920), **Passions of Paradise** (Reef Fleet Terminal, Ph: 07 4050 0676) and **Seastar Cruises** (Finger D, Pier Marina, Ph: 07 4041 6218) day tour to Michaelmas Cay and Reef. Ocean Spirit Cruises, **Ecstasea** (Finger E, Pier Marina, Ph: 07 4041 3055) and **Falla Silver Sail Cruises** (Finger D, Pier Marina, Ph: 07 4041 2001) sail to Upolu Cay, where visitors can snorkel and dive in its pristine coral gardens.

Diving off the beach at Upolu Cay Nearby Oyster Reef shelters an abundance of sea life.

Michaelmas Cay's sandy beach is the interface between the coral underworld and the sea bird rookeries.

Commercial operators offer different ways to see and experience the reef. Most operators design tours that are flexible with people's different comfort zones.

Reef and Islands

Sea Turtles

Six of the world's seven species of marine turtle live on the reef. Four of them, the Green, Loggerhead, Flatback and Hawksbill Turtle, breed in its waters and nest on secluded beaches along the tropical coast.

Having travelled far to mate, females come ashore at night at fortnightly intervals (Nov–Feb) to nest and lay several successive clutches of eggs before returning to their distant feeding grounds. Dragging themselves high up the beach, usually into dune vegetation, the females dig egg chambers in the sand to lay their leathery, "ping-pong ball" eggs. They cover these with sand and then return to the sea.

Two or three months later (Jan–Apr), masses of turtle hatchlings dig their way out of the sand and instinctively scramble towards the ocean, dodging land predators (like Silver Gulls) and then reef fish. Only a few ever cross the reef to the deep water of the open ocean.

Once there, they spend the early years of their long lives feeding on plankton before returning to the reef's rich feeding grounds. They reach sexual maturity at 30–50 years of age. Protected marine environments are essential to sea turtles' survival.

Female turtles return to the sea after nesting.

Green Turtles are listed as a vulnerable species.

Eggs being laid into the incubation chamber.

A Green Turtle hatchling runs the dangerous gauntlet to the sea.

A female Loggerhead Turtle cries "tears" of salt.

Sea Snakes

Banded Sea Krait

Living in the reef's warm waters are about 15 species of sea snake and sea krait. Their modified nasal passages, enlarged lungs, salt excretion glands and flattened tails are remarkably well-adapted for aquatic life. Giving birth to live young at sea, sea snakes do not need to come ashore; however, sea kraits regularly do so to rest, digest their food and lay their eggs.

Like many land snakes, most sea snakes and kraits have hollow fangs to inject venom, rapidly paralysing prey. Their venom is more deadly than that of the most dangerous land snakes, but they pose little threat to humans. The Olive Sea Snake (*bottom left*) is the most common and may swim up to divers; however, they are reluctant to strike unless provoked.

Olive Sea Snakes forage for prey in reef crevices.

Unlike sea snakes, sea kraits are adept on land.

45

Reef and Islands

Fitzroy Island National Park

Fitzroy Island, the closest continental island to Cairns, is actually a high coastal mountain range that, with its cargo of plant and animal life intact, was cut off from the mainland by a rise in sea level some 8000 years ago. **Little Fitzroy Island**, to the north, was formed at the same time. The islands' landscapes are rugged with spectacular granite outcrops breaking through the vegetation. With open eucalypt woodland interspersed among lush tropical rainforest and mangroves, this 339 ha national park protects a diversity of flora and fauna.

Named by Lieutenant James Cook in 1770, Fitzroy Island was used as a quarantine station in the 1930s for leprosy sufferers and later as part of **Yarrabah Aboriginal Reserve**. Little Fitzroy Island was the site of the islands' first lighthouse, a carbide gaslight established in 1923. Twenty years later, a lighthouse was built on the ridge near the lighthouse keeper's residence on Fitzroy Island. In 1970 the lighthouse that currently houses the visitor centre was constructed — Australia's last purpose-built, staffed lighthouse. With technological advances, Little Fitzroy Island was again chosen as the site for the modern automated lighthouse.

Together with their fringing reefs, Fitzroy Island and Little Fitzroy Island, traditionally used and cared for by the Kunggandji people, are part of the **Great Barrier Reef World Heritage Area**.

Fitzroy Island jetty Palm trees, white sand and crystalline water greet visitors as they arrive. The resort lies secluded in the grove of coconut palms behind the beach.

Fitzroy Island and Little Fitzroy Island from the air. Over the past 80 years, both islands have been the site of different lighthouses. The current lighthouse is just visible on the ridge of Fitzroy Island overlooking Little Fitzroy.

The life aquatic Many people visit Fitzroy Island to snorkel on its fringing reefs, where the clear waters teem with spectacular tropical marine life.

Outstanding Attractions

Only 29 km to the south-east of Cairns, **Fitzroy Island** is the city's most accessible continental island and a popular place to enjoy walks and explore the marine life of the fringing reefs just off the beach. A series of tracks traverse the island, providing many opportunities for birdwatching.

The **Secret Garden Walk** (1 km return) is especially picturesque as it passes through complex rainforest; interpretive signs impart helpful information. Those wanting a longer walk can take the **Summit Trail** (3.6 km return, past the ruins of the wartime lighthouse), walk to the lighthouse along **Lighthouse Road** (3.6 km return) or visit both on the **Circuit Walk** (8.5 km). The summit offers spectacular 360° views. **Nudey Beach** (1.2 km return) is another favourite destination.

With over 750 varieties of coral and fish, Fitzroy Island's fringing reefs are a popular snorkelling and diving destination. Colourful fish, hard and soft corals, Giant Clams, crayfish, sea stars, sea turtles and sharks are regularly seen — Manta Rays and Humpback Whales visit the area between June and September. Kayaking around the island is another popular activity; kayaks, catamarans and other water sports equipment are available for hire (**Fitzroy Island Resort**, Ph: 07 4051 9588). For those wanting a more leisurely visit, there are beaches and a resort pool for lazing and relaxing. Fitzroy Island's close proximity to Cairns means private boat-owners often visit the island.

Reef and Islands

Nudey Beach Azure waters, blinding white sand and dense forest make this a paradise for yachties and sun-worshippers alike.

Tours

Departing from the **Reef Fleet Terminal** (1 Spence St, Cairns), **Fitzroy Island Reef Cruises** provides full- and half-day cruises to **Fitzroy Island**, with glass-bottom boat coral viewing and snorkelling, and island transfers for guests of **Fitzroy Island Resort**. **Raging Thunder** (Ph: 07 4030 7900) hosts full-day sea kayaking adventures that visit secluded beaches on Fitzroy and **Little Fitzroy** Islands, which are accessible only by kayak. **Fitzroy Island Dive** (Ph: 07 4051 9588) offers certified dives and provides instruction for novices who want to learn to dive in the waters and around the complex fringing reefs of this beautiful island environment. Raging Thunder's **Thunderbolt Cruise** combines the best of both worlds, with combined Fitzroy Island and outer reef day tours. Further information is available from **Fitzroy Island HQ** (Shields St, Cairns, Ph: 07 4030 7097).

Things to See and Do

1. Relax in the tropical ambience.
2. Enjoy a walk on the beach or marked trail.
3. Snorkel at Welcome or Sharkfin Bay, Nudey Beach or the Playground.
4. Sail in style around the island.
5. Scuba dive on the fringing reefs.
6. Hire a sea kayak.
7. For further information contact QPWS Cairns 5B Sheridan St (Ph: 07 4046 6600).

Island Wildlife

Fitzroy Island's plant communities support innumerable wildlife species. Ulysses Butterflies (*below*) are commonly seen. Quiet walkers may observe Emerald Doves and Orange-footed Scrubfowl on the forest floor. Sulphur-crested Cockatoos cry noisily and Osprey and White-bellied Sea-Eagles (*right*) nest around the islands.

Seasonal migrants, Buff-breasted Paradise-Kingfishers nest in termite mounds and Pied Imperial-Pigeons nest in the treetops, feeding in mainland rainforest. Several gecko and skink species live in the forests, sunning on granite outcrops during the day.

Reef and Islands

Deciding on a Reef Charter

A few guidelines to help find a tour that suits you:
1. How many people will be on the boat/reef with you?
2. What activities are you comfortable with? Does the tour provide equipment?
3. How many hours will you spend on the reef?
4. Are there marine biologists on board?
5. Is the boat comfortable?
6. What type of boat is it?

Divers will most likely choose according to:
1. Group size.
2. Dive locations.
3. Number of dives.
4. Boat style and comfort.
5. Equipment and insurance provided.
6. The company's experience and qualifications.

Further information: www.divingcairns.com

Diving opens up a whole world of wonders, possibilities and challenges.

A diver lines up a Common Lionfish. The reef provides a dazzling palette for the art of underwater photography.

Diving the Outer Reef

The **Great Barrier Reef** boasts some of the world's best dive locations. The reef's maze of possible sites includes platform reefs, lagoons, channels and "ribbon reefs", the long narrow breakwaters on the continental shelf. The northern reef is up to 80 km wide and is only 30–60 km offshore.

Dive Charters from Cairns

A flotilla of charter vessels departs the **Reef Fleet Terminal** each morning. Snorkelling, introductory and certified dives are all on offer and many companies have reef pontoons, viewing areas and glass-bottomed boats. Marine biologists host seminars and help identify fish and coral. Sailing tour operators include **Ecstasea** (112 Hervey Rd, Redlynch, Ph: 07 4041 3055), **New Horizon Sail & Dive Adventures** (Ph: 07 4055 6130), **Ocean Free** (Reef Fleet Terminal, Ph: 07 4053 5888) and **Passions of Paradise** (Reef Fleet Terminal, Ph: 1800 111 346). Other operators include **Cairns Dive Centre** (121 Abbott St, Ph: 07 4051 0294 or 1800 642 591), **Compass Cruises** (100 Abbott St, Ph: 07 4051 5777), **Deep Sea Divers Den** (319 Draper St, Ph: 07 4046 7333), **Down Under Cruise & Dive** (287 Draper St, Ph: 07 4052 8300 or 1800 079 099), **Great Adventures** (Reef Fleet Terminal, Ph: 07 4044 9944 or 1800 079 080), **Quicksilver Cruises** (Reef Fleet Terminal, Ph: 07 4087 2100), **Reef Magic Cruises** (Reef Fleet Terminal, Ph: 1300 666 700), **Seastar** (Pier E14, Marlin Marina, Ph: 07 4041 6218), **Sunlover Reef Cruises** (Ph: 07 4050 1333) and **Tusa Dive** (Cnr Shields St & the Esplanade, Ph: 07 4040 6464).

Some operators also allow for live-aboard trips, complete with night dives. Countless fish and invertebrate species (from giant Humphead Maori Wrasse to eye-catching flatworms) are seen on wall dives, drift dives, canyons and swim-throughs. June and July bring the chance to swim with Minke Whales. Contact **Explorer Ventures** (206 Draper St, Ph: 07 4031 5566), **Mike Ball Dive Expeditions** (143 Lake St, Ph: 07 4053 0500), **Pro Dive** (116 Spence St, Ph: 1800 353 213), **Reef Encounter** (100 Abbott St, Ph: 07 4051 5777 or 1800 815 811), **Spirit of Freedom** (C/- Tusa Dive Shop, Cnr the Esplanade & Shields St, Ph: 07 4047 9150), **Taka Dive Adventures** (131 Lake St, Ph: 07 4051 8722), **Vagabond** (D Finger 16, Marlin Marina, Ph: 07 4051 8722), or those listed above.

With **Undersea Explorer** (3 Dixie St, Port Douglas, Ph: 07 4099 5911) and **Reefwatch Air Tours** (Captain Cook Hwy, Ph: 07 4035 9808) visitors can contribute to research and surveillance of this magnificent ecosystem.

All levels of diving experience are catered for on the Great Barrier Reef.

A scuba diver explores a coral bommie This one houses a family of Pink Anemonefish.

Reef and Islands

The Scuba Diving Experience

Scuba diving can be strange and disconcerting at first; however, once new divers become comfortable with their scuba gear and relax into the weightless underwater environment, the sensation is fantastic. A myriad of sea creatures, not evident from the surface, cohabit this incredible world.

During the day, in good visibility, divers see 15–20 m. As light passes through sea water, wavelengths are absorbed selectively, meaning that with increasing depth the colours progressively lose their vibrancy — first red, then orange, yellow, green and, lastly, blue. Near the surface, fish and corals come in every hue. Magnificent examples live along steep-walled reef edges. Deeper down, sea anemones, feather stars and soft corals, like gorgonian fans, dwell enveloped in the cobalt water, and Coral Cod and lionfish lurk in camouflage. Deeper still, other carnivores patrol caves beneath ledges, waiting for darkness.

Night reveals a different side of the reef. Coral polyps filter food through their extended tentacles, and crayfish, moray eels, sharks and predatory fish emerge on feeding forays.

Diving on the reef can become addictive — every dive is different. Diving during coral spawning (mid to late November) is awe-inspiring.

Visit the famous "Cod Hole" among the Ribbon Reefs off Lizard Island on one of several dive charters. Here it is possible to get up-close-and-personal with curious, charismatic (and extremely imposing) Potato Cod.

Capturing the moment The desire to record underwater experiences prompts many divers to take up photography. Although a photo's two-dimensional instant can never replace reality, it can nonetheless feed our memories and inspire our imaginations.

Documenting the Depths

The underwater world presents new challenges for avid photographers and a wealth of complex equipment is available. Particularly important is a good flash. An electronic flash gives accurate colour and sharp focus for brightly coloured fish and coral.

The best results are obtained by using the flash as a fill-in (using the camera's automatic flash settings so that the flash balances natural light and softens the contrast between light and shadow), or by using two flashes. At night, artificial lighting is imperative; a large range of equipment is available to divers.

Lenses are also extremely important. Micro lenses allow fine details of colour and texture to be captured and are necessary for successful close-up photography of fish, coral and other marine life. Macro lenses are perfect for larger subjects. Wide-angle lenses give the best results when photographing larger fish, fish in schools or underwater scenes.

Regardless of the equipment, the best results are obtained by photographers who are confident divers and who have taken the time to familiarise themselves with the behaviour of fish and invertebrates.

Twin strobes being used to photograph colourful soft corals.

When photographing dangerous fish or invertebrates (such as this Common Lionfish) an extendable light is useful for keeping distance.

Reef and Islands

Fish Watching

Teeming with life, each hectare of coral on the Great Barrier Reef provides food and habitat for more than 200 fish species. Ranging in size from tiny gobies about 10 mm long to enormous sharks and rays, reef fish are generally brightly coloured with bold patterns, and many have bizarre body shapes or appendages. Not only are they awe-inspiring in their number, beauty and diversity, but their intriguing lifestyles, habits and interactions make them fascinating to observe.

Taking refuge among the coral labyrinths are the smaller species and juveniles, often seen in schools. Many medium-sized fish feed around the reef or lurk under coral ledges. The sea floor is home to countless fish from the tiniest blennies to large stingrays and wobbegongs. Other fish prefer the reef flats and slopes, while others swim in the deeper waters between reefs. Large predators, such as sharks, often patrol the reef edges. Many fish are territorial and defend their territory aggressively.

Survival strategies are many and varied and colouration plays a number of important roles. Apart from advertising gender, colour and pattern are used as warning and camouflage tactics — from false eye-spots on dorsal fins and strong patterns disguising body outline to flashy colours that advertise toxicity. With so many fish exhibiting so many ingenious adaptations to the reef environment, it is little wonder many divers become addicted to fish watching.

Observing Relationships

The reef is full of fascinating relationships between different animals, all of which provide constant amusement and astonishment for divers. Although most fish find the stinging cells of sea anemones lethal, anemonefish are commonly seen swimming among their tentacles and using them for protection. In a symbiotic arrangement, the anemonefish lures other small fish into the anemone's tentacles and feeds on the scraps from the anemone's meals. Anemonefish also eat growths on anemones' skin and guard their hosts from potential predators such as butterflyfish.

Similarly, many fish live among the branches of corals, taking protection from their stinging cells. Tiny Seawhip Gobies use the Seawhip Coral as a ladder, enabling them to leave the sea floor and find food with a degree of safety. Of the many gobies that live in burrows in the sea floor, a variety of shrimp gobies share their burrows with alpheid shrimps, which build and maintain the burrows while the gobies acts as sentinels. Other fish ensure their safety by mimicking poisonous fish.

Top and bottom: From a young age, anemonefish coat themselves with mucus from anemone tentacles. In time, the anemone is unable to distinguish the fish from itself.

One of the reef's covert operatives, a Trumpetfish, loiters alongside Moses Perch, awaiting the right moment to launch itself at any unsuspecting prey.

Common Cleanerfish (*above*) are small wrasse whose invaluable service to the reef community guarantees their safety from predators such as Coral Trout (*above*). Groups of Common Cleanerfish establish recognised "cleaning stations" where large fish regularly queue to have parasites and fungi removed from their scales, gills, mouths and throats. In this way, cleanerfish (and certain species of shrimp) play an extremely important role in maintaining the health of the reef ecosystem.

The Blacksaddle Filefish (*right*) is a harmless species whose colouration and patterning is nearly identical to that of the poisonous Blacksaddle Toby (*left*) beside it.

Reef and Islands

Deceptive Blends

Many reef fish change colour and pattern to match their surroundings by expanding or contracting the pigment cells beneath their transparent scales. This is a particularly helpful camouflage tactic for smaller fish. Displaying bright colours during the day, they fade and tuck themselves into the reef's crevices to sleep at night, thus ensuring their safety from sharks and other nocturnal predators.

Other fish undergo colour changes with "mood". When nesting, Coral Trout change colour, advertising their intention to spawn. Cleanerfish induce colour changes in Coral Cods when they rub their ventral fins over the larger fish's body, lulling them into a relaxed state. Male Moon Wrasses turn blue before displaying aggression, and Trumpetfish employ colour changes to camouflage themselves while hunting smaller fish.

Some other species change colour as they mature. Emperor Angelfish undergo startling colour and pattern changes between juvenile and adult stages. Parrotfish and Blotched Fairy Basslets change colour after changing sex.

Feeding Behaviour

Although some reef fish eat plankton, unicellular floating plants and animals, or the algae that grows on the reef and inside coral, most are carnivorous, using thousands of tactics to catch their prey.

Damselfish and fairy basslets pick copepods from the zooplankton in the water one by one; some butterflyfish snip polyps from the corals using specialised snouts and teeth; goatfish probe reef crevices in search of small fish and crustaceans. Trumpetfish, masters of disguise, dart down from above to suck victims up through their tubular snouts, or lurk alongside larger fish, launching ambushes when close enough. Lionfish (*below left*) use the vanes of their spectacular fins to "herd" shrimps to their demise. Larger predatory fish either lie in wait or pursue prey through the water. Predators and prey often school, either as a mode of offence or defence. Barracuda and trevally species feed in numbers. Conversely, the fry of many prey species mass together for safety. Moray eels forage for molluscs, crabs and fish, while sharks use stealth and blistering speed to catch their prey.

Dangerous Fish

Divers need to recognise the few fish whose survival tactics pose a threat to human safety.

The most venomous fish in the world is the stonefish. It ambushes small fish and shrimps by lying on the sea bed, camouflaged as an encrusted rock and waiting. Passing prey is swallowed with lightning speed. Vulnerable to attack by bottom-feeding sharks and rays, stonefish have a row of 13 venomous spines along their backs as their primary defense. Downward pressure on these spines releases venom into the offending animal. In humans, the result is excruciating pain, temporary paralysis and, occasionally, death.

Several other fish use venomous spines as protection against predators; however, they are more mobile and prefer to evade threats. These include lionfish and catfish. Stingrays defend themselves by lashing out with barbed, whip-like tails. The stings of all these animals are extremely painful and can lead to unconsciousness, even death. Although not normally aggressive unless provoked, moray eels have been known to bite divers. Hand-feeding has led to aggression from large reef fish such as the Potato Cod and Queensland Groper.

Pufferfish (*above*), which inflate when provoked, contain a deadly toxin. They and their relatives, porcupinefish, cowfish, boxfish, tobies and sunfish, should never be eaten.

Top and bottom: Black-tipped Fusiliers are brightly coloured during the day but less conspicuous at night. These mid-water plankton feeders live in schools.

Parrotfish scrape algae from coral and, in the process, ingest a lot of coral that is ground up and discarded in regular clouds of sand-like faeces.

Top and bottom: Wear thick-soled shoes in tidal waters and tread carefully to avoid extremely toxic, well-camouflaged Reef Stonefish. Also be careful overturning any rocks.

Black-tip Reef Sharks sometimes cruise the reef edge. Although they may be curious, they are generally timid and rarely attack. Divers should treat all sharks with caution.

51

Reef and Islands

What Fish Is That?

With the sheer number of fish on the reef, it can be overwhelming trying to identify and learn about them. However, a few tips help to identify groups of distinctive fish according to their body shapes and habits. Damselfish are small and stocky with a "typical" fish shape. They hover in large schools above the reef feeding on plankton. Wrasse and parrotfish are cigar-shaped and their tails are an extension of the body; they appear to "fly" through the water. Angelfish are disc-shaped with spines on their gills, usually brightly coloured and patterned. Butterflyfish and batfish are disc-shaped, striped over the eyes, and lack a gill-spine. Boxfish (*left*) derive their name from their angular frames and tough, armoured skin. Triggerfish are bottle-shaped and slightly flattened. They swim with their bodies rigid, using their rear fins rather than their tails. Reef charters generally carry identification charts and reference books for divers. Remembering and researching just two new species each dive is one way to familiarise yourself with fish species.

Stripey Snapper *Lutjanus carponotatus* **(Grows to 40 cm)** During the day these fish form tightly packed "resting" schools, which are always found in the same location.

Chinamanfish *Symphorus nematophorus* **(Grows to 80 cm)** Large specimens have been implicated in cases of ciguatera poisoning. Young fish lose their distinctive "plumage" as adults.

Moorish Idol *Zanclus cornutus* **(Grows to 22 cm)** The greatly elongated and whip-like dorsal fin distinguishes this species, which is a popular aquarium fish.

Red Emperor *Lutjanus sebae* **(Grows to 1.2 m)** The striking bands on juvenile Red Emperor gradually fade as these fish grow into adults and adopt a more uniform red colour.

Emperor Angelfish *Pomacanthus imperator* **(Grows to 38 cm)** One of the most beautiful fishes on the Great Barrier Reef, the Emperor Angelfish is notoriously difficult to rear in aquariums.

Bluethroat Wrasse *Notolabrus tetricus* **(Grows to 60 cm)** Adults of this species are usually encountered on rocky reefs at depths of around 40 m. They are often erroneously called "parrotfish".

Moses Perch *Lutjanus russelli* **(Grows to 50 cm)** Also called "Fingermark Bream" because of the distinct "fingerprint" located toward the back of the body.

Spotted Sweetlip *Plectorhinchus chaetodonoides* **(Grows to 70 cm)** Using mimickry as a defence, young spotted sweetlips are bright orange and look and swim like poisonous flatworms.

Reef and Islands

Barramundi Cod *Cromileptes altivelis* **(Grows to 66 cm)** Once a prized catch for reef anglers, these fish are now protected on the Great Barrier Reef.

Banded Goatfish *Parupeneus multifasciatus* **(Grows to 35 cm)** A goatfish uses the "barbels" under its chin to sift through sand on the sea floor and as sensors to detect food.

Humphead Parrotfish *Bolbometopon muricatum* **(Grows to 1.3 m)** With powerful grinding plates in its throat, a single parrotfish consumes over a square metre of coral every year.

Ringtail Cardinalfish *Apogon aureus* **(Grows to 12 cm)** Despite its small size, this fish has a comparatively large mouth, which the male uses as a brood chamber to incubate eggs.

Leaf Scorpionfish *Taenianotus triacanthus* **(Grows to 10 cm)** The sail-like, overarching dorsal fin makes this curious-looking reef fish easy to identify.

Diana's Hogfish *Bodianus Diana* **(Grows to 25 cm)**
Common Cleanerfish *Labroides dimidiatus* **(Grows to 11.5 cm)** Both these fish are a species of wrasse.

Spotted Sea Bream *Gymnocranius* sp. **(Grows to 45 cm)** Also referred to by anglers as "Iodine Bream", the flesh of this fish has a strong antiseptic odour.

Eyestripe Surgeonfish *Acanthurus dussumieri* **(Grows to 50 cm)** Surgeonfish derive their name from a scalpel-like spine found on each side of the tail.

Dick's Damsel *Plectroglyphidodon dickii* **(Grows to 11 cm)** Despite their diminutive stature, damselfishes are a common sight around crevices on the Great Barrier Reef.

Harlequin Tuskfish *Choerodon fasciatus* **(Grows to 25 cm)** This fish is easily identified by its remarkable colouring and prominent, blue, tusk-like teeth, which change to pink when it is threatened.

53

Reef and Islands

Discovering the Reef's Invertebrate Wildlife

With the vast majority of the Great Barrier Reef's inhabitants being soft-bodied or possessing an external skeleton (rather than an internal skeleton of bone or cartilage), exploring the reef environment with a focus on these creatures can be very exciting. Among the hundreds of species of coral live an incredible diversity of worms, molluscs, sea stars and other invertebrates. A staggering 4000 species of sponges and an amazing number of crustaceans await discovery.

Each species occupies a different niche within the reef environment. While the reef flats are home to some anemones, crustaceans, shellfish and the hardiest corals, shallow lagoons contain a greater variety of corals, sea stars, sea cucumbers and sea urchins. When diving, visitors can see invertebrates that inhabit deeper waters. These include different anemones and soft corals, particularly the distinctive, filigreed gorgonian fans, feather stars, nudibranchs, sponges, various worms, shrimps and crayfish.

Invertebrates survive in fascinating relationships — mutual, symbiotic, parasitic and predatory. Some anemones hitch rides on snail shells inhabited by hermit crabs, lending the protection of their stinging cells in exchange for mobility. Hard corals could not survive without the zooxanthellae that live within their tissues and transfer the sun's energy to the coral. Members of one group of nudibranchs that feed on hydroid and coral polyps protect themselves by concentrating undischarged stinging cells from the polyps in the spiky projections on their backs. Many worms are parasitic, invading the flesh, intestines, gills or skin of fish, crustaceans, shellfish and sea stars. With their insatiable appetite for coral polyps, Crown-of-Thorns starfish cause considerable damage to the reef. Only a tiny proportion of this staggering diverse invertebrate community can possibly be encountered on a single visit to the reef.

Stationary Invertebrates

Most cnidarians (corals, anemones, hydroids and tube anemones); poriferans (sponges, bryozoans — moss animals called lace corals — although they are not corals); ascidians (sea squirts) and even some worms and crustaceans spend their lives attached to the reef or the sea floor. Many live beneath ledges and inside caves and crevices. They feed opportunistically, capturing whatever food flows past on the currents.

Hard corals generally live in shallower waters with plenty of light for their zooxanthellae to photosynthesise. Soft corals and anemones, whose bodies contain support structures called "sclerites", can live at greater depths. Anemones feed like corals, paralysing prey and drawing it in with their tentacles. Filter-feeding sponges and sea squirts are common — sponges playing an important role in the reef-building process.

Tube-dwelling worms extend tentacles into the current to feed, as do barnacles.

Christmas Tree Worms (a kind of tube worm) live on hard corals.

Pink Tube Sponge

A mixed colony of invertebrates forms an intriguing undersea forest.

Sunshine Coral

Reef and Islands

Mobile Invertebrates

Molluscs (shells, octopuses and squids), echinoderms (sea stars, feather stars, brittle stars, basket stars, urchins and sea cucumbers), crustaceans (crabs, crays, prawns and shrimps) and annelids (worms) form the main groups of mobile invertebrates. The most mobile and intelligent are the cephalopods (octopuses, squids and cuttles), thought to have a level of intelligence similar to that of domestic cats!

The reef is home to 4000 species of shell-producing molluscs, the most incredible being the Giant Clam. At over 1 m in length, and weighing up to 200 kg, it is the largest bivalve in the world.

Slugs (or nudibranchs), snails, cowries, balers and cone shells crawl across the reef, feeding on corals, fish, sea stars, worms and crustaceans as they go. The reef also abounds with crustaceans ranging from tiny shrimp to the Painted Spiny Lobster. Some 800 species of echinoderms (with their symmetrical five-part bodies) lend grace to the reef. The most conspicuous are Blue Sea Stars. Flatworms, ribbon worms and segmented worms (such as bristle worms) add to the diversity.

Commensal relationship — a Porcelain Crab and anemone.

Flatworms often sport dramatic warning colours.

Rose Sea Stars prey on other invertebrates.

Snorkelling is a great way to observe invertebrates.

Feather stars on a gorgonian sea fan.

Dangerous Invertebrates

Among the invertebrate life on the reef are several species whose attack and defence mechanisms are harmful to humans. The most troublesome are the ubiquitous "marine stingers", found around the coast between November and May. They are increasingly found on the reef itself.

Bluebottles, Portuguese Man-o-Wars, Pacific Man-o-Wars, Irukandji, Box Jellyfish and other invertebrates all have stinging cells on their long tentacles. Their stings can cause serious injury, sometimes death. Many other reef occupants should definitely be avoided. Fire corals and hydroids use stinging cells to catch prey and can also inflict severe pain upon overly inquisitive humans. Some sea anemones can also cause severe stings.

Sea urchins and Crown-of-Thorns sea stars have venom-tipped spines. Bristle worms, living under rocks or inside coral tunnels, possess venomous bristles. Cone shells feed on worms, other molluscs and fish, harpooning their prey before injecting their powerful venom through a long proboscis. Cone shell venom is extremely complex and potentially deadly to humans.

Although small in size, the Blue-ringed Octopus (*right*) is the most deadly octopus in the world. They live in shallow water, generally in sheltered rock pools and crevices, but can also be found dwelling in abandoned cans and bottles. Normally yellowish-brown in colour, their rings flash a livid blue colour as a warning when threatened. If provoked, they will bite with their beak-like jaws. Their saliva contains a fast-acting toxin that enters the wound and, if undetected, quickly leads to paralysis.

Because of these dangers, extreme care should be taken when observing reef invertebrates. The safest policy is "look but don't touch". Children should always be closely supervised and thick footwear should always be worn.

North of Cairns

Remote and exceptionally diverse, the region north of Cairns offers everything from luxury resorts and eco-adventures to remote camping and self-sufficiency. Wildlife sanctuaries and environmental discovery tours, rainforest hotels, shops and restaurants, tropical fruit and tea plantations, sugarcane farms, and long secluded beaches make this a fascinating area to explore. This region is the focus of much of Cairns' ecotourism activity. Hundreds of thousands of tourists stream to the region annually to marvel at the wonders of the Daintree and to enjoy the region's many different tropical tastes, colours, textures, aromas and sounds.

Female Eclectus Parrot

Where Rainforest Meets Reef

In this region, the **Great Dividing Range** is very close to the coast and the coastal flood plains are diminished. Rivers coursing from the high ranges journey through upland and lowland rainforests, down to the forested coastal ranges and into mangroves before opening into the sea. This is the traditional country of the Kuku Yalanji and Yirrganydji Aboriginal people, who traditionally fished and traded along the coastline and river systems. Despite more recent lifestyle changes, they have maintained their spiritual connection with the landscape. It is also cassowary and crocodile country, largely protected within the **Wet Tropics World Heritage Area**. A wealth of plant and animal species live in the rainforests, mangroves and drier forests of this region, and in the **Great Barrier Reef** not far offshore. This is the only place on earth where two World Heritage Areas converge — an area of exceptional natural beauty and extraordinary biodiversity.

The Deep North

The scenic **Captain Cook Highway** hugs the shores of the Coral Sea, presenting motorists with sweeping coastal views, before skirting slightly inland and passing a number of small communities. **Port Douglas**, with its understated glamour and promise of adventure, is the centre of the region. Some 20 km to the north is the sugar and service town of Mossman. Another 35 km further on lies tiny Daintree Village. Across the Daintree River are a number of close-knit and self-sufficient communities that, until the construction of the Cape Tribulation Road in the 1960s, were completely isolated except by boat. Despite construction of an inland route, Cooktown (250 km north of Cairns) still remains somewhat of a north Queensland outpost.

Cooktown

The charismatic, historic town of Cooktown has grown up on the riverside location where, in 1770, James Cook repaired HM Bark *Endeavour* after running aground on reef off Cape Tribulation. One hundred years later, as the port for the Palmer River Goldfields, "Cook's Town" flourished, becoming Queensland's second largest port after Brisbane. Although the gold rush was short-lived, the town maintained a small population which slowly grew. Each year thousands of tourists visit Cooktown to soak up its frontier atmosphere and history.

Top to bottom: **Port Douglas; Fan Palm Forest, Daintree; Cape Tribulation; Mossman Gorge** Mountains, rainforests, and reef meet here in the north.

North of Cairns

North of Cairns

Port Douglas

The peaceful, relaxed atmosphere of Port Douglas belies its bustling origins. Known originally as "Island Point", the town was conceived in the 1870s as a port for the nearby **Palmer River** and **Hogdkinson goldfields,** in a frenzy of building activity. These were heady days for the town. Within two years Island Point had eighteen hotels, a number of banks, a community hospital, two newspapers and numerous government services. Regular race meetings were held along Four Mile Beach.

For more than ten years the town boomed, but its heyday was short-lived. The government's decision in 1884 to establish Cairns as the terminus for a railway to the Herberton tin fields struck a decisive economic blow, and even though a cane tramway was constructed from the **Mossman Sugar Mill** to Port Douglas in 1900, the town was eventually bypassed altogether.

Subsiding in regional importance, "Port" hibernated as a sleepy town with an atmosphere of island-like seclusion. Home only to a small fishing industry and resident population, it was re-discovered as a tourist destination in the 1970s. The subsequent tourism and real estate boom energised the town with a newfound purpose. With its world-class marina facilities, Port Douglas has become the focus of tourist activities north of Cairns. Everything from birdwatching, game fishing, horse riding, sailing, diving, scenic flights and mangrove excursions are available to satisfy the specific bent of willing adventurers. The **Port Douglas Information Centre** (Ph: 07 4099 5599) is a convenient trove of information.

Port Douglas from the north The historic Council Wharf, constructed in 1904 as the sugar tramway terminus, sits like a welcome beacon at the entrance to Dicksons Inlet and the marina (*foreground right*). To its left is the popular foreshore park where locals and visitors enjoy sunset over the Daintree. The main town centre occupies the middle of the peninsula, with the straight Four Mile Beach on the other side. At the summit of the peninsula, a popular lookout at Flagstaff Hill (Island Point Road, Port Douglas) provides sweeping coastal views.

Local Leisure

The character of its buildings and colourful gardens make Port Douglas a charming place to relax and luxuriate. Port Douglas' main shopping and dining precinct is centred around **Macrossan Street.** The eclectic mix of shops, galleries, spas, therapy centres, restaurants, cafés and bars offer sophisticated menus and alfresco dining, lending the town an air of stylish indulgence.

The town's famed Sunday markets (8 a.m. – 12 noon) are held in the shade of the Poincianas and figs in Anzac Park on the foreshore of Dicksons Inlet, adjacent to the historic (c.1880) landmark church, St Mary's by the Sea. In this picturesque bayside setting visitors can choose from a wide selection of fresh, locally grown produce and quality art and craft items. Each May, Port Douglas hosts the **Reef and Rainforest Carnivale** (Ph: 07 4099 4308), a showcase of the region's gastronomical and artistic talents.

Macrossan St, Port Douglas The main street of this delightful tropical town is a relaxed setting for shopping and alfresco dining. The people are pleasant, the pace is slow and the architecture and gardens exude serenity.

Court House Hotel, one of Port's historic buildings, built in the classic north Queensland style, with wide verandahs and high ceilings. A cyclone in 1911 destroyed many of the town's original buildings.

North of Cairns

Clockwise from top: **Marina Mirage; Sheraton Mirage; Playing golf at a resort; Four Mile Beach** Port Douglas is blessed with stunning natural scenery and a climate conducive to outdoor living. Obeying the lure of the tropics, residents and visitors luxuriate in the relaxing surrounds, taking advantage of the pools, gyms, world-class golf links and other sporting facilities offered by the town's many resorts and tourism operators.

Offshore Adventure

With its natural features and tourist facilities, Port Douglas is a veritable playground. **Four Mile Beach** has been a popular recreational venue from the beginning and **Dicksons Inlet** is a safe boating harbour, a short distance from the Low Isles and other unspoilt Great Barrier Reef destinations. Innumerable commercial operators depart **Marina Mirage** (Ph: 07 4099 5775) for snorkelling, diving, fishing and sailing tours — **Sailaway** (Ph: 1800 085 674); the authentic Chinese junk, **Shaolin** (Ph: 07 4099 4772); **Aristocat** (Ph: 07 4099 4727); **Calypso** (Ph: 1800 005 966); **Haba Dive & Snorkel** (Ph: 07 4098 5000); **Phantom Charters** (Ph: 07 4094 1220); **Tech Dive Academy** (Ph: 07 4099 6880), to name just a few.

Rainforest Habitat

At Rainforest Habitat Wildlife Sanctuary (Port Douglas Rd, Ph: 07 4099 3235) visitors can immerse themselves in naturally-reproduced rainforest, wetland and grassland habitats, complete with over 180 species of native wildlife. The animals move freely through the enclosures, providing visitors with the perfect opportunity to watch them performing their natural behaviours, and interact with them. Taking breakfast with the birds is an especially enjoyable experience. Another is gaining a close view of Koalas, tree-kangaroos and other creatures notoriously difficult to observe in the wild. The sanctuary is open daily.

Below: Visitors enjoy the chance to see a variety of wildlife while strolling along elevated boardwalks through the cool tropical rainforest. *Below left:* Eastern Reef Egrets.

North of Cairns

Rainforest for All

Much of Daintree National Park is inaccessible wilderness, yet Mossman Gorge, with its network of easy walking tracks, is one of the most accessible places to really experience the Wet Tropics rainforest. Solo exploration enhances the peace and purity but sharing the experience in a group can be thrilling. Specialist guides are a great option for those seeking a more educative encounter with nature.

Mature Strangler Fig (with exaggerated buttress roots) in rainforest at Mossman Gorge.

Mossman River Every year thousands of visitors head north to enjoy its mythical beauty.

Local knowledge Interpretive signs enhance a visit to Mossman Gorge.

A world apart Guided walks reveal the intricate details of the rainforest.

The Daintree — Mossman

The Daintree has become part of the Australian consciousness. Indeed, it is world renowned, this region of treasured rainforest and inaccessible wilderness hidden safely away in Tropical North Queensland. Made famous by protests during the construction of the **Cape Tribulation to Bloomfield River Track** in the early 1980s and through its status as part of the 894,000 ha Wet Tropics World Heritage Area (conferred in December 1988), some 750,000 tourists visit the Daintree annually to marvel at its majesty and share in the rainforests' celebration of life.

Situated just 80 km north of Cairns and 20 km north of Port Douglas, Mossman is the gateway to the Daintree. The lush, rainforest-clad mountains that form an imposing backdrop to the town mark the **Mossman Gorge Section of Daintree National Park**. The Daintree River and ferry crossing, which provides access to Cape Tribulation and its ancient vegetation, is a mere 29 km away. **Daintree Village** is but a few kilometres to the west. As the last main town before the Daintree River, Mossman is a handy service centre for people venturing further north.

The Township

Mossman, the administrative centre of the Douglas Shire, is a typical Queensland small country town. With many buildings exemplifying a true north Queensland style, it is not hard to re-imagine Mossman as the sugar milling and gold mining town it was in the 1890s. Visitors enjoy country hospitality in the shops, cafés and historic hotels along the main street. **Karnak Playhouse** (Upper Whyanbeel Rd, Whyanbeel Valley, Ph: 07 4098 8111) hosts excellent theatrical productions.

A range of accommodation is available from luxurious rainforest lodges to camping. Try the **Wonga Beach Caravan Park** (Wonga Beach Esplanade, Ph; 07 4098 7704), **Mossman Caravan Park** (Front St, Mossman, Ph: 07 4098 2627) or **Newell Beach Caravan Park** (44 Marine Pde, Ph: 07 4098 1331).

The mountains of Mossman Gorge loom large beyond Mossman's town centre.

A northern touch Many of the town's houses exemplify older north Queensland architecture.

The Exchange Hotel, built in 1935, after a cyclone claimed the earlier building.

Trackside Discoveries

Inside the forest, life is colourful, varied and abundant. A short walk will reveal over 100 different species of tropical plants.

Greeting visitors at the forest's edge is the magnificent Ulysses Butterfly — a conspicuous denizen with its electric blue wings. From any vantage point overlooking the water a variety of invertebrates and fish may be seen. The distinctive calls of Wompoo Pigeons, Spotted Catbirds and Noisy Pittas are often heard. Trekkers can occasionally observe reptiles such as the Amethystine Python, Australia's largest snake, and Boyd's Forest Dragon (*left*).

60

North of Cairns

Aboriginal Culture

Mossman Gorge is integral to the spirituality and lifestyle of the Kuku Yalanji Aboriginal people who have lived around, and cared for, the gorge for aeons. These custodians offer guided tours along a traditional walking trail, visiting rock art and special sites along the way. Through storytelling, dance and displays, they share their cultural heritage — in particular, their relationship with their country (visit **Kuku Yalanji Dreamtime Walks & Cultural Centre** (Mossman Gorge Rd, Mossman, Ph: 07 4098 2595). Further information is available from **Mossman Gorge Community Rangers** (Mossman Gorge, Ph: 07 4098 1305).

Alternative authentic cultural experiences around Mossman include Coastal Walks and Night-spearing with **Kuku Yalanji Cultural Habitat Tours** (Cooya Beach, Ph: 07 4098 3437), and **Flames of the Forest** (3 Quaid St, Mossman, Ph: 07 4098 3144), a theatrical and enchanting dinner show.

Mossman Section The Rainforest Circuit Track (2.7 km) lets visitors explore the rainforest and discover its magic at their own pace. Within the dense tangle of buttress roots, strangler figs, clinging epiphytes and vines is a remarkable profusion of life.

Things to See and Do

1. Visit Mossman Gorge to experience the magic of the tropical rainforest and wild river environment.
2. Take a tour with a traditional Kuku Yalanji custodian.
3. Stroll around the main street of Mossman. Sample organically grown, local tropical fruits in its cafés.
4. Enjoy horse riding along picturesque Wonga Beach (Ph: 07 4098 7583).
5. Join a small group birdwatching or take a wildlife safari with specialist guides.
6. For more information contact Fine Feather Tours (Ph: 07 4904 1199), Mangrove Man Tours (Ph: 07 4098 2066) or Australian Natural History Safari (Ph: 07 4094 1600).

Daintree National Park — Mossman Gorge Section

The Mossman Gorge section of Daintree National Park is a 56,500 ha rugged wilderness on the slopes of the **Mount Carbine** and **Mount Windsor Tablelands**. The upper mountains are covered in stunted forest, which merges into open forest on the drier north-western slopes, and tall dense rainforests in the sheltered river valleys and lowlands behind Mossman.

Its gateway is the unforgettable Mossman Gorge. It is a special story place, associated with ancient creation legends that feature the gorge's peaks and geological formations. To its custodians, the twin-peaked mountain behind Mossman (Mt Demi or *Manjal Dimbi*) is the protector spirit, and The Bluff (or *Wurumbu*) represents a threatening spirit.

Here, the forest air is dank and earthy — a fecund atmosphere that resonates in birdsong and heaves the slow and ceaseless breath of passing time.

Left, top to bottom: **Mossman River** The Rex Creek suspension bridge; A number of platforms along walking trails have views of the surrounding area. *Below:* Over the aeons, the Mossman River (swimming is not recommended), has carved the Mossman Gorge.

61

North of Cairns

The Daintree River

The Daintree River is world renowned for its spectacular scenery and abundance of wildlife. Commencing in the **Main Range** behind Mossman, the river flows some 135 km before reaching the Coral Sea. With its headwaters and many tributaries rising in areas of extremely high rainfall, it is one of the largest and wettest catchments in the region. Diverse forests blanket the landscape from valley to mountaintop and, despite logging between the 1870s and 1980s, the catchment area remains largely inaccessible virgin wilderness and a crucial refuge for wildlife.

The river was named after Richard Daintree, an early government geologist, in 1873 by Sir George Elphinstone Dalrymple, who was one of the earliest Europeans to explore the area. Dalrymple described the Daintree River as "the finest river scenery in the colony", meaning Queensland.

The Daintree River's estuary, the region where freshwater and saltwater meet, is some 22 km long. The only major river on the eastern seaboard with its mouth facing south-east, the estuary receives large amounts of flotsam and jetsam, including seeds and seedpods, courtesy of the predominant south-easterly winds and oceanic currents. Consequently, the mangrove forests lining these lower reaches are among the most diverse in Australia, with 30 of Australia's 36 mangrove species occurring along this stretch of waterway.

The Daintree River estuary Aerial view of the river mouth. Snapper Island sits just off Cape Kimberley to the north. The Daintree River Ferry and Daintree Village lie several kilometres upstream.

Traditional Custodians

This rich environment is the traditional country of the Kuku Yalanji people. Visitors can gain a glimpse into their cultural traditions by participating in Kuku Yalanji guided tours at the **Daintree Eco Lodge and Spa** (20 Daintree Road, Daintree, Ph: 07 4098 6100). During the Indigenous Guided Rainforest Walk guides showcase features of the rainforest environment and explore Aboriginal foods and medicines while conveying a sense of the Kuku Yalanji connection with this country. During an Aboriginal art workshop, participants paint their own artwork while enjoying stories that illuminate Kuku Yalanji history, culture and traditions.

Daintree Village & Ferry

The quaint hamlet of Daintree Village, a thriving timber and dairy town between the 1880s and 1950s, is now a quiet community whose livelihood centres around tourism. Teahouses and restaurants, gift shops and the **Daintree Timber Museum & Gallery** (12 Stewart St, Daintree, Ph: 07 4098 6224) line the main street, providing retail and refreshments for the many thousands of visitors who participate in river cruises every year. A number of B&Bs and eco-lodges provide secluded accommodation in rainforest close to the village. Camping facilities are also centrally located (Daintree Riverview Caravan Park, 2 Stewart St, Daintree, Ph: 07 4098 6119). The Daintree Tourist Information Centre (Stewart St, Daintree, Ph: 1800 658 833) provides guidance with tours and accommodation.

Top to bottom: Waiting to take the Daintree River Ferry into cassowary and crocodile country, visitors come face-to-face with a life-size cassowary replica; The Big Barramundi Barbeque Garden (Ph: 07 4098 6186).

North of Cairns

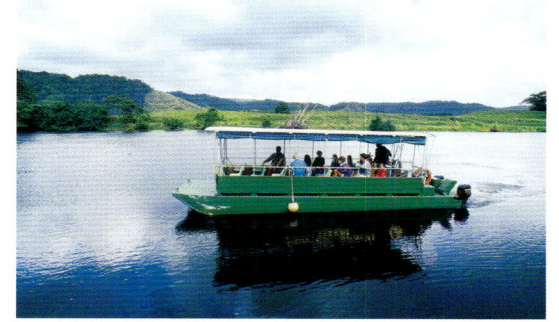

Clockwise from top left: **Reflections on a glassed-out Daintree River; Daintree Croc Spot Tours; one of the smaller wildlife tours** A number of tour operators traverse the river. Before the road to Mossman was completed in 1933 the only access to Daintree Village was via the river, which is best experienced in the early morning and evening.

River Expeditions

A cruise on the Daintree River is a special experience. Around Daintree Village the rainforests extend to the river's edge alongside grasslands, providing a mosaic of habitats for resident bird species. Downstream, salt- and freshwater meet and the rainforest blends into mangroves. This reach, with its small, rainforested islands and numerous sand bars (exposed at low tide), is frequented by birds and, especially in cooler months, crocodiles. In the lower reaches, toward the river mouth, the banks are dominated by mangroves that form a nursery for juvenile marine fish.

A myriad of tour operators offer cruises along the Daintree River and, at certain times of the day, the stretch between Daintree Village and the Daintree Ferry is heavy with water-borne traffic. Companies offering small group cruises, which focus on spotting wildlife in quieter locations, include Bruce Belcher's **Daintree River Cruises** (Ph: 07 4098 7717); **Daintree Croc Spot Tours** (Ph: 07 4098 6146); **Electric Boat Cruises** (Ph: 1800 686 103); **Chris Dahlberg's Daintree River Tours** (Ph: 07 4098 7997); and **Dan Irby's Mangrove Adventures** (Ph: 07 4098 7017).

Things to See and Do

1. Enjoy the Wild Wings & Swampy Things experience (Barratt Creek, Daintree, Ph: 07 4098 6155) — a 40 ha wildlife refuge of reclaimed farmland.
2. Hire a boat (Daintree River Boat Hire, 3 Forest Creek Rd, Daintree, Ph: 07 4090 7789).
3. Take the Daintree Rainforest River Train (Ph: 07 4090 7676) on a journey through the mangroves.
4. Stay in one of the B&Bs or spas near Daintree Village and join one of the many wilderness or wildlife tours (Tranquility Tours, Ph: 07 4098 6000).

Riverside Wildlife

The Daintree River's rich ecosystems support a diversity of forest and riverine wildlife. The 22 km estuary contains some 200 fish species and 70 crustacean species — a healthy source of prey for the area's many waterbirds and riverside animals. Waders such as Royal Spoonbills and Great-billed Herons spear prey in the shallows, while darters, cormorants and Black Bitterns dry off on riverside branches after their fishing excursions. Agile kingfishers strafe the water and Ospreys torpedo their prey from lofty heights. Estuarine Crocodiles bask on sand bars during the day. All manner of forest birds from Double-eyed Fig Parrots and Shining Flycatchers to Helmeted Friarbirds, Metallic Starlings and Sulphur-crested Cockatoos feed on mangrove flowers and fruits, and predatory birds such as Black Butcherbirds, commonly raid their nests. A large colony of Spectacled Flying-foxes (*left*) fly out over the river at sunset, and visitors cruising the river may be rewarded with the sight of a Nankeen Night Heron (*above right*), Papuan Frogmouth, Amethystine Python or Estuarine Crocodile. The Daintree Mangroves Wildlife Sanctuary (Ph: 07 4098 7272) showcases many of the region's most iconic animals.

North of Cairns

Crocodiles

Crocodiles are a much-maligned, poorly understood group of reptiles. The threat these creatures (potentially) pose to human life and limb evokes in most people a deep primordial fear. Yet, biologically speaking, crocodiles are simply large carnivorous reptiles that behave very much like other reptiles. Australia has only two of the world's 22 equatorial crocodile species.

The Freshwater Crocodile (*Crocodylus johnstoni*), a shy fish eater, poses little danger to humans. Occupying both the fast-flowing gorges and quieter, lily-covered reaches of most river systems across northern Australia, it generally prefers waters beyond the reach of its larger cousin, the Estuarine Crocodile (*Crocodylus porosus*). Where they do overlap, Estuarine Crocodiles frequently kill (and occasionally eat) their freshwater relatives.

The Estuarine Crocodile, the largest living reptile, is ranked among the top predators on the planet. Although predominantly a fish-eating species, larger individuals supplement their diets with reptiles, birds and mammals such as Dingoes, wallabies, feral pigs and flying-foxes. Rarely do members of this species kill humans — such an occurrence is thought to be linked to the compromised integrity of the crocodile's natural ecosystem and resultant changes to the normal food chain.

A highly mobile species, the Estuarine Crocodile has a wide distribution, from northern Australia, where the greatest population exists, to India and the islands of the western Pacific. In many countries these ancient reptiles were hunted to the point of near or complete local extinction, but today they are internationally protected. In Australia, where commercial hunting ceased in the early 1970s, populations are rapidly recovering. Commercial farms now breed crocodiles for their attractive leather — favoured for accessories such as shoes and handbags.

Despite being at the top of the food chain in Australia, the Estuarine Crocodile has a surprising number of predators. Females lay their hard-shelled eggs in grassy nests beside waterholes. During the 11–12 week incubation period before their young hatch, constant vigilance is required of the females to protect their nests against marauding feral pigs and monitor lizards. Even after their babies hatch, protection must continue for another week or two as mothers introduce their young to their aquatic habitat.

The first year of life is the most hazardous for young Estuarine Crocodiles, as they are prey for Barramundi, sharks, catfish, Whistling Kites, White-bellied Sea-Eagles, Water Pythons, Yellow-spotted Monitors and larger Estuarine Crocodiles. Less than one percent of the eggs laid hatch; even fewer young crocs survive to adulthood — but, given the right conditions, adult crocodiles may live up to 100 years!

The Freshwater Crocodile (top) and the Saltwater Crocodile (bottom).

Finding and Watching Crocs

Estuarine Crocodiles, commonly known as Saltwater Crocodiles or "salties", are not difficult to locate and make compulsive and fascinating subjects for observation. Surprisingly tolerant of humans — once they establish no harm is intended — they tend to go on about their daily lives unperturbed. However, like all wild animals, crocodiles need their personal space. Never approach a crocodile too closely.

Unlike birds or mammals, which maintain a constant body temperature, a crocodile's body temperature and energy levels are determined by its external environment. They are great energy conservers, spending much of their day basking in the sun. In the late afternoon they may be seen moving into the shadows, and at night they stealthily cruise their territory in search of food.

Most crocodile viewing is undertaken from the safety of boats, particularly specialist wildlife or crocodile-spotting cruises conducted in or near national parks across northern Australia.

The Estuarine Crocodile is an iconic reptile of north Queensland It features in many advertising campaigns and replicas are found throughout the region.

A plethora of companies offer crocodile cruises on the Daintree River, enabling vistors to marvel at this ferocious, prehistoric predator.

One of the more brightly coloured tourist operators sticks close to the mangroves to catch a glimpse of the awe-inspiring beast.

North of Cairns

Estuarine (Saltwater) Crocodiles

Distribution
The Estuarine Crocodile may be found anywhere between India and northern Australia and throughout the islands of the western Pacific. Australia has the greatest population of these formidable and ancient reptiles.

Habitat
Although they are seen mostly in the tidal reaches of rivers, Estuarine Crocodiles are as comfortable in freshwater billabongs as they are in mangrove-lined estuaries. Large individuals migrate long distances upriver to the freshwater reaches to establish territories. All of the major river systems in northern Australia are inhabited by Estuarine Crocodiles, some having considerable populations.

Behaviour
During breeding season, male crocodiles can travel long distances in search of females. Confrontations between roaming males are common, but usually short-lived, mostly consisting of bluff and intimidation from the resident male. Battles, on the rare occasions they ensue, are spectacular, driven by the instinct to keep or acquire the disputed territory. Once the breeding season has passed, Estuarine Crocodiles are more relaxed, spending the majority of their time basking or resting in shady retreats by day, and fishing at night.

Diet
Crocodiles of all sizes eat fish, hunting particularly during the incoming tide. As the tide rises over the mudflats, schools of mullet and Salmon Catfish move upstream in the shallows, filtering the muddy water for small nutrients. Behind them swim Barramundi and Threadfin Salmon awaiting their chance to eat the mullet. Visibility is poor in the muddy water, and many of the incoming fish collide with crocodiles that have angled themselves strategically against the banks. The crocodiles respond in an instant, expending a small amount of energy to capture their prize.

Features
Crocodiles have tough, scaly skin, greenish-grey to almost-black in colour, with black and yellow chequering and blotches. Two rows of horny plates extend from the upper neck down to the tail.

Total Length
Males up to 7 metres.
Females up to 4 metres.

Status
Secure.

Salties inhabit freshwater billabongs as well as estuarine areas.

Crocodiles are armed with 64–68 cone-shaped teeth and can snap their jaws shut with incredible force.

Being cold-blooded, crocodiles are energy-efficient animals that spend a lot of time absorbing sun.

Crocodiles have adapted superbly to a range of different tropical habitats.

Croc nests can be inundated by floodwaters.

How Dangerous Are Estuarine Crocodiles?

Since Estuarine and Freshwater Crocodiles live together in many places in northern Australia, caution is required at all times in crocodile territory. Although most Estuarine Crocodiles avoid humans, the occasional few will, for any of a number of reasons, attack. Aboriginal people have co-existed with Estuarine Crocodiles in Australia for thousands of years because they know and respect the ways of these giant reptiles. Visitors are guided by warning signs and rules, but occasional attacks still occur — mainly through ignorance. With an abundant supply of natural food, crocodiles are less likely to attack. However, hungry crocodiles rarely pass up the offer for an easy meal. Being opportunistic predators, crocodiles will prey on people should they ever put themselves in a position that will afford these animals a chance to attack. Crocodiles are also extremely territorial. During breeding season males doggedly guard against unwanted trespassers. Female crocodiles fearlessly defend their nests against any potential threat to their young.

65

North of Cairns

Daintree Discovery Centre

During a visit to Tropical North Queensland in the 1980s, Ron and Pam Birkett found interpretive information about the lowland rainforests north of the Daintree River virtually non-existent. Soon after, they decided to build an environment centre of their own to make it easier for the region's visitors to understand the ecology of the surrounding rainforests. Several years of negotiation and consultation with the Queensland Parks & Wildlife Service, CSIRO, the local Shire Council, and numerous research and educational centres ensued, before the Daintree Environment Centre (with its iconic Canopy Tower), opened in 1989. Today, the **Daintree Discovery Centre**, as it is now known, is a world-class, multi-award-winning tourist attraction that receives approximately 80,000 Australian and international visitors annually.

The Daintree Discovery Centre is designed for visitors of all ages to access every level of the rainforest — safely, comfortably and enjoyably. The aim is to allow visitors to immerse themselves in the rainforest environment and discover something of its wonder for themselves. As a private enterprise, monies from entry fees are devoted to the ongoing development of the centre.

The Daintree Discovery Centre (Tulip Oak Rd, Cow Bay, Ph: 07 4098 9171, open daily 8.30 a.m. – 5.00 p.m.) is situated in an unspoiled pocket of lowland rainforest nestled into the northern side of the **Alexandra Range**, 10 km north of the Daintree River Ferry crossing.

The Daintree Discovery Centre has 400 metres of elevated rainforest boardwalks with numerous viewing platforms overlooking various tiers of the rainforest. They provide visitors with the opportunity to explore the interactions between plants and animals living on the forest floor and in the middle and upper tiers of the forest. They also invite visitors to share the rainforest's special ambience.

Rainforest Experience

The centre has a number of facilities to help visitors get up-close-and-personal with the rainforest. The wheelchair-accessible Aerial Walkway allows visitors to rise above the forest floor and engage with the mid-canopy of the forest, with its impressive epiphytes, orchids and resident birds. Using information provided in the Interpretive Guide Book (included in the admission fee) visitors can learn about the natural interplay between the rainforest's distinctive plants and their diverse inhabitants.

The 23 m **Canopy Tower**, rising five storeys, allows visitors to discover more about the forest's layers of life. Interpretive signs at each level point out wildlife and plants of particular interest. From the top of the tower, it is possible to observe birds and butterflies feeding, or to see beyond the canopy.

Complementing these two experiences are the elevated rainforest boardwalks — the **Cassowary Circuit** and the **Bush Tucker Trail**. The former explores the food plants and other features of the Southern Cassowary's forest habitat. As the centre is part of an established cassowary corridor, visitors often witness these astonishing birds searching for food on the forest floor. The Bush Tucker Trail, with its lively historical anecdotes, highlights many of the plants used by Aboriginal people and early European settlers for food, medicine and utility items.

North of Cairns

The Visitor Centre

An accredited Wet Tropics Visitor Centre, the large open plan **Display Centre** has an extensive range of interpretive displays and resources that provide easy access to up-to-date, accurate and easy-to-understand information about the surrounding lowland rainforest. With colourful materials covering topics such as the geological history of the region, the impact of tropical cyclones, prized rainforest timbers, dangerous plants/animals and cassowary conservation, the displays provide an excellent introduction to the wonders of these ecosystems. Detailed pictorial information is provided on forest wildlife and there are live displays featuring the larvae of various moths and butterflies. Freshwater fish can be seen in a display highlighting the ecology of the Daintree region's freshwater creeks as they flow from the mountains through the rainforests to the mangroves at the edge of the Coral Sea.

Audiovisual presentations accessed via state-of-the-art touch screens, along with a small theatre, provide information on a variety of topics from conservation to crocodiles, further complementing the learning experience. The centre also has a reference library and a collection of preserved specimens. Its sweeping, all-weather verandahs are both the perfect place to relax and learn, and a handy refuge during wet weather.

The Interpretive Display Centre provides a wealth of information to support visitors' experiences on the boardwalks. Identification displays and interactive installations give visitors the chance to learn more about the rainforest's inhabitants and their global ecological significance. The Canopy Tower, with its five viewing platforms, provides an easy and comfortable way to see and experience the different levels of the rainforest.

Jindalba Boardwalk

A short distance from the Daintree Discovery Centre is the Jindalba Boardwalk. Here, an elevated boardwalk (650 m) passes through majestic rainforest, highlighting buttressed trees, Crows Nests, Fan Palms, tree-ferns, vines and other vegetation. Along the way there is a series of secluded nooks and crannies where visitors can sit and relax.

Here, a rocky stream trickles through the forest lined with palms and tree-ferns that glisten in the dappled light (*left*); there, a grove of Zamias and King Ferns lend their grace to a darkened corner. Birds call from the canopy (*above*) or come close to investigate, colourful fruit brightens the forest floor and fungi add striking colour to rotting logs. This forest is home to cassowaries and tree-kangaroos, which light-footed visitors may be fortunate enough to glimpse.

North of Cairs

Northern Quoll

Wildlife of the Daintree Region

The rainforests of the Daintree region are the ancestral remnants of forests through which dinosaurs roamed when Australia was part of the massive supercontinent Gondwana. These treasure troves of plant and animal species have survived relatively unchanged for millions of years — they are living museums, providing a glimpse into the processes that have shaped life on Earth. In contrast, the rainforests of most of the world's other tropical areas are of relatively recent origin, and have fewer plant and animal species with such primitive heritage.

As Australia's most flora-rich region, the Wet Tropics covers less than 0.1% of the Australian landscape, yet the region's forests are home to 65% of Australia's fern species, 37% of its conifer species, 30% of its orchids and 21% of the country's cycads. Almost one-quarter of the region's plants are found nowhere else on the planet. Not surprisingly, the Wet Tropics is also home to an astonishingly high proportion of Australia's animal species, many of which are also endemic to the area. A large number (76 species) of these are considered to be rare, vulnerable or endangered.

Considered one of the world's most biodiverse ecosystems (alongside the Great Barrier Reef), the Wet Tropics rainforests are jam-packed with an unbelievable array of life-forms filling every available niche, and intricately woven into a dynamic web of life.

Although many species occur across the entire region, some species are confined to specific areas, such as the mountaintops in the Daintree and to the south of Cairns. The Daintree has at least seven species of endemic vertebrates — Bennett's Tree-kangaroo, the Thornton Peak Uromys, four species of frog and an undescribed species of skink — with the possibility of many more species yet to be discovered.

Amphibians

One-quarter (that is, approximately 50) of Australia's frog species live in the rainforests of the Wet Tropics, and of these approximately half occur nowhere else. The White-Lipped Tree-frog (*left*) is the largest, measuring up to 140 mm in length. Ground-dwelling frogs commonly spotted in the marshes and coastal forests of the Daintree area include the Spotted Grass Frog, the Ornate and Striped Burrowing Frogs, the Marbled Frog and the large Northern Barred Frog. The Rocket Frog and Lesieur's Frog are common around rainforest streams, also inhabited by waterfall frogs, mist-frogs, the Australian Lace-lid, the Northern Tinker Frog and the Sharp-snouted Day-frog. The Tapping, Rattling and Mountain-top Nursery-frogs are endemic to the mountain peaks in the region where the Northern and White-browed Whistle-frogs, found only in the Wet Tropics, also occur. A wide variety of tree-frogs also inhabit the rainforests, including the Common Green Tree-frog, Northern Dwarf Tree-frog and Orange-eyed Tree-frog (*right*). In coastal forests near water, the Red Tree-frog, Roth's Tree-frog and green and gold Graceful Tree-frog may be encountered.

As in other parts of the world, several upland rainforest stream species have not been seen since 1991. Their disappearance may be related to the occurrence of a virus, apparently released with infected aquarium fish into streams. At the same time, various frog hospitals throughout the region report an increase in the incidence of disease among lowland frogs. As frogs are useful environmental barometers, concern exists about both situations.

Reptiles

The Wet Tropics are home to almost one-quarter (162 species) of Australia's reptiles, with 22 species endemic to the region. One of the larger and more striking endemic rainforest reptiles is the Boyd's Forest Dragon, commonly seen clinging to tree trunks. Eastern Water Dragons are also found near water in rainforest areas. The Chameleon Gecko and Northern Leaf-tailed Gecko (*right*) are relics of Gondwana times. A number of skink species are endemic to the area, including the Thornton Peak Skink, known only from restricted areas around Thornton Peak, and the seldom seen Prickly Forest Skink.

Of more than 50 snake species recorded in the Wet Tropics, the Northern Crowned Snake, an inoffensive skink-eater, is the only endemic species. The Amethystine Python, Australia's largest snake, which can measure over 5 metres in length, constricts its prey — usually rats, bandicoots, wallabies, possums, flying-foxes and some birds, especially domestic chickens — before swallowing it. In contrast, the small burrowing blind snakes, which feed on termites and ants, are only 18–40 cm long. Most of the snakes in the Daintree are non-poisonous, such as the Brown Tree Snake (*above left*). Krefft's Turtles (*right*) inhabit the rivers and streams and northern Australia's most infamous reptile, the Estuarine Crocodile, inhabits river, estuarine and coastal waters of the Daintree region.

North of Cairns

Insects

Tropical rainforests are generally inhabited by an amazing number of insects and the Daintree is no exception. Interestingly, many insects are restricted to mountaintops, each mountaintop having its own characteristic "suite" of invertebrates.

The Daintree area is home to an endemic stag beetle whose closest relatives live in South America, and an incredible array of other colourful beetles. The Peppermint Stick Insect spends its days hiding among the leaf bases of Pandanus trees. Half of Australia's species of king-crickets occur commonly through the rainforest. Green Tree-ants are particularly prolific; colonies live in football-sized nests sewn together by adult ants using silk produced by their larvae. Although hyper-aggressive, instantly swarming people who accidentally disturb their nests, their sting is mild and leaves no after-effects.

Two hundred butterfly species, approximately 60% of Australia's total, live in the Wet Tropics, feeding on and pollinating the rainforest's flowering plants. Among the myriad of colours and markings, particularly conspicuous are the electric blue Ulysses Butterfly and the gigantic Cairns Birdwing Butterfly. The region is also home to numerous moths, many of them endemic. Australia's largest, the Hercules Moth, with a wingspan of 25 cm, is distributed throughout the Wet Tropics and on Cape York.

Flower Beetle

Male Cairns Birdwing

Australian Lurcher

Female Common Eggfly

Male Common Eggfly

Mammals

Mammals are also well represented in the Daintree's rainforests. The Wet Tropics contains 36% of Australia's mammal species, including 30% of the marsupials, 25% of the rodents and 58% of the bat species. The small, dark Musky Rat-kangaroo, probably the most primitive kangaroo species, inhabits the forest floor at high and low altitudes. Bennett's Tree-kangaroo is confined to isolated rainforests north of the Daintree River and the Lumholtz's Tree-kangaroo dwells at altitudes above 500 m in rainforest south of the river. The Striped Possum lives in lowland rainforests. The Long-tailed Pygmy-possum occurs throughout the Daintree area and the Daintree River Ringtail Possum lives only in the headwaters of the Daintree and Mossman Rivers and on Thornton Peak.

The Daintree's other marsupials include the Common and Long-nosed Bandicoot (*below*), both common in the Daintree lowlands, and the endangered Spotted-tailed Quoll — more common in the upland rainforests around the headwaters of the Daintree River. A dozen different bush rat species, including the White-tailed Rat, are found in the area, and Red-legged Pademelons (*above left*) and Swamp Wallabies are sometimes seen.

The Spectacled Flying-fox, a regional endemic, is common in the Daintree area, as are Blossom Bats. Less commonly seen are the Little Red and Black Flying-foxes. The Daintree is also home to some 30 species of small insectivorous bats.

Wildlife Tours

For visitors seeking a close look at the fauna of the Daintree area, there are a number of eco-accredited wildlife safaris to choose from. Specialist local guides lead bushwalks and river cruises, exposing the daily routines of rainforest and wetland inhabitants. Birdwatching tours operate in the early mornings when avian fauna is most active, and nocturnal creatures may be seen on spotlighting expeditions (*right*).

Guided walking tours are conducted by **Mason's Tours** (Cape Tribulation Rd, Cape Tribulation, Ph: 07 4098 0070); **Crocodylus Village Walking Tours** (Buchanan Creek Road, Cow Bay, Ph: 07 4098 9166); **Heritage Lodge** (Turpentine Road, Cape Tribulation, Ph: 07 4098 9138); **Cooper Creek Wilderness** (Ph: 07 4098 9126) and **Odyssey Safaris** (C/- Coconut Beach Rainforest Lodge, Cape Tribulation Rd, Cape Tribulation, Ph: 07 4098 0033 or 1300 134 044). **Cape Tribulation Wilderness Cruises** (Thornton Beach, Cape Tribulation, Ph: 07 4033 2052) offer day and night cruises on Cooper Creek.

North of Cairns

Birds of the Wet Tropics

With its mixture of habitats, including rainforests, open forests, grasslands, wetlands, mangroves and estuarine areas, the Wet Tropics is home to half of Australia's bird species — thirteen of which are found nowhere else. It is little wonder the region acts as a magnet for international birdwatchers.

The Daintree itself is one of few areas where nine of Australia's ten kingfisher species occur, ranging in size from the Laughing Kookaburra to the miniature Little Kingfisher. Over half of Australia's pigeons and most of the country's cuckoos and owls can be observed in the Daintree.

The Orange-footed Scrubfowl and the Australian Brush-turkey, both of which incubate their eggs in large mounds of leaf litter, are commonly seen scratching and feeding on the forest floor. More elusive ground-dwellers are the Southern Cassowary and the shy Noisy Pittas and Emerald Doves that fly off with a flash of colour when startled. The rainforest mid-canopy is inhabited by a variety of smaller forest birds including fantails, scrubwrens, monarchs, flycatchers and cuckoos. The Spotted Catbird, with its raucous cry, and the curious Black Butcherbird are easily identified.

Yellow-spotted Honeyeater

Two distinctive canopy and under-storey birds are the beautifully coloured Yellow-bellied Sunbird, the females commonly building their pendulous nests around buildings, and Victoria's Riflebird, the males sometimes seen in full courtship display with their chests puffed and wings spread out in a fan shape.

The most common of the nocturnal rainforest birds is the Large-tailed Nightjar. Although the Rufous Owl, Barking Owl, Lesser Sooty Owl and Papuan Frogmouth all occur in the area, they are less commonly seen.

In summer, the Wet Tropics is visited by a number of migrant species — most notably the Pied Imperial-Pigeon, which nests offshore and commutes to the rainforest every day to feed, and the spectacular Buff-breasted Paradise-Kingfisher, which nests in termite mounds on the forest floor. While both of these migrants are restricted to the lowlands, along with some of the resident birds, the bowerbirds are found only in the upland areas. The smallest of these, the Golden Bowerbird, builds the largest and most elaborate of bowers, up to 3 m tall, and is found only at high altitudes in the Daintree and Mt Bartle Frere area south of Cairns.

Rose-Crowned Fruit-Dove Feeding on fruit in the canopy and under-storey, this plump, colourful bird is difficult to see. It is most often located by its accelerating call, or by the sight of falling fruit.

Brown Cuckoo-Dove This large, rusty-brown, long-tailed pigeon is easy to identify. It is often seen around forest margins or walking tracks. Like many other pigeons its nest is a flimsy twig platform.

Pied Imperial-Pigeon Nesting on surrounding continental islands between August and April, flocks of these majestic pigeons fly to and from the lowland rainforests to feed in the canopy.

Red-winged Parrot Colourful but nervous, these medium-sized parrots usually feed in pairs or small flocks on fruit, seeds, nectar and insects among drier forests and rainforest margins.

Male Eclectus Parrot Unusual in that the female is more colourful than the male, this magnificent Cape York parrot can be seen up-close-and-personal in wildlife sanctuaries throughout the area.

Male King-Parrot Reasonably common through eastern Australia, this shy parrot is easily recognised by its colours, which are brighter in males than females. At 43 cm it is one of Australia's largest parrots.

North of Cairns

Spotted Catbird With its grating, meowing call (a characteristic sound of the rainforest), this mid-canopy bird is found only in Tropical North Queensland. It is often heard but not so readily seen.

Rainbow Lorikeet A favourite across much of Australia, these colourful, gregarious and noisy parrots feed on fruit, nectar, blossoms and seeds in many types of habitats.

Male Forest Kingfisher Although somewhat elusive, this small and handsome kingfisher can be spied near streams as it hunts for small fish. It nests in termite mounds in trees.

Some Birdwatching and Photography Tips

As the upland rainforests are largely inaccessible, birdwatching in the Daintree is generally carried out at sea-level. Although fruitful at any time of year, October to November (coinciding with the arrival of the last of the regular migrant species) is considered prime birdwatching season.

Although nocturnal species are encountered after dark, the best birdwatching times are during the early morning and late afternoon. Waterholes and fruiting or flowering trees are often the best place to begin searching for birds. Silence and patience are virtues. Once the observer relaxes into the scenery, some curious birds often come closer to investigate. Many species of rainforest and mangrove birds can be seen and heard along the rainforest and mangrove boardwalks (*above left*) through the Cape Tribulation Section of Daintree National Park, or along the mid-canopy section of the Daintree Discovery Centre's Aerial Walkway (*above right*). When photographing birds in the rainforest it is particularly helpful to have a telephoto lens with a focal length between 300 and 600 mm. As birds move quickly it is best to use a camera's automatic focus and light-metering functions. A tripod is particularly helpful in compensating for low light levels.

Male Satin Bowerbird This iridescent mimic forages widely for fruit and insects. After decorating his bower with blue trinkets, the male performs an elaborate courtship display.

Crimson Rosella This parrot, conspicuous by its colouring, is nevertheless shy and quiet. Identified by its gentle call and dipping flight pattern, it is a seed-eater.

Figbird A gregarious and gymnastic bird, the figbird has a wide range. It feeds on fruit, particularly figs, in the canopies of the Daintree's rainforests and wetlands, dispersing fig seeds as it moves about.

North of Cairns

Living Museum

The rainforests of the Cape Tribulation area are remnants of ancient rainforests that covered much of Australia over a hundred million years ago when it was part of the supercontinent Gondwana. This wild, beautiful and biodiverse landscape — home to some of the most primitive flora and fauna in the world — is believed to be a key for unlocking many evolutionary secrets.

Storm clouds break up over the Daintree River and Thornton Peak (1374 m).

Thornton Peak Granite outcrops and tors characterise this mountainous area.

Daintree River An aerial view showing the river mouth.

Indian Almond *Terminalia catappa* is a common coastal plant of the tropics.

The Daintree — Cape Tribulation

On the northern side of the Daintree River, the **Cape Tribulation Section** of Daintree National Park is one of unsurpassed beauty. Here, the rugged coastal ranges, with their lush tropical rainforests, plunge into the Coral Sea and the Great Barrier Reef. With its mountain peaks often obscured by cloud, this is an area of high rainfall and numerous creeks and waterfalls. Of inestimable global ecological value, this 17,100 ha refuge contains Australia's largest remnant of lowland rainforest, and the oldest continuously surviving rainforests in the world. Amazingly, this area has remained unscathed from numerous periods of volcanic activity and sea level and climatic changes, with its forests and their collection of primitive plant species intact. The area's mangrove forests are among Australia's most complex and diverse.

Driving the Daintree

Of the many scenic routes through the Wet Tropics rainforests, **Cape Tribulation Road** is one of the prettiest. Passing through the endangered lowland rainforests, and crossing a multitude of mangrove-lined creeks, the road winds up the **Alexandra Range** to its lookout (*Walu Wugirriga*) with its magnificent views over the Daintree River mouth and the mountain ranges towards Cairns. This section is lined with ferns and many waterfalls spill onto the road in the wet season, requiring caution. North of the lookout it passes tea and tropical fruit plantations, and the hamlets of **Cow Bay** and **Alexandra Bay** before approaching **Cape Tribulation**.

Roadside Wildlife

Caution is required for another reason along Cape Tribulation Road — motorists sometimes encounter cassowaries and other wildlife. The lowland rainforests and swamps are home to Swamp Wallabies, Striped Possums, White-tailed Rats, Boyd's Forest Dragons, a variety of skinks and geckoes, Amethystine Pythons and Green Tree Snakes.

Estuarine Crocodiles inhabit many of the swamps and streams of the lowlands, feeding on the diversity of frogs, fish and turtles living there. Birds of all shapes, sizes, colours and habits feed on the forests' nectar, fruit, insects and other invertebrates.

Female Swamp Wallaby Common over much of eastern Australia, in rainforests, sclerophyll forests, woodlands and heath country, these wallabies are distinguished by their dark fur and diurnal habits.

Fan Palm Walks

Plentiful throughout Tropical North Queensland before clearing for sugarcane farms in the 1870s, stands of the magnificent Fan Palm are now rare, restricted to pockets in the Daintree and Mission Beach areas.

With their flexible stems and large fronds, these palms are adapted to withstand cyclonic conditions. Visitors can enjoy a cathedral-like stand of these glorious palms at Fan Palm Boardwalk Café (80 Cape Tribulation Road, Ph: 07 4098 9119). Several resorts in the area also proudly showcase small stands.

North of Cairns

Marrdja Boardwalk

For visitors wishing to safely and comfortably experience the wonder of the exceptionally diverse Daintree mangroves, the **Marrdja Boardwalk** at Oliver Creek is just the place. Passing through rainforest and mangrove communities, this boardwalk provides a glimpse into the dynamics and evolution of these wonderfully complex ecosystems.

Interpretive signs take visitors back in time to a world where dinosaurs roamed among ancient ferns, cycads and conifers. Many of these plants exist relatively unchanged in Australia's rainforests today. Sometime in the past, primitive flowering plants evolved, revolutionising the plant kingdom. Nineteen families of these angiosperms still survive across the world. Incredibly, thirteen of these are represented in Cape Tribulation's lowland rainforests. The very rare, primitive Green Dinosaur (*Idiospermum australiense*), also called Ribbonwood or Idiot Fruit, can be seen along the Marrdja Boardwalk.

Top to bottom: **Noah Creek; Oliver Creek** Views from the boardwalks.

Things to See and Do

1. Take time to explore the Cape Tribulation environment and participate in some of the locally organised eco-tours.
2. Enjoy the scenic drive along Cape Tribulation Road, being sure to watch for wildlife and stop at the beaches along the way.
3. Walk the Marrdja, Dubuji and Jindalba Boardwalks to experience and learn more about the significance of the rainforests and mangroves, and why they are World-Heritage-listed.
4. Spend some time at Cape Tribulation itself. Walk the Kulki Boardwalk and enjoy the views over Cape Tribulation Beach and the Coral Sea.
5. Take care at all times, being sure not to harm plants or wildlife in this precious environment.

Cassowary Country

The Southern Cassowary, a grand, flightless bird measuring up to 1.7 metres in height, is unique to the lowland rainforests, woodlands and swamps of Tropical North Queensland and New Guinea. Its coarse black plumage, large beak, prominent helmet-like casque, brightly coloured wattle and thick, scaly legs give it a somewhat prehistoric appearance. Although adults can weigh up to 85 kg, males average 38 kg and the slightly larger females average 47 kg.

Males and females are usually difficult to distinguish except in breeding season. Generally shy, solitary and territorial, they tolerate each other only during courtship and mating, which lasts for several weeks. The male takes full responsibility for the parenting, incubating the large dark green eggs for 50 days, often going without food and water for long periods. He then cares for his cream and brown striped chicks for a further nine to twelve months. The chicks' plumage slowly loses the stripes, then darkens as their wattles and casques develop. They are sexually mature at three years of age.

Although they eat fungi, flowers and a variety of small forest animals, cassowaries forage predominantly on fallen fruit. Their droppings contain a cache of rainforest seeds, ready to germinate, and many large-fruited rainforest trees depend on cassowaries for their regeneration.

Above: Cassowaries are sometimes seen along Daintree roads. Visitors are warned to keep their distance and resist feeding these unpredictable birds. *Left:* Road signs warn of the danger, both to humans and cassowaries, posed by collisions.

73

North of Cairns

International Recognition

Cape Tribulation formed the battleground for a major conflict between environmentalists and the Douglas Shire Council in the 1980s. The council's decision to push a road through the national park generated a storm of protests and the construction of the Bloomfield Track soon attracted international attention. In 1988, World-Heritage-listing was rightfully inscribed to this vital tract of lowland rainforest.

Historic Cape Tribulation

Named by Captain (then Lieutenant) James Cook in June 1770, when the HM Bark *Endeavour* ran aground on the reef 35 km to the north-east, **Cape Tribulation** was at the time occupied by Kuku Yalanji Aboriginal people who travelled the coastline according to the seasons. One hundred years later, Daintree Village was settled by Europeans in search of red cedar, and following clearing north of the Daintree River at **Bailey Creek**, now known as Cow Bay, settlers moved in to commence banana and pineapple farming. In the 1930s, a number of settlers, most notably the Mason family, pioneered the settlement at Cape Tribulation — their farms cleared with assistance from Kuku Yalanji people.

Settlers experienced extreme hardship, with prolonged wet seasons, disease, crop failure, low prices and extremely hard work all taking their toll. Only the hardiest of pioneers remained, isolated except by Aboriginal walking trails and supply boats, until the first real road north of the river reached Cape Tribulation in the early 1960s.

Aerial view of Cape Tribulation, so named by Lieutenant James Cook in 1770, when the HM Bark *Endeavour* struck an offshore reef, but known to its Kuku Yalanji custodians as *Kulki*.

Village in the Mist

Many of the tourists visiting the Cape Tribulation Section of Daintree National Park choose to stay in the area, taking time to explore and soak up the rainforests' sites and significance. Eco-resorts, lodges, backpackers' hostels and campgrounds provide a variety of accommodation options. Some popular retreats are **Koala Beach Resort Daintree** (Cape Kimberley Rd, Ph: 07 4090 7500); **Lync-Haven Rainforest Retreat** (Cape Tribulation Rd, Ph: 07 4098 9155); **QPWS Noah Beach Campground** (Cape Tribulation Rd, Noah Beach, Ph: 131 304 or at www.qld.gov.au/camping); **Cape Tribulation Camping** (Ph: 07 4098 0077); **Ferntree Rainforest Lodge** (Lot 36 Camelot Cl, Cape Tribulation, Ph: 1300 134 044) and **PK's Jungle Village** (Cape Tribulation Rd, Cape Tribulation, Ph: 1800 232 333).

The abundant tropical environment is complemented by culinary treats such as exotic fruits, ice cream and tea produced by local plantations, luxurious restaurant dining, and indulgent spas. The photography and botanical illustrations at **Floravilla Art Gallery** (Baileys Creek Rd, Cow Bay, Ph: 07 4098 9100) present a visual feast, while shops and services cater for practical needs and **Cape Tribulation Tourist Information Centre & Shop** (Mason's Store) (Cape Tribulation Rd, Cape Tribulation, Ph: 07 4098 0070) provides guidance regarding tours and attractions.

In peak tourist season, June to September, when the National Park walking tracks can be crowded, visitors may find relative peace on rainforest trails on private lands. The **Fan Palm Boardwalk Café** is a particularly enjoyable walk through lowland rainforest, its highlight being a majestic stand of Licuala Fan Palms. Several resorts and lodges, including Crocodylus Village (Ph: 07 4098 9166) and Daintree–Cape Tribulation Heritage Lodge (Turpentine Rd, Cape Tribulation, Ph: 07 4098 9138) have self-guided walks available to guests. For information on swimming holes, visit the Cape Tribulation Tourist Information Centre & Shop.

Golden Orchid, one of the largest of the 90-odd orchid species that grow throughout the Daintree–Cape Tribulation area.

Red Beech, a common, distinctive tree with its dark, flaky bark and yellow flowers.

North of Cairns

Cape Tribulation Reef Daytrips

Along the Cape Tribulation coastline is a large collection of extremely biodiverse fringing reefs (*below left*). Their existence adjacent to rainforest is unique in Australia, occurring in only two other places in the world. The main body of the Great Barrier Reef is a series of ribbon reefs situated 20–50 km offshore.

Taking advantage of this incomparable location are Rum Runner IX (Ph: 1300 556 332) and Odyssey H$_2$0 (Ph: 07 4098 0033 or 1300 134 044) which offer small group snorkelling and diving cruises (*right, top and bottom*). Sea turtles, nudibranchs, anemonefish, Giant Clams, a colourful range of corals, reef sharks and Spotted Blue Rays are regularly seen.

A World of Adventure

Cape Tribulation is an eco-adventure hub, with a host of possibilities awaiting exploration. Wildlife spotting is on the agenda for many visitors and the wide selection of wildlife tours (see page 71 for a sample), plus a visit to the **Daintree Entomological Museum** (Turpentine Rd, Cape Tribulation, Ph: 07 4098 9045), **The Bat House Environment Centre** (Lot 2 Cape Tribulation Rd, Cape Tribulation, Ph: 07 4098 0063), and the small wildlife sanctuary at **Lync-Haven Rainforest Retreat** (Cape Tribulation Rd, Ph: 07 4098 9155) are bound to satiate the curiosity of eager nature lovers.

Horse riding on the beach is a popular option (**Cape Trib Horserides**, C/- Rainforest Hideaway, Lot 19 Camelot Cl, Cape Tribulation, Ph: 07 4098 0108), as is sea kayaking. Kayaking tours are offered by **Tropical Sea Kayaks** (C/- Crocodylus Village, Ph: 07 4098 9166); **Paddle Trek** (15 Camelot Cl, Cape Tribulation, Ph: 07 4098 0131) and **Cape Trib Sea Kayaking** (Lot 11 Cape Tribulation Rd, Cape Tribulation, Ph: 07 4098 0077). Alternatively, kayaks can be hired from **Cape Trib Beach House** (Ph: 07 4098 0030) and **Cape Tribulation Camping** (Ph: 07 4098 0077). **Cape Trib Jungle Surfing Canopy Tours** (Lot 24 Camelot Cl, Cape Tribulation, Ph: 07 4098 0090) deliver the ultimate rainforest adventure — the exhilaration of gliding through the treetops on a series of aerial cableways.

Left and right: Cape Tribulation Beach, where the rainforest meets the reef. Daytrippers embark on their own discovery tours or participate in guided 4WD or coach tours from Cairns, Port Douglas or Mossman. Eco-accredited operators include Australian Wilderness Experience (Ph: 07 4098 1666 or 1300 134 044); Billy Tea Bush Safaris (Ph: 07 4032 0077); Daintree Safaris (Ph: 07 4094 1351); Gary's Safaris (Ph: 07 4098 2699); Odyssey Tours & Safaris (Ph: 1300 134 044); Oz Tours Safaris (Ph: 1800 079 006); Personal Adventures (Ph: 07 4036 2484); Tropical Horizons Day Tours (Ph: 07 4058 1244) and Wait-a-While Rainforest Tours (Ph: 07 4098 2422).

North of Cairns

Cape Tribulation to Cooktown

The Wet Tropics World Heritage Area encompasses most of the rainforest and also dry forest and heath country between Cape Tribulation and Cooktown. This is the coastline James Cook and his crew struggled up in the incapacitated *Endeavour* in June 1770. The names of several landmarks bear testimony to the expedition's low morale — **Weary Bay, Mount Sorrow, Mount Misery**.

Kuku Yalanji traditional custodians traversed this country seasonally hunting, fishing and gathering bush tucker as they went. With the Palmer River gold rush and Cooktown's boom, Ayton was founded (with its own access track) some 80 km south of Cooktown. Aborigines, Chinese, Malays and Pacific Islanders carved settlements out of the forest there. By the 1880s, the Daintree coast to the south was frequented by tin miners, timber-getters, itinerant workers and mission workers on the Bloomfield River. Access to the area was by the Aboriginal walking trails and coastal supply boats. Japanese and Malay bêche-de-mer fishermen visited the coastline as well.

The controversial **Cape Tribulation to Bloomfield River Track** was first forged through lowland rainforest in 1968, then again in 1976 and 1979, just prior to the declaration of the Cape Tribulation Section of Daintree National Park. Regrowth and washouts rendered it a walking track, which, in time, gained a mythical status in European and North American bushwalking circles. In the 1980s the road was widened amid vehement protests citing potential environmental impact.

Care should be exercised when travelling this rough, and sometimes steep, 4WD route, especially at creek crossings. The road is generally impassable in the wet season (Dec–Apr). In the dry season (May–Nov), it is wise to check road conditions and obtain information on necessary equipment and safety provisions with **RACQ** (Ph: 1300 130 595, www.racq.com.au) before departing.

The route is sparsely inhabited with settlements at **Wujal Wujal Aboriginal Community** (the former Bloomfield Mission), **Ayton, Rossville** and **Helenvale**. The main tourist attractions are **Bloomfield Falls** accessed by **Walker Family Tours** (Wujal Wujal, Ph: 07 4060 8069) and the historic **Lions Den Hotel** (Helenvale, Ph: 07 4060 3911), built in 1880, which served as an important stop on the supply route from Cooktown to the **Annan River** tin fields. Shady campgrounds, sporting facilities and walking tracks around **Home Rule Falls** (8.5 km) and **Cedar Bay National Park** make **Home Rule Rainforest Lodge** well worth a visit, especially during the **Wallaby Creek Music Festival** (held in September).

Top left: **Bloomfield Falls** is known by its Kuku Yalanji custodians as *Wujal Wujal*, the great waterfall from which their ancestors originated. To them it is a special, healing place. Visitors can learn more about the cultural significance of the falls and see its beauty through Aboriginal eyes, via the traditional cultural stories shared by local custodian-guides. *Above, left to right:* **Donovan Point Lookout; Glimpses of coastal scenery** are caught in several places along the first part of the Bloomfield Track.

North of Cairns

Black Mountain National Park

Situated 25 km outside Cooktown, at the junction of the coastal and inland roads, is Black Mountain (*Kalkajaka*) National Park. Marking the boundary between the Wet Tropics World Heritage Area and the drier savannah-woodland country of Cape York, this rugged mountain is composed of giant piles of black granite boulders (*below*).

In a rare phenomenon, blue-green algae grow over the granite, giving the rocks their dark appearance, the lighter colour underneath only exposed when the boulders explode during times of extreme heat. The mountain is home to plenty of plants and animals, many of them endemic.

Interpretive signs (*right*) at the QPWS carpark provide information on this traditional meeting place of the Kuku Yalanji people.

Cedar Bay National Park

Halfway between Cape Tribulation and Cooktown is Cedar Bay (*Mangkal-Mangkalba*) National Park. Accessed only by boat or a difficult walking track (17 km one way) from Home Rule Rainforest Lodge (Rossville, Ph: 07 4060 3925), the mountainous hinterland is mostly cloaked in dense, virgin rainforest, fringed by sandy beaches and coral reefs protected by the Great Barrier Reef Marine Park.

Cedar Bay is a story place of cultural significance to the Kuku Yalanji Aboriginal people. In the 1870s, tin mining was carried out in the area, with remains still visible in places.

The pristine rainforest environment (*right*) is valuable habitat for the Bennett's Tree-kangaroo (*below*) which is endemic to the Daintree River–Cedar Bay area.

77

North of Cairs

Heritage River & Town

Cooktown (*Waymuurr*) and its surrounds are within the traditional country of the Guugu Yimithirr Aboriginal people. Safe anchorage in the Endeavour River (*Birri Wahalumbaal*) attracted Lieutenant Cook in 1770, and, in 1873, a shipload of gold diggers and officials arrived to establish Cook's Town as a port. Traditionally a rich hunting ground, the river is still the scene of a vibrant fishing and sailing industry.

The waterfront is the scene of much of Cooktown's historical heritage and present-day life.

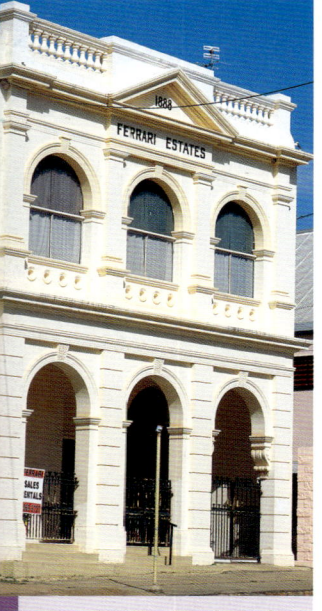

Ferrari Estates, now the Bank of North Queensland, built in 1886, is a stately monument of Cooktown's gold rush era.

Further Information:

Cooktown Booking Centre
132 Charlotte St
(Ph: 07 4069 5381).

Visitor Information Centre
Nature's PowerHouse
(Ph: 1800 174 895).

Cooktown Chamber of Commerce and Tourism
www.cooktowns.com
info@cooktowns.com
(Ph: 07 4069 5381).

Cooktown and Surrounds

On 23 October 1873, just one month after the discovery of gold in the Palmer River catchment, Cook's Town, named in honour of Captain James Cook, was established as a port and supply town for the goldfields. Within months, hundreds of iron and wood buildings lined the main street. Miners swarmed to the goldfields and the town's population quickly soared to around 30,000. Money poured in, and colonial buildings were constructed. However, by 1888, despite hopes to the contrary, output from the goldfields had declined and the town's fleeting glory was soon just a memory. By 1900, the population had shrunk to only a few thousand. Today Cooktown is a quiet and relaxed frontier town, with a visible heritage and palpable sense of history.

Heritage Walks & Museums

Various heritage walks around Cooktown bring the town's past to life. Along the waterfront is the **River of Life Path**, with monuments detailing European exploration of the area. The **East Town Walk** visits several heritage buildings — reminders of the town's heyday — and the **Cooktown Cemetery** is a veritable microcosm of the town's multicultural history.

The **Chinese Shrine** celebrates the contribution made by the Chinese community, who, at the peak of the gold rush, comprised two-thirds of the 15,000 miners on the goldfields. Containing fascinating memorabilia and relics from the *Endeavour*, the **James Cook Historical Museum** (Cnr Furneaux & Helen Sts, Ph: 07 4069 5386, open 9.30 a.m. – 4.00 p.m.) documents the region's maritime, Indigenous and Chinese history. **Cooktown's Old Bank** (122 Charlotte St, Ph: 07 4069 5888) holds photographic displays of aspects of the town's history. **Nature's PowerHouse** (Cooktown Botanic Gardens, Ph: 07 4069 6004) showcases a number of exhibitions, including Vera-Scarth Johnson's glorious botanical illustrations and specimens from Charles Tanner's intriguing wildlife collection.

Bronze memorial to Captain James Cook who explored and named the Endeavour River in June 1770. His crew took six weeks to repair the damage sustained to the HM Bark *Endeavour* after it ran aground on a reef off Cape Tribulation.

Natural & Cultural Attractions

The Cooktown area boasts a number of natural attractions. The **Cooktown Scenic Rim Walking Trail** traverses a variety of terrain, visiting **Mt Cook** (431 m), the heritage-listed Botanic Gardens (Finch Bay Rd, Cooktown) and

Grassy Hill provides panoramic views of Cooktown, the Endeavour River, and the surrounding ranges. This scene has changed little since Lieutenant Cook climbed the hill to chart a safe passage through the surrounding reefs. Several memorials commemorate his visits. The quaint lighthouse was built in England and shipped to Cooktown in 1885, where it ensured safe navigation for 100 years before being made obsolete.

North of Cairns

Grassy Hill. Birdwatching is fruitful at **Keatings Lagoon** (*Mulbabidgee*) **Conservation Park** (Cooktown Development Rd), an important habitat for waterbirds particularly during the dry season, and at **Barretts Lagoon** (Endeavour Valley Rd). Waterfall enthusiasts will enjoy **Trevethan Falls** (Mt Amos Rd, 4WD only), **Endeavour Falls** (access via Endeavour Falls Tourist Park, Endeavour Valley Rd, Endeavour, Ph: 07 4069 5431) and **Isabella Falls** (Battle Camp Rd, Battle Camp).

To the north, the beautiful natural environs of Hopevale, accessible by permits available from the Hopevale Aboriginal Community Council (Muni St, Hopevale, Ph: 07 4060 9133), may be explored via a number of Aboriginal cultural tours. **Guurrbi Tours** (Ph: 07 4069 6259) host tours of local rock art sites, **Maaramaka Tours** (Ph: 07 4060 9389) offer a guided rainforest walk and bush feast. Tours of the Cape Bedford area and Elim Beach, with its coloured sands, may be undertaken with **Malabama Tours** (Ph: 0429 898 367). The Aboriginal guides share their cultural stories and teach visitors about bush foods and medicines and Aboriginal bushcraft. Visitors are also welcome at the **Hopevale Art and Cultural Centre** (Ph: 07 4060 9111; opening times vary).

Scenic river cruises, croc-spotting excursions, and a selection of fishing and reef charter trips are available, including **Barradise Lodge** (Ph: 07 4069 5005); **Cooktown Catch-a-Crab** (C/- Cooktown Booking Centre, Ph: 07 4069 6289 or 0418 643 272); **Cooktown Cruises & Boat Hire** (C/- Cooktown Booking Centre, Ph: 07 4069 5712; **Cooktown Paradise Getaways** (Ph: 07 4069 5500); **Cooktown Reefsports** (Ph: 07 4069 5815); and **Gone Fishing** (Ph: 07 4069 5980). For those wishing to camp, **Elim Beach** has two campgrounds (Ph: 07 4060 9223 or 0429 898 367 for permits) and camping is available at many caravan parks in Cooktown.

Above: **The Milbi Wall,** a story mosaic completed by the Gungarde Aboriginal Community, tells the history of Cooktown from the Aboriginal perspective. The waterfront is the focus of Cooktown's social and cultural life. Each June (Queen's Birthday Weekend), during the Discovery Festival, Bicentennial Park is the setting for the annual re-enactment of Cook's landing and first contact with the Guugu Yimithirr Aboriginal people. Nearby are Cooktown's Wharf and Powder Magazine — constructed in 1874, it is believed to be the oldest brick building in Cape York.

Endeavour River NP

The woodlands, heathlands, mangroves and dunes of the middle and lower catchments of the Endeavour River are protected in this national park opposite Cooktown. The landscape has changed little since 1770, when botanists Banks and Solander amassed an extensive collection of plant specimens during the 48-day stopover to repair the HM Bark *Endeavour*. It was during this time that Lieutenant Cook and his crew encountered two clans of the Guugu Yimithirr Aboriginal people and recorded their use of the word, *gangarru*. These collections and observations formed the English aristocracy's first impressions of the Australian environment and its inhabitants.

Things to See and Do

1. Admire the panoramas from Grassy Hill, or take a scenic flight.
2. Absorb the town's European history along its heritage walkways.
3. For further information on Aboriginal culture visit Cook Museum, contact Cooktown Booking Centre (Ph: 07 4069 5381) or contact Gungarde Aboriginal Corporation (Ph: 07 4069 5412).
4. Enjoy fish & chips on the waterfront.
5. Explore Cooktown's natural surrounds by foot, boat or 4WD.
6. Horse-riding adventures can be enjoyed at Hidden Valley Trail Rides (C/- Cooktown Booking Centre, Ph: 07 4069 5381 or 07 4069 6073).
7. Cape Air Transport (Ph: 07 4069 5649) offers scenic flights over the Cooktown area.
8. Safaris of Cooktown and its surrounds are offered by locally operated Barts Bush Adventures (Ph: 07 4069 6229) and Cooktown Tours (Ph: 07 4069 5125).
9. Several coach and 4WD safaris to Cooktown and surrounds depart from Cairns (Adventure North Australia, 287 Draper St, Cairns, Ph: 07 4052 8300; Queensland Adventure Safaris, 306 Severin St, Parramatta Park, Ph: 07 4041 0133; Wilderness Challenge, 11 Morrisson St, Portsmith, Ph: 1800 354 486 or 07 4035 4488).

North of Cairns

A billabong on the Archer River, Cape York.

Termite mounds and stunted trees abound.

Dunes and sand flats rise from the coastline.

Cape Melville National Park

One of Queensland's most remote protected areas, Cape Melville National Park features rugged landscapes, from the rocky headlands of Cape Melville to the granite boulders of the Melville Range and the sandstone escarpments of the Altonmoui Range. Situated on the eastern end of Bathurst Bay, some 130 km north-west of Cooktown, the park protects parts of the traditional country of several Aboriginal groups who have lived in the area for thousands of years.

Complete with tropical rainforests, woodlands, heathlands, grasslands, mangroves and other wetlands, this diverse landscape is home to a great variety of plants and animals, many of them occurring nowhere else. One endemic plant, the Foxtail Palm, has become a popular garden plant throughout northern Australia. The park has many kilometres of pristine coastline and its fringing reefs are protected in the Great Barrier Reef Marine Park. Freshwater Crocodiles inhabit the park's creeks and rivers and Estuarine Crocodiles frequent these freshwater habitats as well as coastal waters. Visitors should exercise with extreme caution.

Cape Melville is accessible by 4WD vehicles, in dry weather only (generally Aug–Dec). The access road from the west enters the park via Lakefield National Park and Kalpower Station (280 km). The southern route via Cooktown and Starcke Homestead (250 km) is very difficult and travellers are advised to contact **QPWS Cooktown** (Ph: 07 4069 5777) to seek road condition advice before departing.

Camping is permitted at Cape Melville, with permits and further information available from **QPWS Lakefield** (Ph: 07 4060 3271). Alternatively pre-book (Ph: 131 304 or www.qld.gov.au/camping).

Brolga

Green Turtle

Quinkan Rock Art

Considered by the UNESCO International Committee on Rock Art to be one of the most significant rock art areas in the world, the collection of Aboriginal paintings in rock shelters in and around the **Quinkan Aboriginal Reserve** near Laura are amazingly well-preserved.

The paintings, many of them featuring animals and hunting scenes, record details of the material and spiritual lives of the area's inhabitants. Particularly distinctive are the "Quinkans" — spirit figures central to the Dreamtime mythologies of the area.

With a number of sites also illustrating early encounters with European explorers and settlers, the Quinkan Rock Art is one of few examples in the world where contact with another culture is recorded in pictorial images. Consequently, they have attracted international attention and been extensively studied by archaeologists. These Aboriginal art galleries are recognised as some of the oldest examples of rock art in the world. A variety of colours have been used and older paintings are evident underneath.

Many of the rock art sites are protected in the Quinkan Aboriginal Reserve, approximately 140 km from Cooktown. Visitor access is provided at Split Rock Gallery by a fairly steep rough bush track (900 m, 10–15 minutes) complete with interpretive signage. Private tours to Split Rock Gallery and other easily accessible sites can be organised through **Quinkan & Regional Cultural Centre** (Lot 2, Peninsula Development Rd, Laura, Ph: 07 4060 3457).

The endlessly stretching coast of the Cape.

Paintings depict emus, kangaroos and many other animals.

North of Cairns

Every second June, Cape York's many Aboriginal tribal groups gather outside Laura, a traditional Aboriginal meeting place, for the **Laura Aboriginal Dance Festival**. On-site camping is available to visitors who wish to absorb this lively forum of traditional dance, music and art. Further information about the rock art and the dance festival is available at the **Quinkan and Regional Cultural Centre**, which also interprets the European history of the Laura–Maytown area, particularly during the days of the Palmer River gold rush, between 1873 and 1888. Visitors interested in the historic and cultural heritage of the Laura–Maytown district can also walk the **Laura Heritage Trail** (Deighton Rd, Laura).

Right: Nankeen Kestrel clinging to a termite mound. *Left, top to bottom:* Heading inland leads through a desolate wilderness of Outback; Small craggy islands and headlands jut out from the Cape York coastline.

Lizard Island National Park

Approximately 90 km north-east of Cooktown is the awe-inspiring Lizard Island Group, five continental islands set among the turquoise waters of the outer Great Barrier Reef. Cloaked mainly in grasslands, but with some wooded slopes and mangroves, Lizard Island abounds with Gould's Sand Monitors, hence the name bestowed by (then Lieutenant) James Cook in August 1770, when he climbed the island's peak to sight a way through the surrounding reefs and shoals.

Lizard Island (1013 ha) is a significant cultural site for its traditional custodians, the Dingaal Aboriginal people, who have inhabited the surrounding area for many thousands of years. The island was also the scene of a bêche-de-mer industry in the late 1800s. Since the 1970s, it has been a favoured island hideaway and the site of an Australian Museum Research Station.

The islands are home to eleven species of lizard, a variety of geckoes and skinks, as well as several snake species. Insectivorous bats and a Black Flying-fox colony constitute the mammalian population. Over 40 bird species frequent the islands, which are important nesting grounds for terns. White-bellied Sea-Eagles, Ospreys, Bar-shouldered Doves, Pheasant Coucals and Yellow-bellied Sunbirds are commonly seen. Seasonal visitors include Pied Imperial-Pigeons, White-tailed Tropicbirds, Dollarbirds and Rainbow Bee-eaters.

Campgrounds (Ph: 131 304 or www.qld.gov.au/camping) and a series of short walking tracks (**Chinamans Ridge**, 340 m one way; **Watsons Cottage & Pandanus Track**, 685 m one way; **Watsons Walk**, 520 m one way; **Cooks Look**, 2.25 km return; **Research Road**, 2.2 km one way; Blue Lagoon, 450 m return) are available. The islands are accessed via regular and charter flights from Cairns (**Hinterland Aviation**, Tom McDonald Dr, Cairns, Ph: 07 4035 9323) and charter vessels from Cairns, Port Douglas and Cooktown.

The fringing reefs of the Lizard Island Group are intricate and complex ecosystems. The Blue Lagoon (*top*), with its easy beach or dinghy access, is a favoured site for snorkelling. Feather stars, sea pens, sponges and a plethora of fish-life, including the Potato Cod (*centre*) can be seen, along with more than 200 species of hard coral (*above*).

West of Cairns

To the west of Cairns on the Hann, Atherton and Evelyn Tablelands lies the tropical landscape known as "the Tablelands" or "Cairns Outback". The traditional country of many Aboriginal tribal groups, the Tablelands is an area of exceptional natural diversity. In the north-west, the red soil, blue cloudless skies and dry eucalypt forests stretch into the sunset. Not far to the south is the luxuriant Atherton Tableland, covered in a green patchwork of World-Heritage-listed rainforests and small crops. The Evelyn Tableland, just a little further south, combines the best of both — the lush rainforests and dairying country on the eastern side giving way to dry hills cloaked with eucalypt forest and eventually to the savannah country. This area has a rich Aboriginal and European heritage. Its stark contrasts, rural charms and colourful history make it a great region to explore.

Rufous Hare Wallaby

Cultural Heritage

For many thousands of years, rainforest Aboriginal people dwelled on the **Atherton Tableland,** moving seasonally to enjoy the area's abundance of food, medicines and natural assets. Different tribal groups lived similar hunter–gatherer lifestyles in the drier areas. Although their daily existence has changed considerably, these traditional custodians have retained their intimate knowledge of, and spiritual ties to, their country. In many places tours and visitor centres share insights into these rich cultures.

European Settlement

With a geological history that has blessed the area with mineral ores, limestone caves, fossilised remains, crater lakes, cinder cones, lava tubes, lush rainforests and rich volcanic soils, it is little wonder the area has proven popular with Europeans. The 1876 discovery of gold in the **Hodgkinson River** basin kick-started European occupation of the Tablelands, with timber-getters and pastoralists close on the prospectors' heels. By the 1890s, the Tablelands was scattered with thriving townships sustained by the bounty of mining and farming. Since the 1930s and 1940s, tourism has been forging a niche in the area. Today the Tablelands is a medley of towns and communities, each with its own distinct character.

Waterfalls and Wildlife

Closer to Mareeba, Emerald Creek Falls (QPWS, 83 Main St, Atherton, Ph: 07 4091 1844), is a popular retreat for swimming and picnicking. The Falls Walk (700 m) leads to the top of the waterfall with its extensive views over the valley looking towards Mareeba. Camping is not permitted. Waterfalls and wildlife can also be enjoyed at Granite Gorge Nature Park (Paglietta Rd, Mt Abbott via Mareeba, Ph: 07 4093 2259 or 07 4093 2174). Estuarine crocodiles can be seen at Melaleua Crocodile Farm (301 Peters Rd, Mareeba, Ph: 07 4093 2580) and waterbirds such as the Nankeen Night Heron (*right*) can be observed at Nardello's Lagoon (Kennedy Hwy, Walkamin).

Top to bottom: Atherton Tableland; Millaa Millaa Falls; Lake Barrine Cruise; Hou Wang Temple, Atherton.

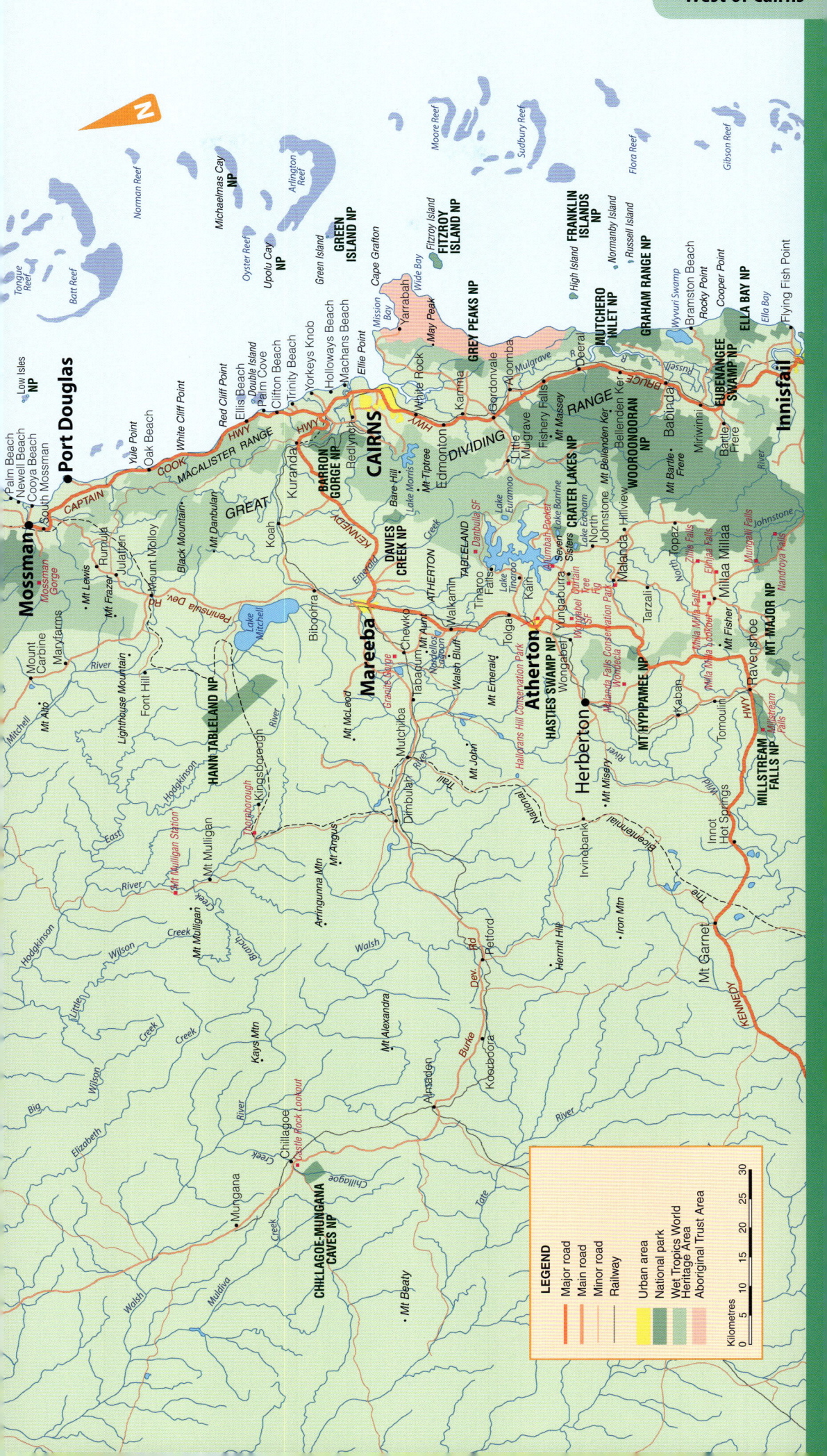

West of Cairns

West of Cairns

Gateway to the Outback

A dry region of dramatic landscapes — rugged mountains, underground caves and spectacular rock formations — the weather and terrain of the tropical outback are perfect for all manner of adventures, from hot-air ballooning to 4WD touring. Once a thriving mining and tobacco-growing district, the Mareeba area is dotted with eye-catching features and remnants of bygone eras.

Top and bottom: **Davies Creek National Park** Vista from the lookout at the top of Davies Creek Falls; Davies Creek cascades over time-worn granite boulders.

Top to bottom: **Highlander Hotel, Mareeba** Built in 1930, this is the third hotel on its site — the previous two buildings were destroyed by fire; **Mareeba's icon, the Brahman Bull,** commemorates the role of this hardy breed in the northern beef industry.

84

Mareeba to Chillagoe

In the 1870s, reports of gold attracted thousands of optimistic prospectors to the Hodgkinson River, 80 km to the north-west of Mareeba. In the heart of Kuku Djungan country, the township of **Thornborough** blossomed. After the gold rush, miners dispersed to new mineral-rich areas, including the **Herberton tin fields**. As a result, the administrative centre of the region was moved to **Mareeba** in 1919.

Mareeba

From humble beginnings as a tent town for teamsters, prospectors and railway workers in the 1880s, Granite Creek, later renamed Mareeba, developed into a prosperous town supporting the local timber, livestock and dairying industries. It was well established as a key link on the railway between the **Chillagoe Smelter** and **Cairns**, completed in 1901, before being chosen as the shire's administrative centre. During World War II the town was assumed as a military base. After the construction of the **Dimbulah** and **Walsh River** irrigation schemes in the 1950s, farming expanded, and while the tobacco industry failed, livestock, fruit and fodder have proven to be reliable.

Nowadays, Mareeba is a relaxed tropical country centre, its broad main avenue lined with cafés, shops and services. The community's main events are its annual **Mareeba Rodeo** (July, Kerribee Park, Mareeba, Ph: 07 4092 1583) and **Mareeba Multicultural Festival** (August, Arnold Park, Mareeba, Ph: 0418 770 095). The surrounding area is a scenic agricultural area, renowned for its coffee plantations and boutique wineries.

Davies Creek (Dinden) National Park

To the north-east of Mareeba is **Davies Creek National Park**, set among tall, dry eucalypt forest in a deep valley. Walking tracks follow the creek to the scenic lookout over the falls and valley. Picnic and camping facilities are provided (pre-book at www.qld.gov.au/camping or Ph: 131 304, or self-register on site). 4WDs are recommended.

Top and bottom: **Mareeba Heritage Museum & Tourist Information Centre** is open daily and makes for an educational time trip (Centenary Park, 345 Byrnes St, Mareeba, Ph: 07 4092 5674).

Mareeba Wetland Reserve

This 2000 ha reserve is one of Australia's most ambitious artificial habitat projects. A series of interpretive walking trails overlook 140 ha of wetlands, and guided Twilight Safaris, electric boat cruises, canoe hire and camping can be arranged at the Mareeba Wetland Foundation Visitor Centre (Pickford Rd, Biboohra, Ph: 07 4093 2514). A selection of waterbirds can be seen around the lily-covered waterways, including Black Swans, Magpie Geese, Brolgas and Sarus Cranes. The Foundation supports the Gouldian Finch reintroduction program.

West of Cairns

The Road to Chillagoe

In homage to the nomadic prospectors who roamed the gold, tin and copper fields pushing wheelbarrows containing their essential possessions, the road from Mareeba to Chillagoe is known as **Wheelbarrow Way**. South-west of Mareeba the road passes through a series of small country towns, once important stops along the railway line to Chillagoe, with several historic buildings and displays.

The **Thornborough Cemetery, Canton Hotel** and **Court House** foundations mark all that remains of Thornborough — one-time capital of the district. Nearby, **Tyrconnell Outback Experience and Historic Gold Mine** (399 Thornborough Valley Rd, Ph: 07 4093 5177) arranges tours of the Thornborough Cemetery and the historic **Tyrconnell Mine** and battery. Gold panning, bushwalks and luxury camping or cottage accommodation make this a genuine outback encounter.

Mt Mulligan Station (Mt Mulligan Rd, Mt Mulligan, Ph: 1800 359 798) offers camping, farmstay accommodation and outdoor activities. Known to its Kuku Djungan custodians as *Ngarrabullgan*, beautiful **Mount Mulligan** can be experienced with **Djungan Ngarrabullgan Cultural Tours** (Ph: 07 4092 4908).

In the early 1900s Chillagoe enjoyed bourgeoning prosperity due to mining magnate John Moffat's Chillagoe Smelter. Political machinations and a series of closures saw the state government take control of the smelter in 1919 and continue operations until 1943. During its lifetime the smelter processed 1.25 million tons of mineral ore.

Chillagoe Creek Homestead (Airport Rd, Ph: 07 4094 7160) offers camping along Chillagoe Creek, access to a private fossil collection and guided tours. The **Heritage Smelter Walk** takes in the smelter site and the **Historical Town Walk** visits the town's old buildings and traces its vibrant history. Visitors can enjoy stargazing at **Chillagoe Observatory & Eco Lodge** (Hospital Rd, Ph: 07 4094 7155). Fishing and swimming are also popular distractions in this dry and dusty clime. The town's signature events (both in May) are the **Chillagoe Big Weekend** (Ph: 07 4094 7087) and the 149 km **Wheelbarrow Race** from Mareeba.

Chillagoe is reached via car, bus — **Chillagoe Bus Service** (Hospital Rd, Ph: 07 4094 7155) connects in Mareeba with **Whitecar Coaches** (Ph: 07 4091 1855) — or train (**Savannahlander**, Queensland Rail, Ph: 131 617). **Coral Coaches** (Ph: 07 4031 7577) makes day tours to Mount Mulligan and Tyrconnell Mine.

Top to bottom: **Historic smelter site** on the hill overlooking Chillagoe; **Chillagoe Hub Information Centre** (23 Queen St, Ph: 07 4094 7111).

Rock Oddities

Below, left to right: Undara Volcanic National Park, Chillagoe caves; Balancing Rock, Chillagoe–Mungana National Park.

On the western side of the Great Dividing Range, a curious geological evolution has formed the world's longest lava tubes and a spectacular network of caves. Some 400 million years ago, Chillagoe lay at the bottom of an ancient inland sea strewn with extensive coral reefs. With time, the limestone deposits of the Chillagoe region were compressed, upthrust by the movements in the Earth's crust, then slowly eroded to form pinnacles towering up to 40 m above the surrounding plains. Falling rain, combined with carbon dioxide, has seeped through the cracks over time, eroding the insides of the bluffs as well as the outside and forming a series of spectacular caves.

Some 150 km to the south, approximately 190 million years ago, Undara volcano erupted. Molten lava flowed over an area of 1550 km^2, cooled, and left over 160 km of lava tubes. Used as shelter by specific Aboriginal groups, the Chillagoe–Mungana cave system and Undara Lava Tubes were discovered by European settlers in the 1890s and 1910s respectively.

West of Cairns

Around Yungaburra & Malanda

The Atherton Tableland is an area of awe-inspiring scenery. Remnant World-Heritage-listed rainforest is set among a fertile, green patchwork of farmlands — local produce thrives on the area's nutrient-rich red soils. Interspersed among farm and forest are volcanic lakes and hills that bear testimony to the area's recent geological upheavals. In this area of high rainfall rise the headwaters of many of the regions' large rivers — their creeks, swamps and tributaries supporting diverse wildlife and forming magnificent aquatic playgrounds.

Yungaburra

In the early 1900s, Yungaburra was the administrative and business centre for the rich timber and farming area of the eastern Tablelands, and, after the opening of the Gillies Highway in 1926, the town became the Tablelands' prime tourist destination. Now primarily a tourist detour and rural retreat, Yungaburra has lost none of its historic charm. Its quaint, wooden buildings, many crafted from local timbers, house a range of art galleries, craft shops, classic cottage accommodation and distinctive, award-winning restaurants. Situated in the heartland of the region's prime natural attractions, it makes a perfect base for Tablelands exploration. Oozing rustic personality, Yungaburra forms a picturesque and mellow setting for visitors looking to escape the coast and relax into country life.

Brixie's Cakes, now known as Cedars Coffee Shop, Yungaburra. Residents and visitors can enjoy a taste of Yungaburra's heritage while perusing locally handcrafted items and sipping coffees on the deck.

Peterson Creek Wildlife and Botanical Walk

Commencing at Petersen Creek Bridge on the outskirts of Yungaburra, the Peterson Creek Wildlife and Botanical Walk (2.5 km) provides easy access to wildlife and historical sites. Platypuses (*below*) are often seen in the creek from the viewing platform beside the bridge. The path meanders along the creek to the viewing platform at Allumbah Pocket, one of the area's earliest settlements, where Pioneer Cemetery is located.

Curtain Fig Tree Starting life as a tiny seed dropped by a bird in the host tree's canopy, this iconic and much-observed fig gradually overwhelmed its host over the years. Its extensive "curtain" of aerial roots drop about 15 m to the forest floor.

Lake Eacham Hotel, Yungaburra Constructed in 1910, the Lake Eacham Hotel was a tourism hub for many years. Its interior, crafted from local rainforest timbers, is still largely in its original form. Early horse hitching posts and street lamps remain outside.

West of Cairns

Old World Charm

As the largest National Trust village in Queensland, Yungaburra is delightful. Residents live and work around eighteen heritage-listed timber buildings that hearken back to Yungaburra's early years, and visitors can enjoy them while dining, shopping or relaxing in the village.

One of the oldest buildings is the **Yungaburra Community Centre**, constructed in 1910 and used originally as a dance venue, then as a cinema, before assuming its current mantle. The **St Mark's Anglican Church** (Eacham Rd, Yungaburra) and **St Patrick's Catholic Church** (Mulgrave Rd, Yungaburra) date to 1911 and 1913, respectively. The **Yungaburra Butcher Shop** (Eacham Rd, Yungaburra, Ph: 07 4095 3592) and some of the village's other shops date to the 1920s, including the building that houses the Burra Inn Restaurant (1 Cedar St, Yungaburra, Ph: 07 4095 3657). A private residence known as **Cedrella**, constructed around 1914, along with its gardens and tennis courts, was for many years the social centre of the district. In 1988 it was auctioned and redesigned as **Eden House Heritage Restaurant** (Eacham St, Yungaburra, Ph: 07 4095 3355). Outside Yungaburra the **Peeramon Hotel** (Yungaburra–Malanda Rd, Yungaburra, Ph: 07 4096 5873), which dates to 1908, is the oldest hotel on the Atherton Tableland.

Burra Inn Restaurant is said to be the Atherton Tableland's oldest BYO restaurant. Originally a barber's shop (constructed in 1926), it was used for a variety of commercial purposes, including a fish and chip shop and clothes shop, before becoming a restaurant.

Things to See & Do

1. Explore the village centre with its heritage buildings via The Old Town Loop Walk.
2. Marvel at the rainforest folk in the Chalet Rainforest Gallery (Gillies Highway, Yungaburra, Ph: 07 4095 2144).
3. Try your hand at fishing or enjoy Lake Tinaroo at sunset with Gerry's Wildlife Cruise & Fishing (Ph: 07 4095 3658 or 0417 646 088).
4. Hire a houseboat from Tinaroo Tropical Houseboats (191 Xhafer Road, Tinaroo, Ph: 07 4095 8322).

Lake Tinaroo, with its sublime natural vistas, is a perennially popular retreat.

Above: **Lake Tinaroo** The lake is the result of a large dam built in 1959 across the Barron River.

Playtime on Lake Tinaroo

Since the construction of **Tinaroo Dam**, **Lake Tinaroo** has been a popular boating, waterskiing, canoeing, windsurfing, fishing and camping venue. Access and camping facilities are provided in several places along its 200 km shoreline, including **Lake Tinaroo Holiday Park** (Dam Rd, Ph: 07 4095 8232). Campsites along the unsealed Danbulla Forest Drive are also extremely popular. Contact QPWS (Ph: 07 4046 6600) for more information.

Above: Boating on Lake Tinaroo.

West of Cairns

Crater Lakes National Park

Formed some 10,000 years ago by massive explosions of superheated ground water, then subsequently colonised by rainforest and filled with water, **Lake Barrine** and **Lake Eacham** represent unique environments. Their clear waters teem with fish, turtles, eels, crayfish and other freshwater life. The fringing rainforests contain towering Kauri Pines, descendants of species that dominated the Tablelands' forests for thousands of years. These forests provide homes for a multitude of birds, mammals and reptiles. More than 180 species of bird have been recorded in the park.

Crater Lakes National Park, declared in 1934, is the perfect place to unwind and absorb the cool, fresh Tablelands' air. Situated in country traditionally shared between the Ngadjon and Yidindji Aboriginal people, the lakes have always been a favoured place for picnicking and swimming.

Lake Barrine

The largest of the Atherton Tableland's crater lakes (or maars), Lake Barrine sits at an altitude of 730 m above sea level and has an average depth of 65 m. Visitors can enjoy the freshwater and rainforest environment by walking the **Circuit Trail** (5 km) around the lake through complex rainforest that is home to a myriad of wildlife. Buttress roots and epiphytes can be seen on many trees and water dragons and Amethystine Pythons are often seen by the lake edge. A feature of the walk is the **Twin Kauri Pines**. Believed to be well over 1000 years old, each tree's imposing girth is more than 6 m.

Above, left and right: **Lake Barrine** With the Lake Barrine Cruises and Teahouse (Gillies Hwy, Lake Barrine, Ph: 07 4095 3847) operating since the 1880s, taking a Devonshire tea in the teahouse and spotting wildlife while cruising on the lake are both long-standing traditions. The teahouse was used as a convalescent home for returned soldiers during World War II.

Above, left and right: **Lake Eacham** The lake's calm, clear waters and serene setting are often visited and photographed. Lake Eacham served as a military camp during World War II and the rainforest clearing at this time is still evident near the carpark. The lake's depth has not been accurately determined but in places it may plunge down to 150 m.

Lake Eacham

Equally tranquil is Lake Eacham, which has been a popular tourist destination since 1912. Accessed via an enchanting drive through rainforest (where the overarching canopy almost meets), the road then opens onto a large grassy recreation area with picnic and barbecue facilities on the lake's edge. This area, combined with its swimming platforms, make the lake a popular aquatic playground.

Visitors can explore the lake environment at several viewing platforms, or circumnavigate the lake on foot. **The Circuit Walk** (3 km) passes through a variety of rainforest types, where elusive Musky Rat-kangaroos are sometimes seen. About 300 m from Lake Eacham is the unmarked **Vision Falls Walk** (30 minutes), which takes in highland rainforest and a number of small but delightful waterfalls en route to Vision Falls. Alternatively, a self-guided walk through the rainforest leads to the **QPWS Ranger Station** (McLeish Rd, Lake Eacham, Ph: 07 4095 3768) where further information is available.

While touring the lakes region, visitors may enjoy the Tablelands' hospitality at a selection of B&Bs, cottages and cosy cabins tucked away in the surrounding forest. Campsites are available at **Lake Eacham Caravan Park & Self-Contained Cabins** (Lakes Dr, Lake Eacham, Ph: 07 4095 3730) or at the more indulgent **Crater Lakes Rainforest Cottages** (1 Eacham Cl, Ph: 07 4095 2322).

West of Cairns

Wildlife of the Crater Lakes

The rainforests rimming the crater lakes vary according to soil, drainage and disturbance patterns. At Lake Barrine, the complex rainforest is typical of that found on basalt soils at high altitudes, but around Lake Eacham these forests stand alongside simpler rainforests that lack the buttress roots and complexity of life forms, as well as regenerated forests cleared during WWII. Over 180 bird species have been recorded in the park. Notable residents include the Tooth-billed Bowerbird, Bridled Honeyeater and Grey-headed Robin (*below right*). Australian Brush-turkeys (*above right*) and Saw-shelled Turtles (*below*) are commonly seen.

Magical Malanda

In the western shadow of **Mt Bartle Frere**, nestled among rainforest and rolling dairy country, is the township of **Malanda** — one of the Tablelands' busiest towns. Situated in the very heartland of traditional Ngadjon country, the township sprang up around the railway line from **Tolga**, which opened in 1910. The town's economy developed with the logging industry, but soon became synonymous with dairying. By World War II, the cooperative dairy factory was the principal cheese-maker and whole-milk supplier for the Tablelands and, after the closure of the **Millaa Millaa** factory in 1982, its sole dairy facility. **Malanda Dairyfoods** operates the longest milk run in the world!

Starting at the town library, the **Malanda Mosaic Trail**, a commemorative series of nine vibrant mosaics winds through the township and captures the community's rich heritage. Also not to be missed is the **Majestic Theatre** (Cnr Catherine & Lions Sts), built in 1926 and still styled with original, oak-framed canvas bleachers. It is Australia's oldest continuously operating cinema. The innovative **Malanda Dairy Heritage Centre** (8 James St, Malanda, Ph: 07 4095 1234), with its interpretive centre, restaurant and guided tours, celebrates the area's milk heritage. For an excellent stepping-stone to the rainforest, be sure to visit the **Malanda Falls Visitor Centre** (Ph: 07 4096 6957) on the edge of town.

Left to right: Malanda Hotel; Malanda Falls Built by the English family in 1911, the Malanda Hotel was the town's first commercial building and is the largest timber hotel in Australia. Its Silky Oak staircase is considered one of the finest examples of wood craftsmanship in the district. The same pioneering family established Australia's first tropical rainforest interpretation centre at nearby Malanda Falls. Malanda Falls Conservation Park and Scenic Reserve (Malanda–Atherton Rd, Malanda) protects these rainforests and their cultural significance to the Ngadjon people. The rainforest environment and Ngadjon culture are presented at Malanda Falls Visitor Centre where information can be obtained about Ngadjon guided tours.

89

West of Cairns

Friendly Atherton

Named after John Atherton, one of the Tablelands' renowned pioneers, the township of Atherton was established in the 1880s as a support town for the farming, mining and timber industries of the surrounding area.

Known as "the friendly town", it is a tranquil place with many historic buildings and a wide range of antiques. The Barron Valley Hotel (Main St, Atherton, Ph: 07 4091 1222) and Grand Hotel (Cnr Main & Vernon Sts, Atherton, Ph: 07 4091 4899), built in 1939 and 1933 respectively, are historical landmarks and the focal point of the township.

Atherton's neat suburbs and iconic Jacaranda trees often earn it Tidy Town awards.

Top to bottom: **Downtown Atherton, Main Street; The Atherton Court House** was built during World War II, reputedly with bomb shelters underneath.

Tolga Woodworks Gallery & Café in nearby Tolga is a popular tourist destination.

Around Atherton

Commencing as a camp for timber-getters and teamsters at **Priors Pocket** in the 1870s, the township, renamed Atherton in 1886, was well established by the 1890s with government offices, shops, and two hotels. The arrival of the railway in 1903 saw the expansion of the town and its surrounding farming and timber industries. By the 1900s Atherton was the centre of Queensland's prime maize-growing industry, pioneered by Chinese settlers. The beef and dairy industries were also important. During the war years, Atherton was the base for the largest military encampment on the Tablelands — an administration centre, training ground and construction depot. The **Atherton War Memorial** (Main St, Atherton) and **Atherton War Cemetery** (Kennedy Hwy, Atherton) commemorate the town's military history.

With access to some alluring natural areas, and in itself an extremely scenic town, Atherton is visited by large numbers of tourists, particularly during the **Maize Festival** (August, Ph: 07 4091 4222). One popular attraction is **The Crystal Caves** (69 Main St, Atherton, Ph: 07 4091 2365), a subterranean labyrinth housing an extensive collection of crystal formations and fossils. Further information on the area's attractions can be obtained from the **Atherton Information Centre** (Cnr Main St & Silo Rd, Atherton, Ph: 07 4091 4222).

Former Chinatown

Of particular interest is Atherton's former **Chinatown.** In the 1880s, with the decline of the Palmer and Hodgkinson River goldfields, many Chinese moved to the Tablelands to start market gardens and timber-getting ventures. Situated on opposite banks of **Piebald Creek,** Chinatown developed alongside the early European settlement. During the 1920s and 1930s most of the Chinese community left the area — their hands forced by legislation changes.

The **Hou Wang Temple**, built in 1903, survived Chinatown's demise. It is one of the few remaining Chinese temples in Tropical North Queensland, despite the region's large Chinese population and the integral role they played in its history. The heritage-listed temple, which has been fully restored, is part of an archeological site and museum complex where visitors can explore Atherton's Chinese heritage. **Hou Wang Temple & Chinese Museum** (86 Herberton Rd, Atherton, Ph: 07 4091 6945) is open daily from 10 a.m. – 4 p.m. Guided tours are available.

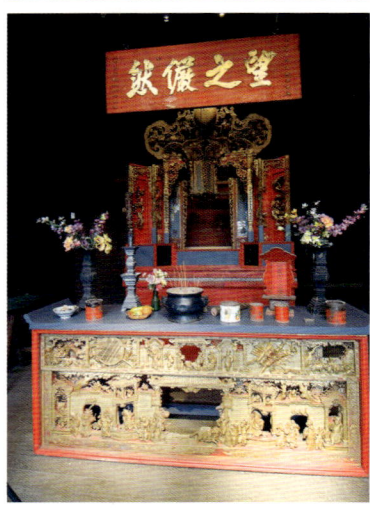

Hou Wang Chinese Temple is the only surviving timber and iron Chinese temple in Queensland. Most of its fittings, carvings and items used for worship were especially made in China.

Tolga

The tiny town of **Tolga**, once busy with timber mills, is home to **Tolga Woodworks Gallery & Café** (Kennedy Hwy, Tolga, Ph: 07 4095 4488), where visitors can peruse a selection of exquisite handcrafted timber pieces. **The Tolga Railway Museum** (Kennedy Hwy, Tolga, Ph: 07 4095 4135 for opening times) has a fascinating collection of memorabilia. **Rocky Creek War Memorial Park** (Kennedy Hwy, Tolga, Ph: 07 4092 0700) is situated on the site of the 2/2 Australian General Hospital laundry and medical stores site.

West of Cairns

Nyleta Wetlands

Five kilometres south of Atherton is Hasties Swamp National Park (Koci Rd, Atherton), which protects 57 ha of the once-extensive Nyleta Wetlands. This mosaic of seasonal freshwater habitats, comprised of open water areas fringed in native reeds and sedges, is bounded by remnants of the open eucalypt woodland and wet sclerophyll forest that once surrounded the swamp.

Its seasonal cycle of wet and dry attracts some 50 species of resident and migratory waterbird, including Magpie Geese (*above right*), Plumed Whistling-Ducks (*below right*), Sarus Cranes, Brolgas, Radjah Shelducks, Black-necked Storks, and a variety of herons, cormorants, sandpipers and dotterels.

A boardwalk meanders through Swamp Mahogany and Blue Gum at the southern end of the wetlands, whose name is a Yidindji word meaning "where the waters meet". The best time to birdwatch is during the dry season (April to November) at dawn or dusk. Over 170 species of forest bird can also be seen, including nine species endemic to the Wet Tropics.

Top to bottom: **Nyleta Wetlands bird hide** A two-storey hide perched over the wetlands offers superb viewing assisted by identification charts and birdwatching tips.

Out and About

Atherton is set among a patchwork of potato, peanut, maize, sugarcane and fruit and vegetable farms in traditional Ngadjon and Yidindji country. Shaped by volcanic forces, and once covered by lush rainforest and dry eucalypt forest, this area is home to an impressive diversity of wildlife. **The Atherton Bat Hospital** (PO Box 685, Atherton, Ph: 07 4091 2683, open by appointment) cares for paralysis-tick-affected flying-foxes roosting in the nearby **Tolga Scrub** — one of the precious few fragments of rainforest known to ecologists as "Complex Notophyll Vine Forest" or to locals as "Mabi Forest".

Bushwalking and birdwatching are popular pastimes. **Platypus Park** (Herberton Rd, Atherton) has picnicking facilities and a wheelchair-accessible rainforest walk along a stream where waterbirds rainforest birds and, of course, the resident Platypus can be seen. **The Atherton Birds of Prey Show** (86 Herberton Rd, Ph: 07 4901 6945) provides an intimate raptorial experience in a natural setting. The steep trail (2 km return) through dry eucalypt forest to the summit of **Mt Baldy** (accessed via Rifle Range Rd) presents panoramic views over the Tablelands. A little further south in **Wongabel State Forest** (Atherton–Ravenshoe Rd) visitors can trek easy trails through Mabi Forest and a Hoop Pine plantation (**Wongabel Heritage Trail**, 800 m return and **Wongabel Botanical Walk**, 2.4 km).

Hallorans Hill On top of a dormant volcanic crater, Hallorans Hill Lookout & Conservation Park (via Wadley Cl, Atherton, open daily, 9 a.m. – 5 p.m.) offers spectacular 360° views over the township, its surrounding patchwork of farms, and The Seven Sisters — a series of volcanic cinder cones 45–60 m high. This wheelchair-accessible parkland, complete with picnic and barbecue facilities and a children's playground, was named after a pioneering family who farmed the hill for many years. Artworks developed by local artists grace the lookout and the trail (30 minutes return) through the Mabi rainforest inside the crater has interpretive signs sharing insights into traditional Aboriginal lifestyle.

West of Cairns

Herberton

To the south-west of Atherton, 900 m above sea level on the eastern edge of the **Great Dividing Range**, is the historic tin mining town of **Herberton**. Tin was discovered in the hills around the **Wild River** in the 1870s and the town, named for its location on the headwaters of the **Herbert River**, developed as prospectors from the declining Palmer River and Hodgkinson goldfields to the north arrived. The first town on the Tablelands to hold a shire council meeting and open a school (both in late 1881), Herberton nevertheless remained a frontier town for a long time, linked to the rest of the Tablelands via rough bush tracks. The **Cairns–Herberton railway line**, which secured Cairns' future, was commenced in 1886 but did not reach Herberton until 1910 — ironically after the tin boom was over. Herberton was finally linked to Innisfail via the Palmerston Highway (completed in 1936). In recent times, the highway has brought a resurgence of visitors and settlers to the area, which, with its cooler climate, continues to attract people wishing to escape the scorching summer heat.

A sleepy but pretty town, with its timber buildings, colourful gardens, sidewalk cafés and friendly residents, Herberton comes to life for the monthly markets at **Wondecla Sports Reserve** (3rd Sunday of the month, Ph: 07 4096 2408) and the **Jacaranda Arts and Crafts Festival** in October (Ph: 07 4091 2181). In August, Herberton is flushed in a fragrant, golden hue with the mass flowering of the town's wattle trees.

Main Street, Herberton Lined with heritage buildings dating back to the town's beginnings, and featuring a large mural portraying prominent characters in the town's development, visiting Herberton's main street is almost like stepping back in time to the early 1900s.

Heritage Village

Although Herberton is located on the side of a steep hill, traversing the town to enjoy its heritage attractions is reasonably easy. Information and brochures are available from the **Herberton Mining and Information Centre** (Jack's Rd, Herberton, Ph: 07 4096 3474). The **Photopost Walk** depicts the main street during the town's heyday, while the **Heritage Walk** visits a number of the town's remaining heritage buildings. The **Herberton School of Arts** building (Grace St, Herberton), the Tablelands' oldest public building, and the **Herberton Camera & Photography Museum and Gallery** (49 Grace St, Herberton, Ph: 07 4096 2092) are a must for history buffs or those wishing to get a feel for the town's heritage (and some cool spy cameras). **Anzac Memorial Park** (Cnr Perkins & Myers Sts, Herberton) and **Upper Grace St Lookout** (1 km) reveal fine views over the river and town.

Mining Heritage

Evidence of mining and remnants of the mining era are visible around the town. At the **Herberton Mining and Information Centre**, which tells the story of tin mining in the surrounding landscape, the **Great Northern Mines Walk** (1 km) explores the relics of the area's rich tin mines. **The Copper Mines Walk** (1.5 km) and **Specimen Hill Lookout Walk** (1.5 km) explore mining country and visit old mine sites. Visitors can also trek longer trails through the Herberton hills (**The Great Northern Walking Trails**) on their own or, for a little adventure, join **Wilderness Expeditions** (3765 Rocca Rd, Herberton, Ph: 07 4096 2266) on a walking and camping trek with pack donkeys.

In nearby **Irvinebank**, the **Loudon House Museum** (16 O'Callaghan St, Irvinebank, Ph: 07 4096 4020), the oldest highset timber home in the north, tells the story of famous Scottish mining entrepreneur John Moffat.

Picnics & Relaxation

Along the **Wild River Walk** (1 km), visitors can picnic, birdwatch, identify plants and relax. Facilities are provided at the **Wild River Lions Park** (River Tce, Herberton). **Wondecla Sports Reserve** is another popular and well-shaded place for picnics.

Top to bottom: Royal Hotel; Post Office, **Herberton** Built in 1880 (the second storey was added in 1914), the Royal Hotel is the sole survivor of the many hotels that once lined Herberton's streets.

West of Cairns

Mt Hypipamee National Park

The volcanic pipe at Mt Hypipamee was formed some 10,000 years ago when the vent of a volcano exploded violently. This event created a sheer-sided crater and released gases and volcanic bombs far across the surrounding landscape. Set amid beautiful highland rainforests, remarkably different from tropical rainforests found elsewhere on the Tablelands, the resultant explosion crater is less than 70 m across, its cliffs dropping 58 m to the algae-covered pool below, which is believed to be 82 m deep.

A short walking track (400 m) leads to a viewing platform (*below left*) where visitors can overlook the crater (*below right*). Nearby, there is a walking trail (1 km) to Dinner Falls (*centre & bottom*), part of the upper Barron River where water cascades over basalt columns formed by solidified lava flows.

The highland rainforest gives way to wet sclerophyll forest and open eucalypt forest at the transition between the Wet Tropics and the outback. This plant diversity ensures a rich variety of fauna, including numerous possums, Lumholtz's Tree-kangaroos and endemic birds such as the Golden Bowerbird, Tooth-billled Bowerbird, Mountain Thornbill, Victoria's Riflebird and Bridled Honeyeater. Other rainforest birds include the Chowchilla, Spotted Catbird, Rose-crowned Fruit-Dove (*above*) and the more common Lewin's Honeyeater and Australian Brush-turkey.

Shared country between several rainforest Aboriginal tribes, Mt Hypipamee is a culturally significant story place. The volcanic activity on the Tablelands is so recent that the lava flows are etched into the cultural repertoire of rainforest Aboriginal people whose stories speak of large black pythons moving over the land and swallowing everything in their paths.

Mt Hypipamee National Park is situated 24 km south of Atherton on the Kennedy Highway to Ravenshoe. Secluded and eerie, particularly at night, it is the ideal place to experience the Tablelands' relatively young volcanic landscape. A range of other forest types is also found in this beautiful national park.

West of Cairns

Nocturnal Adventures in the Forests

With a large proportion of the Wet Tropics' animals being nocturnal, night-time affords the best opportunity to observe many of its wild denizens in their natural states. As the sun goes down and the diurnal species settle for the night, the forests come to life with the sounds of possums and tree-kangaroos moving through the trees, frogs calling for mates, and frogmouths and owls whooping. In the spotlight's beam, insectivorous bats pursue moths as geckoes stalk katydids and a myriad of other insects. King-crickets, worms, snails, slugs and all manner of invertebrates crawl through the leaf litter, especially after rain. Tree-snakes recline in the trees and pythons and other snakes lie in wait for unsuspecting bandicoots or pademelons to blunder into ambushes. In the streams, freshwater prawns and crayfish, fish and eels scavenge for food. Crocodiles lurk in the rivers and night-herons keep a vigil along the banks. At night, just as during the day, the tropical rainforests are literally pulsing with life.

Many of the region's national park walking trails are suitable for spotlighting, which is best undertaken in small, quiet groups commencing just after dark on evenings with little or no moon. With the aid of a good spotlight and a keen pair of eyes, a number of species may be seen. Trained eyes are even better and many of the region's naturalists offer guided spotlighting tours in habitats guaranteed to expose all manner of wildlife. To see the animals and their antics, learn about their lifestyles, and share an evening of adventure, is both a joy and an unforgettable way to experience, completely, the realm of the rainforest.

Spotlighting at Mt Hypipamee reveals mammalian residents such as possums and (if you are lucky) even a Lumholtz's Tree-kangaroo. For information on tours at Mt Hypipamee, contact QPWS (Ph: 07 4091 1844) or the local visitor information centres.

Left to right: The sloth-like Green Ringtail Possum; The Spotted Cuscus. *Below, left to right:* A Herbert River Ringtail; Striped Possum; Lemuroid Ringtail Possum.

True Possums

The Wet Tropics rainforests are important refuges for four species of ringtail possum — the Green, Lemuroid, Herbert River and Daintree River Ringtails. In contrast, the widely distributed Common Ringtail and Common Brushtail Possums adapted to life in drier forests, although they are sometimes seen in rainforests. The Atherton and Evelyn Tablelands, with their mixture of rainforest and drier habitats, have one of the largest concentrations of possums in Australia.

The Green Ringtail is the most common, named for the greenish tinge on its fur. Its diet consists of a selection of common, tough, poisonous leaves, low in energy, which make this animal a great energy-saver. The Lemuroid Possum, which eats leaves low in fibre (thus requiring less energy for digestion) is extremely energetic, leaping from tree to tree over distances of 2–3 m. The Herbert River Ringtail's diet and energy levels lie somewhere between these two extremes. The Daintree River Ringtail, found only in the upland forests of Mount Windsor and Mount Carbine Tablelands, feeds on pioneer species on the rainforest edges.

Long-tailed Pygmy-possum

West of Cairns

The Coppery Brushtail Possum is restricted to the uplands of the Atherton Tableland. Distinguished from the rainforest ringtails by its pointy ears, it eats a variety of leaves, fruits, flowers and insects. Confident on the ground, these possums often scavenge around picnic areas. Only two of the Wet Tropics' endemic possum species are found in the lowlands as well as the uplands. The skunk-like Striped Possum feeds noisily, jumping from tree to tree, crashing on branches, as its forages for fruit, pollen and insects. Its tongue and long fourth finger are exceptionally useful in extracting boring beetles and moth larvae from under the bark and in holes of trees. The Long-tailed Pygmy-possum, with its quaint face and dark eye patches is a spotlighting favourite — although because of its tiny size, this possum can be particularly difficult to locate high in the canopy.

Common Brushtail Possum

Common Ringtail Possum

Look up — There's Roos in the Trees!

Australia's two species of tree-kangaroo are found only in isolated pockets of rainforest on the Atherton Tableland and in the Daintree area. Road signs (*left*) warn motorists to be cautious in tree-kangaroo territory. The Lumholtz's Tree-kangaroo (*below left*) occurs in both regions, although in the Daintree it is restricted to upland forests to the south of the Daintree River. Bennett's Tree-kangaroo (*right*) is endemic to the lowland rainforests of the Daintree River–Cedar Bay area.

Returning to the trees, from where it is believed all kangaroos originated before planting their feet firmly on the ground, tree-kangaroos are a novelty and something of an evolutionary conundrum. The long, cylindrical tail assists with balance in the trees, but is not prehensile. Tree-kangaroos do not match possums' agility. Their legs move independently as they climb or walk, forwards or backwards, along branches. With claws sharp and rounded for grasping branches, the ability to hop from tree to tree, and a diet of leaves and fruit, they are well adapted to their arboreal lifestyle. However, tree-kangaroos do, surprisingly, spend time on the ground. Descending backwards down the trunk before jumping the last two metres to the ground, they then walk, run or hop to their destination.

During the day, both species, which are generally solitary, sleep crouched on tree branches and at night move through the trees feeding. Little is known about the details of their breeding and development. The Bennett's Tree-kangaroo is slightly larger than its cousin, weighing up to 13 kg compared to 10 kg, and males of both species are larger than the females. Elusive and nocturnal, both species are rarely seen except on spotlighting excursions.

Left to right: Greater Glider; Feather-tailed Glider; Squirrel Glider; Sugar Glider.

The Gliding Possums

The eucalypt forests of the Atherton and Evelyn Tablelands are home to a number of glider species, which like possums, sleep by day in tree hollows lined with leaves, and spend their nights feeding on leaves, sap, resin, flowers, buds, fruits or insects. With membranes of skin extending from their forelegs to hind legs and a tail that can be used as a rudder, they are adept at moving gracefully through the trees when startled or in search of food.

The tiny Feather-tailed Glider is extremely fast, agile and manoeuvrable in flight, leaping through the canopy and gliding more than 20 m. The 30–40 cm Sugar Glider and slightly larger Squirrel Glider (*right*), very similar in appearance, are feisty characters, defending their territories noisily and gliding for more than 50 m. The Yellow-bellied Glider, easily distinguished by its yellow chest, can soar staggering distances — up to 120 m. The largest of the family is the Greater Glider, 70–105 cm from head to tail tip, distinguished by its rounded, fluffy ears. The Mahogany Glider, once believed to be extinct, lives in isolated areas around Cardwell and Ingham.

West of Cairns

Waterfall Country

From the Aboriginal word meaning "plenty water" or "waterfall", the township of Millaa Millaa sits in the centre of the well-known and much-visited waterfall circuit. The mountain terrain and abundant rainfall ensure that the falls, set amid lush rainforest, flow year round.

Top to bottom: Millaa Millaa Falls; Elinjaa Falls; Mungalli Falls.

Around Millaa Millaa

On the eastern Evelyn Tableland, at an altitude around 800 m, **Millaa Millaa** is often shrouded in cloud. This cool, lushly rainforested area lies within the traditional country of the Ma:Mu Aboriginal group.

With the verdant hills first settled by European dairy farmers in the early 1900s, the township of Millaa Millaa began its life in 1919, thriving when the completion of the railway from Malanda to Millaa Millaa (in 1921) linked the town to Cairns and facilitated a timber boom. Throughout the 1920s Millaa Millaa was the busiest timber and dairy-loading depot in the region. The **Millaa Millaa Cheese Factory**, opened in 1930, was one of the Australia's first to produce export quality cheese.

Heritage buildings dating from this time include the **Country Womens' Association Hall** (Palm Ave, Millaa Millaa) and the **Millaa Millaa Hospital** (Palm Ave, Millaa Millaa) and stand as testimony to the thriving social life of the district. **The Liberty Theatre** (Main St, Millaa Millaa), constructed in 1939, was a popular venue for movies, dances, wedding receptions and other functions — particularly during WWII when military camps dotted the Tablelands. Sadly, fires, closure of the railway in 1964, and relocation of the dairy factory to Malanda (in 1982) have all changed the face of Millaa Millaa. **The Eacham Historical Society Museum** (Main St, Millaa Millaa, Ph: 07 4097 2147) remains to celebrate the area's lively history.

This fibreglass sculpture epitomises the daily chores of a bygone era in Millaa Millaa.

Dairy cows graze contentedly on pasture near the town of Millaa Millaa.

Waterfall Circuit

Home to the iconic **Millaa Millaa Falls**, with its bridal veil drop set in lush rainforest, the area around Millaa Millaa has another eight large waterfalls to explore. Further along **Teresa Creek Road** are **Zillie** and **Elinjaa Falls**. The scenic route to **Ravenshoe** (Old Bruce Hwy, Millaa Millaa) passes two more — **Souita** and **Papina Falls**. **Mungalli Falls** is situated east of Millaa Millaa along the Palmerston Highway, and further east in the Palmerston Section of **Wooroonooran National Park** are **Nandroya**, **Wallicher** and **Tchupala Falls**.

Millaa Millaa's country roads alternately pass through lush rainforest and offer sweeping views across rolling green hills to Queensland's highest mountain — Mt Bartle Frere (1622 m). **Millaa Millaa Lookout** offers extensive vistas over the Tablelands and coast, arguably the best views on the Tablelands.

Millaa Millaa is along the **Taste of the Tropics Food Trail** (Australian Tropical Foods, Ph: 07 4040 4415) and the region has a biodynamic dairy (Mungalli Creek Dairy, 251 Brooks Rd, Millaa Millaa, Ph: 07 4097 2232), and a number of teahouses and accommodation options for visitors wishing to savour the sights and flavours of the district. Camping facilities are provided at **Millaa Millaa Tourist Park** (Malanda Rd, Millaa Millaa, Ph: 07 4097 2290) and **Mungalli Falls Rainforest Village** (280 Junction Rd, Millaa Millaa, Ph: 07 4097 2358), which also offers bushwalks and a range of other outdoor activities.

Millaa Millaa also accesses the **Hinson Creek** and **Gorrell Trailheads** of the **Misty Mountains Trail** network, which explore the rainforested catchments of the South Johnstone River and its tributaries. For further information contact QPWS (5B Sheridan St, Cairns, Ph: 07 4046 6600).

West of Cairns

Left to right: **Eastern Yellow Robin; Orange-Eyed Tree-frog; Spotted Catbird.**

Wooroonooran National Park

Traditional country of the Ma:Mu people, the Palmerston Section of Wooroonooran National Park is an area of outstanding beauty, and an important part of the Wet Tropics World Heritage Area. Diverse tropical rainforests cover the mountains from uplands to lowlands, streams cascade over sheer drops, and wild rivers flow through steep rainforest-clad gorges. The combination of high rainfall, fertile basalt soils, and favourable topography and temperatures has led to the development of complex rainforests characterised by incredible plant diversity — more than 500 plant species have been recorded.

Various wildlife inhabit these forests, including Wet Tropics and Cape York endemics like the Musky Rat-kangaroo, Spotted-tailed Quoll, Green Ringtail, Lemuroid Ringtail and Herbert River Ringtail Possums, Southern Cassowary, Orange-footed Scrubfowl, Victoria's Riflebird, Golden Bowerbird, Spotted Catbird and Papuan Frogmouth. Platypuses may sometimes be seen in the creeks.

The Palmerston Highway, which follows the traditional route taken by Ma:Mu people who have moved seasonally between the mountains and the coast for many thousands of years, provides easy access to the Palmerston Section of the national park. Visitors can explore the rainforest and experience its beauty and wildlife along a series of walking tracks — Nandroya Falls Circuit (7.2 km), Henrietta Creek–Goolagan's Picnic Area (800 m), Goolagan's Tchupala Falls Entrance (3 km), Tchupala Falls Walk (1.1 km return) and Crawford's Lookout–North Johnstone River (5 km return) — or enjoy the awe-inspiring view over the North Johnstone River Gorge from Crawford's Lookout. Henrietta Creek and Goolagan's Creek are popular for picnicking and swimming. Camping facilities are provided at Henrietta Creek Campground (Ph: 131 304 for bookings).

Tchupala Falls, where crystal clear water flows over a sheer granite rockface to a plunge pool below.

Nandroya Falls In a picturesque forest setting, water falls into a pool over a high narrow drop then over a wider, shorter drop.

One of many cool mountain streams flowing through the Palmerston Section of Wooroonooran National Park.

West of Cairns

Understanding the Rainforest

How the Rainforest Works

Rainforests are dynamic ecosystems, with complex webs of relationships between living and non-living components. Bursting with life, tropical rainforests are literally jam-packed with an extensive list of organisms. Such incredible biodiversity supports more than half of the world's plant and animal species. These fill every available rainforest niche, taking advantage of every opportunity for growth. Consequently, there is little room for waste. Plants continually shed bark and leaves, which are broken down by minions of invertebrates and micro-organisms, converted into nutrients and re-absorbed by plants. Rainforests are stable, self-sustaining communities that maximise their use of the sun's energy and the soil's nutrients.

Change is a normal process in nature and rainforests respond and adapt to a range of environmental stimuli. However, given favourable conditions and lack of major disturbances, such as cyclones, logging or clearing, rainforests can, over time, develop in complexity to reach a "climax forest" state. Such a rainforest environment is said to have reached the cumulative stage, or peak, of its natural evolution. The largest protected remnants of these forests are found on the rugged ranges in the Mossman–Daintree area and in Wooroonooran National Park near Innisfail. Tropical rainforests are, literally, a celebration of the chaos and creativity of life. Symbolically, they are one of the most peaceful and spiritual places on Earth.

Critical biomass In the Wet Tropics World Heritage Area, mountain ranges are cloaked with a dynamic ecosystem that is rainforest.

Australia's only native Rhododendron is found on the summits of Mt Bartle Frere and Mt Bellenden Ker south of Cairns, and on Thornton Peak and other mountains in the Daintree area.

Lilly Pilly Despite a variety of designs, rainforest fruits share one intent — proliferation of their species.

What Rainforest Needs

In general, a rainforest needs optimal conditions to develop and thrive in all its complexity. High and frequent rainfall (1500 mm/year, regularly falling each month) and a warm climate (temperatures over 19° C with little fluctuation) are the two primary precursors. Fertile soils are not a prerequisite, as nutrient cycling in the rainforest is fast and self-sustaining. However, well-drained soil is important, as is the absence of fire, cyclones and human disturbances.

Photosynthesis

Plants use the sun's energy to convert water and carbon dioxide into sugars for their maintenance and growth. Chlorophyll, which is remarkably similar to haemoglobin in human blood, drives this process. A plant's ability to photosynthesise forms the basis for most of the Earth's food chains. Without photosynthesis, the majority of herbivores would not survive.

Leaves

Chlorophyll is the compound that gives leaves their characteristic green colour and their photosynthetic ability. Leaves also help regulate water levels in and around the plant. Transpiration, or evaporation of water from the leaf surface, is a normal process, but in the humid air of rainforests most plants have "drip tips" on the ends of their leaves to hasten this process and drain their leaves after rain.

Buttresses

Buttress roots are a peculiarity of complex rainforests. Whether they support large trees in the rainforests' shallow soils, assist with oxygen intake in wet soils, or perform some other function, the roots decorate the bases of tree trunks and form vast networks across the forest floor.

Flowering Trunks

Technically known as "cauliflory", some tropical rainforest plants (including figs and the Bumpy Satin Ash) sprout flowers from their trunks rather than their branch tips. Being closer to the ground, these fruits attract different animals and are dispersed differently from the majority of rainforest fruits (which are produced in the canopy).

Flowers and Fruits

Flowers are the sexual organs of flowering plants. Tropical rainforests produce a cornucopia of flowers in different colours, shapes and sizes, designed to attract insects, nectarivorous birds and flying-foxes for pollination.

West of Cairns

Seeds and Seed Dispersal

Seeds are the means by which flowering plants reproduce themselves. They contain the genetic material for new individuals, and most rainforest species incorporate means to spread their seeds throughout the forest. Dispersal by wind, water and animals (particularly Musky Rat-kangaroos, flying-foxes, cassowaries, parrots, pigeons and other fruit-eating birds) is a common strategy among rainforest plants.

Food Plants

Tropical rainforests are the source of many of the world's foodstuffs, including chocolate, coffee, fruits (bananas, rambutans and tamarinds) and spices (pepper and nutmeg). In the Wet Tropics these foods constituted the traditional diet of Rainforest Aborigines. Some are used in modern "bush tucker" cuisine.

Striving for Sunlight

In the darkened rainforest, plants use a variety of strategies to reach the sunlight according to their requirements. Pioneer species grow very quickly to reach the canopy in relatively short time, vines and climbers hitch a ride on other plants, and epiphytes disperse their spores on the wind so that they can germinate high on the damp trunks of rainforest trees.

Strangler Figs

Starting life as a seed that germinates in a bird dropping on a host tree, a strangler fig seedling sends roots to the ground. Over time, these roots thicken, join and envelope the host tree. At the same time, the fig's crown grows to overshadow its host's. Eventually, the strangler fig out-competes its host, which slowly rots away to reveal the lattice-like framework of the fig's deadly embrace.

Epiphytes and Parasites

Epiphytes, such as some mosses, lichens, orchids and ferns, hitch a ride on the trunks of rainforest trees to access higher light levels and collect leaf litter for nutrient cycling. In contrast, parasites, such as mistletoe, not only attach themselves to the tree trunks but tap into them, feeding on the plant sugars produced by the rainforest tree.

Recycling

In nature, everything is cycled and recycled, and rainforests are no exception. Their warm temperatures and high moisture levels are extremely conducive to decomposition. These complex forests are supported by a thin layer of leaf litter rapidly recycled by a host of worms, fungi, insects and other organisms living in the soil and leaf litter.

Regrowth and Succession

Following cyclones or clearing, exposed patches receive extra sunlight that stimulates the growth of pioneer species (whose seeds have been lying dormant in the soil). As they grow, pioneers create suitable conditions for more shade-tolerant species, which slowly overtake them. In this way, disturbed areas can become closed forests within 10–20 years.

Chemical Warfare

Plants are rarely passive or benign; they guard their hard-won resources by engaging in chemical warfare and employing poisonous saps, hairs and spines to deter herbivores.

Cluster Fig In a phenomenon unique to tropical rainforests, some plants bear flowers and fruit on their trunks. This profusion of fruit close to the ground attracts different kinds of dispersal animals from those attracted to fruit growing in the canopy.

The rainforest floor is a colourful pastiche of fruit (such as the Cassowary Plum), fungi, leaves, bark and branches, creating a nutrient-rich layer over the rainforest floor.

Rock Orchid An example of a rainforest epiphyte.

A Strangler Fig gets a firm hold on its host tree. These plants begin their lives as seeds lodged in the crevices of their hosts.

West of Cairns

Ravenshoe Timber buildings in the old north Queensland style line the wide main street.

Hotel Tully Falls Built in 1927, this characteristic building is Queensland's highest pub.

Crossroads

Standing at the crossroads of the Evelyn Tableland, the Cardwell Range and Gulf Savannah country, Ravenshoe is the gateway to a number of natural attractions, including the Undara Lava Tubes, Tully Gorge and the Misty Mountains network of long range walking trails.

In the heart of the traditional country of the Jirrbal Aboriginal people, the area is one of exceptional natural diversity, and an abundance of wildlife inhabits the rainforests, eucalypt forest and savannah country.

Contact the Ravenshoe Visitor Centre & Nganyaji Interpretive Centre (24 Moore St, Ph: 07 4097 7700) for more information.

Around Ravenshoe

At 920 m above sea level, Ravenshoe is Queensland's highest town. This quiet, remote town, originally known as **Cedar Creek**, began its life in the 1890s as a timber milling centre when the cedar-getters, having exhausted supplies in the Cairns' region, pressed further afield into the Tablelands in search of the prized "red gold". With the proposed extension of the Cairns–Herberton railway to Ravenshoe, the area was surveyed for agricultural selection, and clearance of the **Evelyn Tableland's** rich stands of cedar, walnut, mahogany and pine followed. With the completion of the railway in 1916, the terminus, renamed Ravenshoe, quickly became the timber and dairying centre for the district.

The **Kennedy Highway** to Cairns and **Palmerston Highway** to Innisfail were completed in 1935 and 1936 respectively, ending the town's isolation. Although the dairy industry moved to Millaa Millaa and Malanda, timber-getting continued with approximately 35 species including walnut, mahogany, maple, silkwood, Kauri Pine, Black Pine and Silky Oak, being milled in the town in the 1940s.

With the declaration of the Wet Tropics World Heritage Area in 1988, most of the logging was stopped. Eco- and heritage tourism are now the key industries in this charming country town with its old timber buildings.

Attractions

Ravenshoe's timber milling heritage is most evident inside the town's older buildings (like the Club Hotel/Motel, built in 1910) and during **Torimba & Festival of the Forest** (first fortnight in October, Ph: 07 4097 6407), featuring its woodcraft competition and timber displays. Woodwork is also available at the town's markets held in the railway yards every fourth Sunday (Ph: 07 4097 6332) and the **Archer Creek Markets**, held second Sunday of the month (Ph: 07 4097 6458). The work of Jirrbal people and other local artists can be seen at several art and crafts venues including **Win's Gallery** (35 Grigg St, Ravenshoe, Ph: 07 4097 6522).

Misty Mountains Trail — Cardwell Range Track

The Misty Mountains Trail network comprises over 130 km of walking tracks, many of them following Jirrbal and Ma:Mu pathways that connect the coastal plain to the Tablelands.

The western end of the Cardwell Range Track (26.7 km one way) can be accessed from Ravenshoe (via Cockram/Gold Coast Rd, off Tully Falls Rd). The hike takes about 2 days to complete, traversing the hills of the Cardwell Range, and takes in untouched rainforest, mesmerising lookouts and waterfalls.

A permit is required to camp overnight and a special Wet Tropics permit is also required should walkers wish to travel along Maple Creek Rd (between Hinson and Gorrell Trailheads). Contact QPWS (Ph: 07 4046 6600) for more information.

Below: A 1925 authentic steam train, the *Millstream Express,* journeys through open eucalypt forest, across trestle bridges over the Millstream River and into Tumoulin — the highest railway station in Queensland. Trains depart Ravenshoe Sat and Sun (1.30 p.m.) from Jan–Apr, (Ph: 07 4097 7402).

West of Cairns

Not far outside the town is **Windy Hill Wind Farm** (Cnr Kennedy Hwy & Glendinning Rd, Ravenshoe, Ph: 07 4097 7700), where 20 turbines atop 44 m steel towers generate electricity for 3500 homes (up to 12 megawatts) on the Tablelands. As north Queensland's only wind farm, Windy Hill makes an interesting diversion.

A number of retreats and B&Bs dot the landscape and camping is available on the edge of town at **Tall Timbers Motel & Caravan Park** (Kennedy Hwy, Ravenshoe, Ph: 07 4097 6325).

Nature on the Doorstep

Millstream Falls National Park is situated just outside Ravenshoe, in dry eucalypt forest on the edge of the Wet Tropics World Heritage Area. The popular **Millstream Falls** is easily accessible (3 km along the Savannah Way) with walking tracks leading to the falls, swimming holes and picnic facilities. At **Little Millstream Falls** (Wooroora Road, 500 m outside Ravenshoe along Tully Falls Road), a short walking track leads to a tranquil, zen-like scene.

To the south of Ravenshoe, Tully Falls Road forges through rugged landscape and different forests en route to **Koombooloomba Dam**. Ten kilometres along the road is the **Wabunga–Wayemba (Charmilla Creek) Rainforest Walk** (3 km) with its delightful waterfall and plunge pool. This walk was developed by the Jirrbal people who sometimes offer guided tours (enquire at the **Ravenshoe Visitor Centre & Nganyaji Interpretive Centre**). Trailheads providing access to the **Misty Mountains Trail** network are a little further on. Some 23 km from Ravenshoe, in **Tully Gorge National Park**, **Tully Gorge Lookout** offers views over the 300 m Tully Falls, which, since the construction of the dam, flow only occasionally in the wet season. At the end of the road is the dam — popular for walking, camping, swimming, canoeing.

At Millstream Falls the Millstream River flows over basalt columns. When in flood, these are Australia's widest falls.

Things to See and Do

1. From Mt Garnet it is possible to travel via unsealed roads south to Blencoe Falls.
2. Dip into the warm waters of Nettle Creek at Innot Hot Springs.
3. Try your luck gem fossicking around Mount Surprise.

Undara Volcanic National Park

Roughly 150 km south-west of Ravenshoe, Undara Volcanic National Park (*below*) protects a series of lava flows formed during volcanic eruptions about 190,000 years ago. Flowing down riverbeds, the lava cooled quickly on the edges, but the fiery inner lava continued to flow. The resultant hollow lava tunnels were subsequently colonised by a distinctive suite of plants and animals.

Undara lava flow — from the Aboriginal name meaning "a long way" — is 160 km long, the planet's longest lava flow from a single volcano. Undara Experience (Savannah Way via Mt Surprise, Ph: 1800 990 992) provides guided tours of the lava tubes and a range of other outdoor bush experiences in the traditional country of the Ewamian Aboriginal people. Visitors can stay in restored railway carriages (*top right*), or choose from a range of camping options.

101

South of Cairns

South of Cairns, the spectacular scenery of the Wet Tropics and Great Barrier Reef World Heritage Areas, with their rugged mountain ranges, diverse rainforests, wild rivers, lush wetlands, palm-lined beaches and offshore islands, cays and reefs, continues for another 200 km all the way to Cardwell. This northern half of the "Great Green Way", which spans the territory between Cairns and Townsville, is a region of outstanding natural beauty. Known as the "Cassowary Coast", in recognition of its important habitats for the Southern Cassowary, the region's high mountains give way to extensive floodplains that support significant wetlands and provide valuable habitats for a multitude of wildlife. Queensland's highest mountains, Mt Bartle Frere (1622 m) and Mt Bellenden Ker (1592 m), protected in the awe-inspiring Wooroonooran National Park, dominate the landscape between Gordonvale and Innisfail. Their summits are home to many species of plants and animals found nowhere else in Australia.

Southern Cassowary

Cassowary Coast

The Cassowary Coast encompasses the traditional country of many Aboriginal groups who, for thousands of years, have maintained a close cultural and spiritual connection to the area. Explored by timber-getters and gold miners in the 1870s, then later developed into a patchwork of sugarcane and banana farms, the region is largely agricultural but has a regular scattering of small towns and beachside communities. Here residents enjoy the simplicity of a modern, tropical, country lifestyle.

Containing some of Tropical North Queensland's best-kept secrets, the area gives visitors the chance to explore the exotic beauty of the tropics in relative seclusion. Wildlife is abundant and there are numerous picnic spots beside crystal-clear streams and freshwater swimming holes (safe from crocodiles and marine stingers and perfect for hot summer days). The region has a network of bushwalks to explore, ranging from short wilderness forays to extended overland treks for more adventurous souls wanting to explore the region's grand mountain areas.

Tully River Rafting

Tully is a region of wild rivers and the setting for some of Australia's best whitewater rafting. Foaming Fury (19–21 Barry St, Cairns, Ph: 1800 801 540) offers half- and full-day tours for beginners or more experienced rafters on the Grade 4 rapids of the Russell and North Johnstone Rivers. But by far the most popular river destination, renowned around the world, is the Tully River.

A series of 44 rapids (Grade 3 to 4) provides the ultimate adrenalin rush for experienced kayakers and thousands of people on commercial rafting tours every year. Tully River whitewater rafting trips are offered by Raging Thunder Pty Ltd (Bruce Hwy, Tully, Ph: 07 4068 3210) and R'n'R Rafting (278 Hartley St, Cairns, Ph: 07 4041 9444). All tours incorporate rainforest walks.

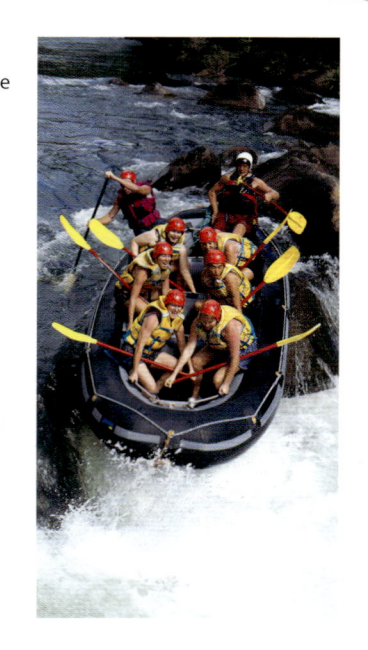

Top to bottom: Josephine Falls; Mt Bartle Frere and foothills; Muggy Muggy Beach, Dunk Island; Hillcock Point, Hinchinbrook Island.

South of Cairns

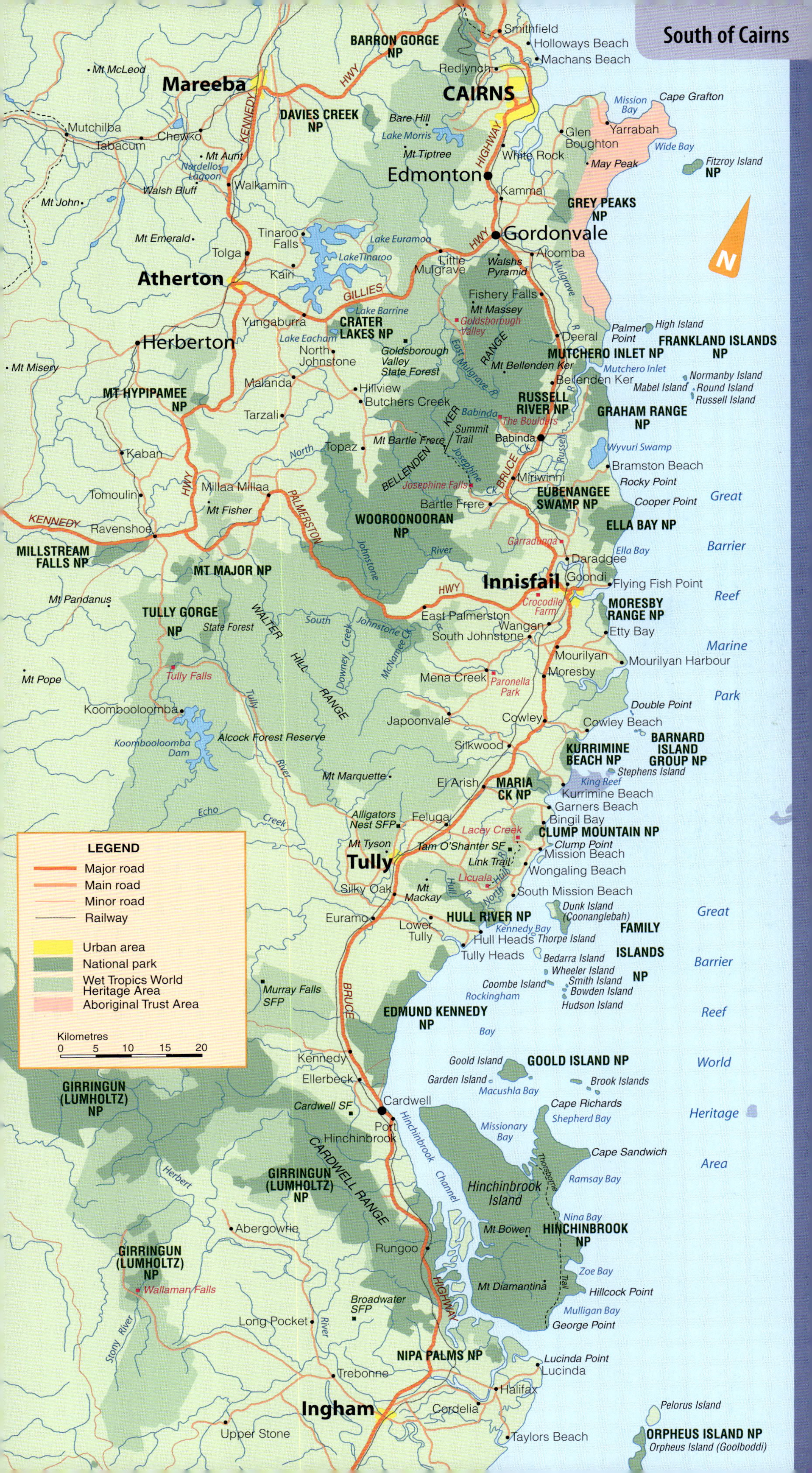

South of Cairns

Gordonvale to Babinda

Between Gordonvale and Babinda the scenery is lush and green, with the sugarcane fields on the floodplains of the Mulgrave and Russell Rivers bounded to the west by the impressive **Walshs Pyramid** and **Bellenden Ker Range** in **Wooroonooran National Park**, and by the lower Thompson and Graham Ranges to the east. An area of high rainfall and seasonal flooding, the vegetation of the region combines with the topography to create a very scenic drive, with small settlements dotting the highway to the south and providing the perfect places to stop for a light snack or a meal.

Frankland Islands National Park

Beyond the coastal ranges are the **Frankland Islands**. These continental islands were part of the coastal mountain ranges, until they were cut off from the mainland by rising sea levels some 8000 years ago. Ancient sedimentary outcrops are backed by dense rainforest that hugs the protected slopes and gullies. Sand spits, which have formed in the lee of the islands, are thick with coastal vegetation, and mangrove swamps and beach rock add to the diversity. Surrounding the islands are coral reefs that, together with the islands' vegetation, support plentiful marine life as well as forest and sea birds.

These five small islands, **High, Normanby, Mabel, Round** and **Russell,** and their fringing reefs have traditionally been used and cared for by several Aboriginal tribal groups. Close to the mainland, the islands and the surrounding sea country represent easily accessible hunting and gathering sites, which retain their cultural significance to this day.

Named after two Lords of the English Admiralty by Lieutenant James Cook in 1770, the Frankland Islands were used by bêche-de-mer fishermen in the 1850s and coastal explorers into the late 1800s. In the early 1900s the islands became popular as fishing and boating destinations for local residents, being declared national parks in 1936 and zoned into the Great Barrier Reef World Heritage Area in 1983.

Top and bottom: Frankland Islands Round and Russell Islands are joined by a sand spit; Frankland Island Cruise and Dive offer an exclusive day tour of Normanby Island's rainforests, rockpools, sandy beaches and fringing reefs. The islands are easily accessible places to enjoy tropical island walks and explore the abundant marine life just off the beach.

The peak of Mt Bellenden Ker (1592 m) Queensland's second highest mountain is vegetated with cloud forest — home to several plant and animal species found only on the mountain and the adjacent Mt Bartle Frere, Queensland's highest peak (1622 m).

Just 10 km offshore from Russell Heads, the islands are easily accessible by boat via the **Mulgrave** and **Russell Rivers. Frankland Island Cruise and Dive** (109 Draper St, Cairns, Ph: 07 4031 6300), the only tour company licensed to visit the uninhabited islands and their fringing reefs, departs daily from Deeral Landing on the Mulgrave River. Their exclusive daytrip to Normanby Island includes snorkelling, diving, glass-bottom boat tours and guided island walks — giving visitors access to the complete range of the island's natural attractions.

For those seeking an extended stay, camping is available on Russell and High Islands, with permits available from QPWS (5B Sheridan St, Cairns, Ph: 07 4046 6600). Facilities are limited and, as Russell Island has no fresh water, campers are required to take their own. Frankland Island Cruise and Dive carry campers to Russell Island.

South of Cairns

Behana Gorge/Fishery Falls/Bellenden Ker

Approximately 5 km south of Walshs Pyramid is **Behana Gorge,** accessed via a turnoff just to the north of the Behana Creek bridge. Rising in the rugged and mist-shrouded Bellenden Ker Range, which dominates the landscape south of Walshs Pyramid, the creek cascades over large granite boulders in an impressive, time-worn and rainforest-clad gorge. A rough vehicle track traverses the gorge to the Cairns City Council (Ph: 07 4044 3044) water supply intake approximately 1.5 km upstream. Walking is permitted along this track, though a degree of fitness is required and there are no guard rails or visitor facilities. Well-prepared hikers will be rewarded with magnificent views of the gorge below.

Fishery Falls is a tiny hamlet, named for the small waterfall at the base of the Bellenden Ker Range, (right on the Bruce Highway, 12 km south of Gordonvale). Although this waterfall is officially closed for water supply purposes, camping is available at **Fishery Falls Caravan Park** (Bruce Hwy, Fishery Falls, Ph: 07 4067 5283). Just over 5 km south is **Deeral** with its service centre and boating access to the Mulgrave River. A small distance further on through the agricultural lands is Bellenden Ker, another modest hamlet named after the imposing mountain range to the west, which lies in the centre of Wooroonooran National Park.

Russell River National Park viewed from Bramston Beach, with Thompson Range in the background. This small park protects lowland rainforest, paperbark swamps and mangroves near the combined estuary of the Russell and Mulgrave Rivers. Estuarine Crocodiles inhabit these waterways. To the north of Bramston Beach is Graham Range.

Coastal National Parks

Unlike Wooroonooran National Park, which at 79,500 ha is one of Queensland's largest national parks, the ranges to the east of the main highway comprise two smaller national parks — the **Grey Peaks** and **Russell River National Parks**. Included in the Wet Tropics World Heritage Area, these unspoilt parks protect important coastal ecosystems.

With no visitor facilities, these areas are uncommon destinations on travellers' itineraries, although bush camping is permitted at **Russell Heads** (self-register on-site and be sure to bring cooking gear). Access is along a 6 km unsealed road to the north of Bramston Beach. The birdwatching in these places is excellent, with miles of far-stretching beaches, wetlands and pristine mangrove habitats; however, be sure to bring insect repellent and be wary of straying too close to waterways — Estuarine Crocodiles inhabit these areas.

Metallic Starlings

One of the unique birds of the Wet Tropics World Heritage Area is the Metallic Starling. From August onwards, the adult birds, with their iridescent green-black plumage and red eyes, form large colonies to rear their chicks. Building large, pendulous, haystack-like nests (*right*), crammed together in conspicuous positions, they can completely inundate their host trees. Branches and nests accumulate, becoming infested with mites and attracting snakes looking for an easy meal. Once the chicks have left their nests, these birds may gather together in flocks of several thousand.

Metallic Starlings generally nest in or near rainforest, where they forage for fruit and nectar. Their habit is to fly as a flock low above the canopy, wheezing and squawking as they go. Although their antics endear them to some people, their colonial behaviour and raucous calls generally make them one of the least popular tropical birds, and many residents keenly await their departure to the islands north of Australia in April.

South of Cairs

Around Babinda

Some 60 km south of Cairns is **Babinda**, a small town famous for being one of the wettest places in Australia. Nestled among lush farmland and tropical rainforest at the base of **Mt Bartle Frere** and **Mt Bellenden Ker**, Babinda receives an average annual rainfall of over 4500 mm. Its name is derived from the Yidindji word for waterfall, *bunna binda*, and the town's backdrop is a long waterfall over a granite rock face on Mt Bartle Frere. Downstream from the falls are **The Boulders**, a popular swimming hole only a few kilometres from Babinda.

Babinda began its life as a sugar milling town with the construction of **Babinda Central Mill** in 1915. A police station, bank and school soon followed, with mill workers' cottages and basic stores lining the main street. The **Babinda State Hotel** (Munro St, Ph: 07 4067 1202), opened in 1916, was the first State-built and State-owned hotel in Queensland. It is still in operation, as is the mill. Other historic buildings include **St Rita's Convent**, completed in 1928, the **Babinda Hospital Nurses' Quarters**, exemplifying a 1950s architectural style, and the **Bartle Frere Masonic Lodge**, dating to 1919.

In March 2006, over 80% of Babinda's buildings and most of its surrounding fruit and cane farms were decimated by Category 5 Tropical Cyclone Larry.

Top and bottom: **Babinda** During the town's Umbrella Festival (June) and Harvest Festival (September) banners decorate Babinda's main street.

Babinda Boulders

Some 7 km west of Babinda, The Boulders is a popular swimming hole and picnic area and a place of spiritual significance to Yidindji Aboriginal people.

Cool, clear water flowing straight from the mountains tumbles over large granite boulders in a creek lined with lush rainforest. A deep pool adjacent to the picnic area provides a shaded swimming hole. The Wonga Track Rainforest Circuit (850 m) and Devil's Pool Walk (1.3 km return) take in the rainforest and creek environment.

At the Devil's Pool, the creek cascades down a series of granite boulders and washpools that have claimed several lives. A Yidindji legend tells of a young woman who, having thrown herself into the creek to avoid being separated from her lover, calls young men to their deaths in the pool.

South of Cairns

Goldfield Trail

Following the discovery of gold on the north-west slopes of Mt Bartle Frere in the 1930s, prospectors used an Aboriginal trail across the saddle between Mt Bartle Frere and Mt Bellenden Ker for access to the goldfields. The 19 km track, which was restored in 1986 by participants of Operation Raleigh, an international volunteer project, passes through complex tropical rainforest between **The Boulders** outside Babinda and the **Goldsborough Valley**, some 20 km from Gordonvale.

This picturesque trail traverses a variety of terrain, crossing numerous creeks before reaching the **East Mulgrave River** causeway and the **Goldsborough Valley State Forest** campground. Vines, Crow's Nests, orchids and other epiphytes, King Ferns and moss-covered rocks by babbling streams are all visible along this delightful walk, and numerous species of rainforest birds can be both seen and heard. The trail is a bush track, rough in places, and caution should be exercised when negotiating this trail. Further information and camping permits are available from **QPWS** (Flying Fish Point Rd, Innisfail, Ph: 07 4061 5901). **Wooroonooran Safaris** (3–5 Warrego St, Cairns, Ph: 07 4051 5512) run guided walks along this trail.

The Goldfield Trail can be negotiated by experienced bushwalkers in 1–2 days. Those seeking a shorter walk can enjoy a return trip part way along the track, which remains flat for the first 3 km, skirting Babinda Creek for a section of the walk.

Bramston Beach

A 24 km scenic drive from Babinda, south to **Miriwinni** and then east through canefields, wetlands and lowland rainforest, brings travellers to the small and sleepy village of **Bramston Beach**. Set upon a glorious sweeping beach with views to the **Frankland Islands** group, Bramston Beach's residents enjoy a quiet life amid their tropical landscape.

Beach walking and fishing are popular local pursuits. Visitors may enjoy a picnic in the shade of large paperbark trees in the lovely park adjacent to the beach, or camp on the beachfront under the trees at **Cairns City Council Campground** (96 Evans Rd, Bramston Beach, Ph: 07 4067 4121) or at **Plantation Village Holiday Resort and Caravan Park** (Evans Rd, Bramston Beach, Ph: 07 4067 4133).

Bramston Beach This long, golden sandy beach is a great place for beachcombing, swimming, walking and fishing.

Baldy Hill overlooks the main freshwater swamp lined with sedges, native grasses and paperbarks. This unique and crucial habitat supports numerous bird species. Its vegetation varies considerably from that seen in other swamps of the region.

Eubenangee Swamp National Park

This internationally recognised coastal wetland is situated on one of the wettest floodplains in Queensland and is the only sizable freshwater lagoon with open water between the Daintree River and Tully during drought periods. Lowland rainforest occurs in the well-drained areas, while sedges and paperbark swamps dominate the wetter areas. As such, it is highly significant for the survival of much of the region's wildlife, including crocodiles, turtles, butterflies and resident birds, as well as visiting migratory birds. Significantly, the Black-necked Stork (or Jabiru) nests in the park every year.

Eubenangee Swamp is easily accessed from Miriwinni, along Bramston Beach Road and Cartwright Road. Home to some 200 bird species and numerous rare and threatened plants and animals, it is one of the premier sites for observing wildlife in the Wet Tropics. A 1 km track passes through riverine vine forest before emerging onto grassy plains and traversing a grassy knoll, with spectacular views over a magnificent open freshwater swamp set in front of Mt Bartle Frere. From this vantage point, a variety of waterbirds, including Greater Egrets, Green Pygmy Geese and Comb-crested Jacanas can be seen. Estuarine Crocodiles can be spotted at night. An extensive range of rainforest and grassland birds is commonly seen and heard along the way, and Swamp Wallabies can also be seen feeding. Species lists and further information are available from QPWS Innisfail (Flying Fish Point Rd, Innisfail, Ph: 07 4061 5901).

South of Cairns

Josephine Falls — Wooroonooran National Park

Approximately 12 km south of Babinda, in Ngadjon country, is **Josephine Falls**. At this popular destination, crystal-clear water flowing straight from Mt Bartle Frere falls over large granite boulders in a creek flanked by luxuriant rainforest. A 600 m walking track passes through the forest toward a series of lookouts, which give superb views over the creek and falls.

The falls are situated at the base of Mt Bartle Frere, only a few kilometres downstream from the summit, which receives an annual rainfall in excess of 10 m. As flash flooding is common, and rocks are extremely slippery, it is wise to obey the numerous warning signs around the creek and lookouts and to keep out of the restricted areas.

The high rainfall and mist from the falls have created a thick tangle of vegetation, where trees, vines and epiphytes clamber all over each other in search of sunlight. A colourful profusion of flowers and fruits is borne by the flowering plants and these, together with the leaf litter, support a wealth of wildlife. On the ground, bandicoots, Musky Rat-kangaroos, Australian Brush-turkeys, frogs, lizards and all manner of invertebrates seek food, shelter and mates. The shrubs and trees provide food and homes to a range of rainforest birds, particularly fruit- and honey-eaters, and masses of different insects. A variety of turtles, fish, crayfish and small invertebrates inhabit the clear cool waters of the creek, feeding on fruit and leaves that drop into the water. The serene, enchanted atmosphere of the place belies the underlying reality — the forest and creek are bursting with life.

Interpretive signs are positioned along the track, and picnic and barbecue facilities situated in the day-use area adjacent to the carpark make this a great spot to absorb the atmosphere.

Above left to right: **Josephine Falls; Wooroonooran National Park** An exceptionally high volume of cold water flows over these falls every year — temperatures are usually 12–15 °C. Josephine Creek is home to a wealth of freshwater life. In the foothills of Mt Bartle Frere, the rainforest is complex and diverse, characterised by tall trees with sprawling buttress roots, countless vines and creepers, and a profusion of shrubs and ferns.

Josephine Falls, with its multiple-tier drop and large plunge pool at the bottom, is one of the most picturesque waterfalls in the region. The large granite slabs lining the creek have been worn smooth by the flow of water over time.

A Crow's Nest fern makes the most of the light levels in its aerial location over the creek. Many epiphytes cling to the rainforest trees hugging Josephine Creek.

South of Cairns

Further information about this beautiful area (and species lists) is available from QPWS (Flying Fish Point Rd, Innisfail, Ph: 07 4061 5900).

Upper Russell River

A mere stone's throw from Josephine Falls is the **Russell River**, which also thunders down the sides of Mt Bartle Frere. Whitewater rafting is a popular pursuit here. Contact **Foaming Fury Whitewater Rafting** (19–21 Barry St, Cairns, Ph: 1800 801 540). The rapids open onto the **Golden Hole** at **Biggs Recreation Area** (Cairns City Council, Ph: 07 4044 3044), which is a popular swimming and picnicking destination. The tiny tropical hamlet of Bartle Frere lies in the shadow of its mountainous namesake nearby.

Musky Rat-kangaroo This diurnal species, seen around Josephine Falls, is Australia's smallest macropod.

Things to See and Do

1. If you're fit enough, experienced enough and game enough, climb Mt Bartle Frere.
2. Experience the thrill of rafting down the Russell River rapids.
3. Soak up the ambient atmosphere at Josephine Falls.
4. Camp at the picturesque and peaceful Ella Bay.
5. For more information on local attractions and Ngadjon and Yidindji culture, visit the Babinda Information Centre (Ph: 07 4067 1008).

Bartle Frere Summit Track

At 1622 m, Mt Bartle Frere is the highest mountain in Queensland. Known to the Ngadjon Aboriginal people, its traditional custodians, as *Chooreechillum*, the summit of the mountain was rarely approached because of its special spiritual significance. First ascended by Europeans in 1886, it is a popular destination for bushwalkers who may be fortunate enough to spy a Golden Bowerbird (*right*), a species unique to this region.

There are two paths to the summit. The eastern trail follows an early tin miners' track, and the western trail follows traditional Aboriginal tracks then diverges to the summit. The trails, both 7.5 km long, are unformed and very steep in places. Only the fittest hikers can ascend and descend the mountain in a single day.

Ella Bay National Park

This 3450 ha park protects lowland rainforest and swamps and the coastline to the south of Bramston Beach. **Ella Bay** itself is extremely picturesque, with large paperbark and rainforest trees converging on its two sweeping sand beaches — popular with walkers. Beach camping facilities are provided (Johnstone Shire Council, Rankin St, Innisfail, Ph: 07 4061 2222). The drive into **Ella Bay** around the rainforested hillsides is also very scenic. This is a dirt road, so caution is necessary. The national park protects wildlife such as the Southern Cassowary and Estuarine Crocodile.

Ella Bay Its long beaches are popular with hikers.

South of Cairns

Around Innisfail

Innisfail's location on the junction of the **North** and **South Johnstone Rivers**, and only kilometres from the coast, gives the town a natural and scenic atmosphere. The town has endured its share of natural adversity. Rebuilt after a Category 5 cyclone virtually razed the entire town in March 1918, half of Innisfail's homes and much of its surrounding farmlands were damaged by Cyclone Larry in March 2006.

Many of Innisfail's buildings date to the 1920s and 1930s and their diversity of styles add justifiable weight to the town's claim to the title of "Art Deco Capital of Australia". The town's charming buildings, beautiful riverfront and gardens, and colourful history combine to make it a fascinating place that can be explored more fully by taking a self-guided walking tour of the town (brochure available from information centre).

Flying Fish Point looking towards Ella Bay.

Cassowary Coast

Situated a mere 90 km south of Cairns, and with a population of 8000, the lively sugar "city" of Innisfail is the centre of the Cassowary Coast.

With picturesque Flying Fish Point, Ella Bay National Park and Etty Bay nearby, as well as several constructed tourist attractions, Innisfail is the perfect base from which to explore the natural attractions of the surrounding area.

Driving into Innisfail reveals wonderful views of Mt Bartle Frere From any direction, this mountain, with its distinctive "Broken Nose", dominates the scenery around Innisfail. Although it is often wreathed in cloud, the summit is visible for many miles on clear days.

Johnstone River Crocodile Farm

Minutes from the centre of Innisfail is the Johnstone River Crocodile Farm (Flying Fish Point Rd, Ph: 07 4061 1121). This farm displays approximately 3500 Estuarine Crocodiles (*right & below right*), which range in size from 30 cm juveniles to a gigantic 5.2 m male known as Gregory, who weighs in at 1200 kg.

Freshwater Crocodiles and American Alligators are also on show. Guides explain the behaviour of the three species and provide insights into the farming of these reptiles. There are also opportunities for close encounters with a variety of native wildlife including kangaroos and wallabies (*bottom left*), pythons, cassowaries, Emus, parrots and other birds.

South of Cairns

Clockwise from above: Aerial of Innisfail and surrounding mosaic of farmland; Innisfail's fishing fleet docked at the waterfront; The modern Clock Tower stands alongside the Innisfail Court House, built in 1939.

Multicultural Flavour

Innisfail is situated in the heart of the traditional country of the Ma:Mu Aboriginal people, and many of the surrounding place names, including **Daradgee**, **Mundoo**, **Wangan** and **Japoonvale**, are derived from their Aboriginal names. In the 1880s an influx of European cedar cutters and Chinese gold prospectors formed the basic stock for a rich "cultural stew" of settling migrants, looking to establish cane farms or strike it rich in the nearby goldfields. Innisfail soon developed into a cosmopolitan town and now serves as the social and business centre for the surrounding farming area.

Innisfail's lively cultural scene features **The Feast of the Senses** (March, jcult@znet.net.au), the **Kulture Karnivale** (August) and the **Innisfail Festival** (October/November). A seasonal calendar of art exhibitions and performances is hosted by the **Sugarama Gallery** at the **Australian Sugar Industry Museum** (Bruce Hwy, Mourilyan, Ph: 07 4063 2656), which explores the cultural and farming heritage of the local area.

Warrina Lakes (Charles St, Innisfail, open daily, Ph: 07 4030 2222) features a botanic gardens, rainforest walk, small lakes, covered picnic and barbecue facilities and the **Ma:Mu Bush Tucker Garden** (Campbell St entrance). The **Lit Sing Gung Chinese Temple** (Owen St, Innisfail, open daily, 8 a.m. – 5 p.m., free entry), which was built after a cyclone destroyed the original temple, is the only Chinese temple still in use as a house of worship in Tropical North Queensland. **The Canecutters Memorial** (Cnr Fitzgerald Esplanade & Edith Sts), erected in 1959, celebrates the town's Italian heritage.

Exploring the Area

From Innisfail it is only 7 km to **Flying Fish Point**, and a further 7 km to Ella Bay National Park. To the south lies the charming beach of **Etty Bay** and **Mourilyan Harbour**, with its bulk sugar terminal. A worthwhile scenic detour is **The Canecutter Way**, which visits the small surrounding townships of **Wangan, South Johnstone, Mena Creek, Japoonvale** and **Silkwood** along the old Bruce Highway, giving a feeling for the area's heritage and lifestyle. Access to the **Misty Mountains Trail** is 10 km (follow the signs) from **Paronella Park** at Mena Creek.

Camping is available at **River Drive Van Park** (7 River Ave, Bruce Highway (south), Innisfail, Ph: 07 4061 2515), **Mango Tree Tourist Park** (6 Couche St, Innisfail, Ph: 07 4061 1656), **August Moon Caravan Park** (Bruce Highway, Innisfail, Ph: 07 4063 2211), **Flying Fish Point Caravan Park** (Elizabeth St, Flying Fish Point, Ph: 07 4061 3131) and **Etty Bay Van Park & Kiosk** (The Esplanade, Etty Bay, Ph: 07 4063 2314).

For further information visit the **Innisfail Information Centre** (Bruce Highway, Mourilyan, Ph: 07 4061 7422).

Things to See and Do

1. Try your hand at fishing. Boat ramps are located in Innisfail, The Coconuts, Flying Fish Point and Mourilyan Harbour.
2. Enjoy a scenic drive along The Canecutter Way, or drive through Garradunga with its historic hotel to Eubenangee Swamp.
3. Visit Australian Sugar Industry Museum & Sugarama Gallery or the Innisfail & District Historical Society's Local History Museum (11 Edith St, Innisfail, 4860, Ph: 07 4061 2731).

The Australian Sugar Industry Museum, Mourilyan honours the sugarcane pioneers of the area.

Etty Bay, Moresby Range National Park, where cassowaries are often encountered.

South of Cairns

The Castle, with its theatre-cum-ballroom, was Paronella's crowning achievement.

The Lower Refreshment Rooms, where Margarita Paronella entertained guests.

Paronella Experiences

Each year over 100,000 visitors experience Paronella Park through a variety of tours. The Dream Continues Tour is a 45-minute guided walk that takes in the park's many highlights and explains Paronella's vision. Bush Tucker Tours are led by Indigenous guides who tell Dreamtime stories and point out local bush tucker. The Darkness Falls Tour is a one-hour tour that uncovers the park's nocturnal secrets.

Paronella Park

In 1929, after making his fortune sugarcane farming, Spanish-born José Paronella purchased a 13 ha property adjacent to **Mena Creek Falls** to pursue his dream. Inspired by childhood memories of Catalonian castles, José, wife Margarita and their labour team, worked intensely for several years to create the pleasure gardens and reception centre. **The Castle, Grand Staircase** and **Lower Refreshment Rooms** (with changing cubicles for swimmers) were constructed of poured concrete reinforced with old railway irons and smeared with a plaster made of clay and cement. Tennis courts were made from crushed termite mounds and more than 7000 trees were planted, including an avenue of Kauri Pines that tower over the gardens. To power the park, north Queensland's first hydroelectric plant was built.

Opened to the public in 1935 — making it one of north Queensland's earliest tourist attractions — Paronella Park was for many years the hub of local social life. Visitors wandered through the gardens, swam, played tennis and enjoyed refreshments. At night there were movies in **the Theatre** and dances in the **Grand Ballroom** with its massive ball of 1270 mirrors, which, when slowly rotated and reflected with spotlights of pink and blue, produced a surreal, snowflake effect around the room.

Unfortunately, in 1946 disaster struck — a mass of logs and a railway bridge swept over the falls during a flood, destroying much of the Park. The Park was reopened, but a series of further setbacks followed. The current owners, who purchased the park in 1993, have revived the dream and obtained National Trust Listing. Today, the unique romantic setting of the park is a popular venue for weddings, receptions and an annual opera event.

Paronella Park (Japoonvale Rd, Mena Creek, Ph: 07 4065 3225), with its café and gift shop, is open daily. Guided tours enable visitors to share Paronella's vision, learn about bush foods and spot nocturnal wildlife. Adjacent to the Park is **Paronella Caravan and Camping Park** (Ph: 07 4065 3225). Across the suspension bridge over the Mena Creek Falls is **Mena Creek Environmental Park** with its picnic facilities and short bush track to the plunge pool at the bottom of the falls.

Fish and turtle viewing are a feature of Paronella Park's regular guided tours.

The Lower Tea Gardens overlook the plunge pool at the base of Mena Creek Falls. Nearby is the hydroelectric plant.

South of Cairns

Heading for Mission Beach

From Innisfail and **Mourilyan**, the Bruce Highway continues south through whispering canefields and small towns with views to the rainforest-clad hills to the west and the coastal ranges to the east. This area of high rainfall is the heartland of the "Cassowary Coast" — "green like you've never seen".

Silkwood and the Canecutter Way

Approximately 30 km south of Innisfail is the township of **Silkwood**, whose usually tiny population swells during the **Festival of the Three Saints** each May (Ph: 07 4065 6214). From Silkwood it is possible to travel back to Innisfail along **The Canecutter Way**, a 40 km scenic drive along the old Bruce Highway through canefields, fruit farms, pockets of lush rainforest and small country towns, which, in their heyday, were thriving sugar towns. This drive accesses the **Gorrell Trailhead** of the **Misty Mountains Trail**, some 10 km outside Mena Creek (follow the signs from Paronella Park or the Mena Creek Hotel). For further information on the **Misty Mountains Trail Network**, contact QPWS (5B Sheridan St, Cairns, Ph: 07 4046 6600)

Silkwood Hotel This graceful old hotel, built in the older north Queensland style, with wide verandahs and timber interiors, lends a touch of country class to its surrounds and reminds visitors of a bygone era.

Cowley Beach is a sleepy fishing village on the coast, which enjoys ocean views to the nearby Barnard Islands. Visitors can stay at Cowley Beach Caravan Park (Bambrook Rd, Cowley Beach, Ph: 07 4065 4806).

Kurrimine Beach

Kurrimine Beach, 36 km south of Innisfail is a popular yet sleepy seaside village inhabited by avid anglers and a handful of dream-seeking sea changers. Its long, coconut-lined beach and foreshore park offer swimming, playground and picnicking facilities. Kurrimine Beach is renowned for **King Reef** not far offshore, excellent fishing and beachcombing opportunities, and sumptuous seafood menus.

Kurrimine Beach Conservation Park protects a 6 ha remnant of lowland rainforest known as "Mesophyll Vine Forest", which although now endangered, once blanketed the area. The **Paddy Illich Track** (600 m), named after a Ma:Mu elder who received a bravery award for rescuing a drowning swimmer, provides access to the park where vines (such as the infamous "wait-a-while"), palms, and large trees (such as Native Nutmeg and Milky Pine) can be seen. Observant visitors may see large land snails, Emerald Doves, Lace Monitors, Green Tree Ants and Orange-footed Scrubfowls and their nests. Further information is available from QPWS Innisfail (Flying Fish Point Rd, Innisfail, Ph: 07 4061 5901). Camping facilities are located at **King Reef Resort Hotel & Caravan Park** (Jacobs Rd, Kurrimine Beach, Ph: 07 4065 6144), **Kurrimine Beach Holiday Park** (Jacobs Rd, Kurrimine Beach, Ph: 07 4065 6166) and the **Johnstone Shire Council Campground** (Jacobs Rd, Kurrimine Beach, Ph: 07 4061 2222).

Barnard Island Group NP

Just off the coast between Mourilyan Harbour and Kurrimine Beach lie the North and South Barnard Islands (*below*), part of the traditional sea country of the Ma:Mu Aboriginal people. Accessible by boat or sea kayak from Mourilyan Harbour or Kurrimine Beach, the seven continental islands are home to many plant and animal species and form important breeding sites for sea birds, particularly Bridled Terns, Crested Terns (*right*), Lesser Crested Terns and Black-naped Terns.

South of Cairns

Tropical Playground
A popular holiday destination, picturesque Mission Beach boasts 14 km of palm-fringed, sandy beaches with shimmering aquamarine waters and views of nearby islands. All manner of beach activities are possible here, including beach walking, sunbathing, swimming, kayaking, windsurfing, sailing and fishing. Then there are the islands to explore, by foot, boat or paddle power.

The glorious golden sands of coconut-lined South Mission Beach.

Windsurfing off Mission Beach with Dunk Island in the background.

Kayaking off Mission Beach Kayaking is a novel way of reaching the nearby islands.

Bingil Bay is a beautiful and secluded hideaway north of Mission Beach.

Mission Beach

Mission Beach is actually four small villages — **Bingil Bay, North** and **South Mission Beach** and **Wongaling Beach** — set among some of the region's most gorgeous natural scenery. Long, golden beaches arc around the glittering Coral Sea, encompassing views of continental islands across the horizon. The majority of the surrounding landscape, part of the traditional country of the Djiru Aboriginal people, is within the Wet Tropics World Heritage Area. Vibrant rainforest-clad ranges merge here with lowland forests and mangroves. These forests and wetlands provide life-sustaining habitats for the endangered Southern Cassowary and a wealth of other wildlife, including the Ulysses Butterfly — a tourism mascot for this area. The **Community for Coastal and Cassowary Conservation Inc.**, or **C4** (Porters Promenade, Mission Beach, Ph: 07 4068 7197) provides information on Djiru culture and local flora and fauna, particularly cassowaries. Further information regarding Djiru culture is available from **Clump Mountain Wilderness Camp** (Cassowary Dr, Mission Beach, Ph: 07 4068 7408) and **Girringun Aboriginal Corporation** (235 Victoria St, Cardwell, Ph: 07 4066 8300).

The villages are home to people from all walks of life, including a contingent of artists who have found their muse in the tropical environment (**Mission Beach Artists and Craftworkers Association**, Porter Promenade, Mission Beach, Ph: 07 4088 6056). Art galleries and shops line the main street of **North Mission Beach**, and fine restaurants and cafés offer gourmet cuisine and tropical delicacies. **Wongaling Beach** has a business and light industrial centre, as well as its share of dining venues and beach bars. **Bingil Bay** and **South Mission Beach** are somewhat quieter and more secluded. The entire area exudes a natural and laid-back charm that captivates visitors.

Although the villages hold regular markets during each month (first Saturday, third Sunday), perhaps the best time to visit Mission Beach is on **Monster Market** day. Mission Beach hosts this extremely large event on the last Saturday of every month, attracting hordes of marketers and shoppers from all over the area. Mission Beach is also especially lively during the annual **Aquatic Festival** in October (Ph: 07 4068 9517) and the **Mission Beach–Dunk Island Sailing Regatta** (also in October, Ph: 07 4068 8201). For further information, contact the **Mission Beach Wet Tropics Visitor Information Centre** (Porter Promenade, Mission Beach, Ph: 07 4068 7099).

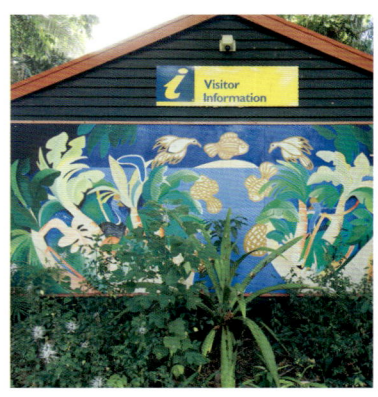

Colourful scenes enliven the Visitor Information Centre at North Mission Beach.

Mission Beach Resort, Wongaling Beach, with its attendant giant cassowary, icon of the area.

Ecotours & Adventures

Mission Beach is abuzz with ecotourism activity — a number of companies offer tours to the reef, rainforest and outlying islands. **Quick Cat Cruises** (Clump Point Jetty, Mission Beach, Ph: 07 4068 7289) are a fast and easy way to explore the islands. Guided rainforest walks and tours are offered by **Wet Tropics Guided Tours** (44 Pacific View Dr, Wongaling, Ph: 07 4068 8037 or 0428 181 494) and **Geoff's Camping and Tours** (Ph: 0409 720 264), which also caters for camping. River cruises for wildlife spotting are conducted by **River Rat Eco Cruises** (Hull River Boat Ramp, Jackey Jackey St, Mission Beach, Ph: 07 4068 8018) and **Crocodari Crocodile Spotting & Eco Tours** (34 Seaview St, Mission Beach, Ph: 07 4088 6154 or 0408 871

South of Cairns

Licuala Fan Palm Forests

The access roads into Mission Beach cut through **Tam O'Shanter State Forest**, where visitors can glimpse cassowaries in their lowland rainforest habitat. Along **El Arish–Mission Beach Road** is **Lacey Creek Recreation Area**, with its picnic facilities, arboretum, display and **Rainforest Walk** (1.1 km return).

At **Licuala Recreation Area**, accessed from Tully-Mission Beach Road, the **Licuala Rainforest Circuit and Boardwalk** (1.8 km circuit) passes through a cathedral-like Fan Palm forest. The **Licuala Children's Walk** (350 m) ends with a suitable surprise. Fit, experienced bushwalkers are bound to enjoy the **Link Trail** (7 km one way) between Licuala and Lacey Creek.

The magnificent Fan Palm, with its eye-catching circular aesthetic, occurs in wetter soils in several places through the Wet Tropics rainforests. Cassowaries relish the palm's fleshy, orange fruit.

Things to See and Do

1. Visit C4 to discover more about the endangered Southern Cassowary, its habitat, and Djiru culture.
2. Enjoy a walk along one of the beach or forest tracks.
3. Be adventurous! Join a diving, sea kayaking, fishing tour, or an evening crocodile spotlighting cruise.
4. Sip coffee or dine in one of Mission Beach's splendid restaurants and cafés.
5. Soak up the sun and relax on the beach.
6. Visit Mission Beach's Monster Markets.

Clump Mountain National Park

Clump Mountain National Park, protecting rare lowland rainforest remnants, is a key cassowary refuge and best viewed along the Bicton Hill Track (3.9 km circuit) accessed from Bingil Bay.

This track accesses several lookouts on Bicton Hill (*below right*), which offer spectacular views over Dunk and the Family Islands. These lookouts were once used by local residents eager for the arrival of supply ships. Cassowaries (*left*) can be spied by walkers, but Emerald Doves and other fruit-eating birds are more commonly seen.

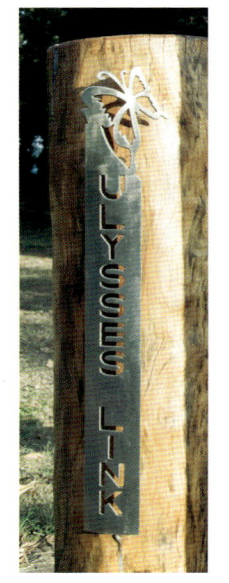

Ulysses Link & Kennedy Walking Trails

Several walking tracks have been developed by the pioneers and residents of Mission Beach. **The Cutten Brothers Walking Track** (1.5 km) near Bingil Bay links the boat ramp at **Clump Point** through mangroves and endangered "Complex Mesophyll Lowland Rainforest" to the **Clump Point Jetty**.

From the Clump Point Jetty it is possible to walk back to the centre of North Mission Beach along the **Ulysses Link**. This walk through the dune vegetation is punctuated by a series of mosaics and artworks produced by the local community to share its history.

The **Edmund Kennedy Memorial Walking Track** is a 9 km walk (one way) along the coastline from the boat ramp at South Mission Beach around **Tam O'Shanter Point** to **Kennedy Bay** and then onto **Hull Heads**. This track was cut in homage to Edmund Kennedy's ill-fated 1848 expedition to Cape York.

Walking paths allow visitors to get close to wildlife.

South of Cairns

Dunk Island and Family Islands

A mere 4.5 km offshore from Mission Beach lies **Dunk Island**, the largest in the Family Islands group, a cluster of continental islands extending some 14 km along the coastline. Traditionally, this is the shared sea country of the Bandjin and Djiru Aboriginal people, who know it as *Coonanglebah*. Dunk Island retains its cultural significance to these groups. Its first non-Aboriginal resident, E J Banfield, who dwelled there with his wife between 1897 and 1923, drew international acclaim to the island through his books about life there — the most famous of which is *Confessions of a Beachcomber*. Contemporary visitors to this beautiful isle enjoy the same timeless tropical charm and opportunities to relax and "get dunked" in the island's entrancing nature.

Exotic Island Paradise

Part national park (730 ha) and part privately owned land (240 ha), the best of Dunk Island is accessible to visitors. Thirteen kilometres of walking tracks beckon exploration, their destinations being **Banfield's Grave** (2 km return, easy), the 271 m summit of **Mt Kootaloo** (7 km return, moderate), **Muggy Muggy Beach** (3 km return, easy) and **Coconut Beach** (7.6 km return, moderate). The **Island Circuit** (10.8 km return, moderate) combines most of these walks (bypassing Muggy Muggy Beach).

Dunk Island, so named by James Cook in 1770, lies off Mission Beach. Purtaboi Island (foreground) is an important sea bird nesting site.

Left and right: **Dunk Island Resort** In this tropical island paradise, visitors spend days in pure relaxation by the pool or beach.

Left to right: **Dunk Island; Muggy Muggy Beach** For the outdoors type, Dunk Island has a multitude of environments to explore and physical activities to enjoy.

Several artists live and work in the island's artist colony — founded in 1974 by the late Bruce Arthur, who was renowned for his tapestries. The island also has a working farm. **Dunk Island Resort** offers luxury accommodation and the full range of resort facilities — boutiques, therapeutic spa and pools, restaurants and bars, watersports and an 18-hole golf course. The **Dunk Island Day Pass** allows day visitors to the island access to the resort's facilities. Camping facilities are also provided on the island (contact Dunk Island Resort, Ph: 07 4068 8199 for permits and information).

South of Cairns

Island Wildlife

Dunk Island's diverse habitats, including creeks, rainforests, eucalypt forests, rocky shores, reef flats, mangroves and beaches support an incredible diversity of wildlife, including Dunk's ubiquitous emblem — the Ulysses Butterfly (*left*). More than 150 bird species live on the island, including White-faced and Striated Herons (*below left & below right*), Ospreys and other raptors, Yellow-bellied Sunbirds (*below centre*) and a variety of other honeyeaters, forest and wading birds have made Dunk home. Particularly conspicuous are the Australian Brush-turkeys and Orange-footed Scrubfowls that incubate their eggs in large mounds of leaf litter on the forest floor. Reptiles, including a variety of monitors, dragons, skinks and geckoes, can be seen during the day, and the island's few mammals, the Fawn-footed Melomys and several flying-fox and insectivorous bat species, are active at night. The island's freshwater creeks are home to Saw-shelled Turtles and fish species, including Jungle Perch, rainbow fish, gobies, and Long-finned Eels. The fringing reef is a coral wonderland, home to countless marine animals.

Family Islands

A total of eleven continental islands comprise the **Family Islands** — so named by the Bandjin people because of their resemblance to a family group headed by father *Coonanglebah* (Dunk) and mother *Bedarra*. Just to the north of Dunk Island lies **Purtaboi Island** with **Kumboola Island** and **Mung-Um-Gnackum Island** nearby. South of Dunk Island are the majority of the group — **Bedarra, Thorpe, Coombe, Wheeler, Hudson, Smith** and **Bowden Islands**.

Unlike Dunk Island, the remainder of the Family Islands, with their distinctive granite boulder formations, rise to rocky peaks no more than 100 m above sea level. Their vegetation is strongly influenced by the prevailing south-easterly winds. On their exposed southern sides, casuarinas, wattles and eucalypts sprawl between the large granite slabs. In contrast, the northern sheltered slopes harbour rainforest with figs, palms, Milky Pine and Satin Ash. The islands also generally have sand spits on their north-western sides, which provide sheltered access points and also support patches of coral.

Bedarra Island with the other southern Family Islands in the background. Bedarra and nearby Thorpe Island are privately owned, with a resort and private residences and vacation accommodation. The southern islands are all protected within the Family Islands National Park along with Purtaboi Island. Self-sufficient camping is permitted on Wheeler and Coombe Islands (permits available from QPWS, www.qld.gov.au/camping or Ph: 131 304). The islands are accessible by boat only, with charters available from Dunk Island, Mission Beach, Cardwell and the Hull or Tully Rivers.

Swimming and snorkelling are possible from many of the beaches around the islands. Dugongs and sea turtles are sometimes seen feeding on the seagrass meadows between the islands, and sea birds feed among the mangroves and across intertidal zones.

Before sea levels rose some 8000 years ago, the islands were connected to the mainland via a coastal plain known to the Aboriginal people as "eastern grey kangaroo country". Once submerged, coral colonised this plain, and the reefs and islands traditionally provided a rich bounty of food and material resources for the Bandjin Aboriginal people, who paddled between them in bark canoes. Shell middens provide evidence of this group's long association with the island.

South of Cairns

Sugar Country

Nestled between Mt Mackay (723 m) and Mt Tyson (687 m), Tully rivals Babinda as the wettest town in Australia. Tully's sugar mill is set against a stunning mountain backdrop and beautiful river scenery in the traditional country of the Gulnay, Girramay and Jirrbal people. Tully's main attractions are its natural wonders and multicultural heritage.

The Hotel Tully, built in 1926, has long been the centre of the town's social life.

Cane trains are a common sight (and sound) during the cane-cutting season (June–Dec).

Butler Street, Tully The main street seemingly melts into the greenery behind.

Hull Heads, Hull River Mouth is a popular fishing spot with locals.

Tully Region

Approximately 140 km south of Cairns is a small but busy rural town that supports its surrounding sugarcane and cattle-farming community. With the **Tully River** settled by Chinese banana growers in the early 1900s, a small settlement known as "Banyan" sprang up along **Banyan Creek**. Sugarcane was firmly established in the area with the construction of the sugar mill in 1925, and when the official township of **Tully** was surveyed in 1927 it was situated near the sugar mill. The town takes its name from Surveyor General William Alcock Tully, who had been a member of the landing party that established the port of **Cardwell** (to the south) in 1864.

A relaxed walk around the town, which has several buildings dating to its early years, gives a feeling for the small multicultural community. The townspeople celebrate their tropical lifestyle during the **Tully Gumboot Festival** (September). Markets are held on the 2nd and 4th Saturdays of the month. **The Tully Visitor and Heritage Centre** (Bruce Hwy, Tully, Ph: 07 4068 2288) provides information on local history and Indigenous culture as well as the various attractions and events of the area.

Close to Tully

The **Mount Tyson, Scouts Rock & Summit Walk** (6 km, 3 hr return, commencing at Brannigan St, Tully) is reserved for very fit and experienced bushwalkers, but allows extensive views of the area. Walkers are requested to notify local authorities before departing as this is a rough bush track. Approximately 7 km north of Tully (via Murray St–Bulgan Rd) is **Alligators Nest State Forest Park** with its enticing swimming hole (safe from crocodiles, despite its name). From Tully it is a short drive to the fishing villages of **Hull Heads** and **Tully Heads**, at the mouths of the **Hull** and **Tully Rivers**.

Murray Falls, where crisp rainforest water flows over time-sculpted stone.

Cultural Heritage

For a glimpse into Jirrbal Aboriginal culture and lifestyle, join traditional custodians for an exclusive walk along an Aboriginal trading route. This walk (8 km return) passes through lush strands of virgin rainforest and cool, crystalline pools in the **Tully Valley** on its way to **Echo Creek**, south-west of Tully. Jirrbal guides point out rainforest species traditionally used for bush tucker and medicines.

Tully Welly

Tully's icon is the 7.9 m Golden Gumboot situated at the entrance to Butler Street. The "welly" signifies the town's highest recorded annual rainfall — a whopping 7.9 m in 1950.

Made of fibreglass, the Golden Gumboot has been sculpted with a gigantic White-lipped Tree-frog, one of the faunal emblems of the region, clinging to the outside. Inside, a spiral staircase leads to an observatory with wonderful views of the town, the mill and Mt Tyson.

Tully's claim as the country's wettest town is justified. It has 150 wet days per year and an average annual rainfall of over 4 m.

118

South of Cairns

Tully Gorge — Alcock State Forest

Some 40 km north-west of Tully is the **Tully Gorge** section of the **Tully River** — world renowned for its thrilling whitewater rafting. After passing through banana plantations and cattle-grazing country, the road skirts the rainforested gorge ending at **Kareeya Hydro** (Cardstone Rd, Ph: 07 4035 0222), 2.4 km downstream from Tully Falls and 15 km downstream from **Koombooloomba Dam**. Along the way, there are several lookouts (**Frank Roberts Lookout**, **Flip Wilson Lookout** and **Cardstone Weir**) with spectacular views of the river, including some rampant stretches of rapids frequented by rafters. **Tully Gorge State Forest Park**, the exit point for rafters, has picnic and camping facilities (Ph: 131 304 or register on www.qld.gov.au/camping), access to the river for swimming and a **Rainforest Butterfly Walk** (375 m return) where swarms of butterflies are often seen between September and February.

Misty Mountains

Nine kilometres along H Road, accessed via Cardstone Road several kilometres before the Frank Roberts Lookout, are the **Cochable Creek** campsite, and the trailheads of the **Cannabullen Creek Track** and **Koolmoon Creek Track**. These trails, which explore the tributaries of the Tully River, form part of the **Misty Mountains Trails**, a 130 km network of short- and long-distance walking trails and roads through Jirrbal and Ma:Mu traditional country. From the campsite it is possible to walk to **Ravenshoe** (36 km), **Mena Creek** (60 km) or the Palmerston Highway between **Millaa Millaa** and **Innisfail** (50 km). For guided tours of the Misty Mountains, contact Tully Visitor and Heritage Centre (Bruce Hwy, Tully, Ph: 07 4068 2288). For further information about the Misty Mountains network, contact QPWS (5B Sheridan St, Cairns, Ph: 07 4046 6600).

Murray Falls State Forest

To the south-west of Tully, in the foothills of the **Kirrama Range**, are the picturesque **Murray Falls**. The **River Boardwalk** (300 m) provides safe viewing of the falls, and the **Rainforest Walk** (1.8 km return) is a pleasant walk through rainforest and eucalypt forest to a lookout overlooking the falls and the **Murray Valley**. Interpretive signs along this walk feature some of the hunting and gathering methods of the traditional custodians, the Girramay Aboriginal people. Picnicking, camping and swimming facilities are all available for use. Contact **QPWS Cardwell** (for information, Ph: 07 4066 8779 or to book permits, Ph: 131 304 or book online at www.qld.gov.au/camping).

Kirrama Range & Blencoe Falls

Further south is the hamlet of **Kennedy**, the gateway to **Kirrama Range Road** and **Blencoe Falls**. The road, built in the late 1930s, passes through World-Heritage-listed rainforest as it winds up the range to **Society Flat**, where there was once a thriving logging community. Along the way, several lookouts provide views over the Kennedy and Murray Valleys. A boardwalk and bushwalk (720 m) feature gigantic Kauri Pines and Rose Gums.

Blencoe Falls, a spectacular 91 m drop, can be reached via a walking track or 4WD track from the **Mt Garnet Road** on top of the range. From the lookout at the top of the falls, visitors can enjoy stunning views of the **Herbert River Gorge**. For information contact QPWS (Ph: 07 4066 8779).

Top to bottom: **Tully River; Whitewater Rafting in Tully Gorge** The Tully River's grade 3 to 4 rapids ensure an action-packed day out.

Things to See and Do

1. Visit the Golden Gumboot right in the centre of Tully.
2. Visit the rainforests and waterfalls close by. Picnic and swim in the designated areas at Alligators Nest and Murray Falls.
3. For thrill-seekers, try whitewater rafting in Tully Gorge, walk to the summit of Mt Tyson, or venture into the Misty Mountains.

Shooting the Rapids

As the river has some very dangerous rapids, independent kayaking is recommended only for experienced paddlers in groups. Professional guides ensure a safe experience. Two companies lead rafting trips on the Tully River.

1. **Raging Thunder** Bruce Highway, Tully (Ph: 07 4068 3210).
2. **R'n'R Rafting** 278 Hartley St, Cairns (Ph: 1800 079 039).

For further information contact the Tully Visitor and Heritage Centre (Bruce Hwy, Tully, Ph: 07 4068 2288) or QPWS Cardwell (Ph: 07 4066 8779).

South of Cairns

For Nature-lovers
Surrounded by World-Heritage-listed forests, wetlands and reef, Cardwell is the launching pad to a vast nature-lover's playground. Bushwalking, photography, swimming, 4WD touring, boating, fishing and diving can all be experienced. With its stunning tropical scenery and location by the sea, Cardwell offers an idyllic getaway. Residents and visitors celebrate the town's natural abundance during the multicultural Cardwell Carnivale (April) and Seafest (August, Ph: 07 4068 8478).

Top and bottom: **Cardwell beaches** Long stretches of sand fringe the mainland side of Hinchinbrook Channel.

Top and bottom: **Port Hinchinbrook** The marina is the focus of boating activity during the day.

Around Cardwell

Cardwell is situated 185 km south of Cairns in the traditional country of the Girramay Aboriginal people, whose culture is showcased alongside other local Aboriginal cultures at the Girringun **Keeping Place** (235 Victoria St, Cardwell, Ph: 07 4066 8300). **The Rainforest & Reef Interpretive Centre** (QPWS, 142 Victoria St, Cardwell, Ph: 07 4066 8601) presents a Girramay creation story of the area and has information on the national parks and wildlife of the region.

The township of Cardwell, initially known as **Port Hinchinbrook**, played a particularly important role in the history of Tropical North Queensland. Settled by Europeans in 1864 as the first port north of Bowen, the town was for many years an important centre for pastoralists across the Cardwell range and for hopeful gold prospectors on their way to the goldfields.

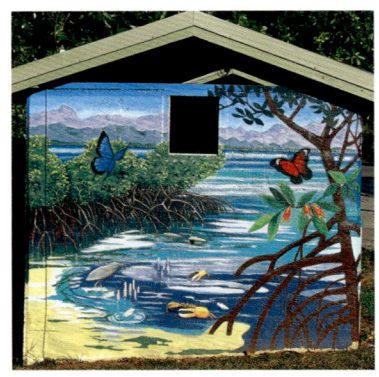

Decorative Cardwell dunnies For more local art visit Hinchinbrook Regional Art Inc. (156 Victoria St, Cardwell, Ph: 07 4066 2475).

The Telegraph Office, opened in 1870, served as a link in the bush telegraph between Townsville, the goldfields and the Gulf. Timber-getting, cattle production and small crops supported the pioneers. As settlement spread north, Cardwell itself was bypassed and the shire's administrative centre was moved to Tully in 1929. The heritage-listed **Cardwell Bush Telegraph Heritage Centre** (53 Victoria St, Cardwell, Ph: 07 4066 2412), and the **Coral Sea Battle Memorial Park** (Coral Sea Dr, Cardwell) along the waterfront, provide a sense of the history of the area, particularly in early May when dignitaries from Australia and the USA commemorate the 1942 Battle of the Coral Sea.

Fishing is enjoyed off **Cardwell Jetty** (the venue for monthly markets, every first Saturday) or via one of the area's many fishing charters. Camping is also popular, with facilities at **Cardwell Van Park** (107 Roma St, Cardwell, Ph: 07 4066 8689), **Cardwell Village Beachcomber Motel & Tourist Park** (43A Marine Pde, Cardwell, Ph: 1800 005 633), **Kookaburra Holiday Park** (175 Bruce Hwy, Cardwell, Ph: 07 4066 8648) and **Meunga Creek Caravan Park** (Ellerbeck Rd, Cardwell, Ph: 07 4066 8710).

Important Habitats

Part of the Great Barrier Reef World Heritage Area, the shallow waters of Hinchinbrook Channel and Rockingham Bay, are important habitats for marine animals including Green Turtles and Dugongs (*below*) — both endangered species. Extensive seagrass beds and the reefs fringing the nearby islands provide abundant food and sheltered waters for breeding. Dugongs and turtles are most often seen when they surface to breathe.

South of Cairns

Nature on the Doorstep

The **Cardwell Forest Drive** (accessed via Brasenose St) is a 26 km scenic route in the foothills behind Cardwell. Its series of walking tracks, lookouts, swimming holes and well-maintained picnic facilities are the perfect place for relaxation and exploration on a hot summer's day. The highlight of the drive is the **Cardwell Lookout**, with its stunning coastal panoramas.

Several kilometres south of Cardwell, similar facilities are provided at **Five Mile State Forest Park**. Nearby, the historic **Dalrymple Gap Walking Track** (8 km) traversing the **Cardwell Range** is suitable for fit and adventurous bushwalkers. Contact QPWS (142 Victoria St, Cardwell, Ph: 07 4066 8601) for permits. Creative visitors who know what they want can tailor adventures with **SWIT Guide** (55 Gregory St, Cardwell, Ph: 0424 210 981).

Island Retreats

A short distance to the north-east of Cardwell, in **Rockingham Bay**, lie two islands perfect for secluded island camping, **Goold Island** (camping facilities provided, Ph: 07 4066 8601 for permits) and **Garden Island** (no facilities, no permit required). Access is via private boat or **Hinchinbrook Island Ferries** (Ph: 07 4066 8585).

Top to bottom: **Zoe Bay; Shepherd Bay** Hinchinbrook Island is a treasure chest of glittering natural jewels.

Hinchinbrook Island An aerial view of magnificent Hinchinbrook Island. Shepherd Bay lies between Cape Richards (*right*) and Cape Sandwich (*left*). Just beyond is Ramsay Bay – one of the features of the Thorsborne Trail. The 32 km track traverses Hinchinbrook's eastern side.

Hinchinbrook Island National Park

Cardwell's most famous attraction is the incomparably beautiful **Hinchinbrook Island**. Australia's largest island national park (39,000 ha), this continental island separated from the mainland by the narrow **Hinchinbrook Channel** is the traditional country of the Bandjin people. Rising from the ocean, its rugged rainforest and heath-covered ridges peak at the granite summits of **Mt Bowen** (1142 m) and **Mt Diamantina** (955 m). The island also contains open forests, woodlands, paperbark and palm wetlands, sandy beaches and rocky headlands. Predominantly wilderness, the island is the region's centrepiece of biodiversity and natural beauty.

Fringing Hinchinbrook Channel and **Missionary Bay** are vast mangrove forests, one of the country's largest remaining stands, spanning kilometres of canopy broken only by a series of tidal creeks. Among the richest and most varied in Australia, with 31 of Australia's 36 species of mangrove plants, they provide habitats and a valuable breeding ground for many marine animal species.

Top to bottom: **Mangrove-lined channels of Missionary Bay; Exploring the mangroves.**

South of Cairns

Trekking the shoreline of Ramsay Bay, part of Hinchinbrook's famous Thorsborne Trail.

Thorsborne Trail

As one of Australia's earliest national parks, protected since 1932, Hinchinbrook Island provides visitors with an unforgettable wilderness experience. Every year over 1000 hikers experience the world-famous **Thorsborne Trail**, 32 km of rugged track following the island's east coast. The track is named after local conservationists Margaret and Arthur Thorsborne, who continually strived to protect the region's ecology.

Generally taking three to five days, walkers experience a wide range of varying topography and native plant communities. Beaches, both sandy and rocky, headlands, swamps and rainforests, river crossings and waterfalls, mountains and valleys all combine to make this the walk of a lifetime. Camping facilities are provided at designated campsites along the way.

As numbers are limited, bookings are generally best made six months in advance (QPWS, 142 Victoria St, Cardwell, Ph: 07 4066 8601). Before departing, walkers are required to view a video about minimal impact bushwalking. April to September, when the weather is mildest, is the best time to visit. Access to the trail is via boat. **Hinchinbrook Island Ferry** & **Hinchinbrook Island Wilderness Lodge** (Port Hinchinbrook, Cardwell, Ph: 07 4066 8270) provide transfers to/from Cardwell and **Hinchinbrook Wilderness Safaris** (Lot 404 Dungeness Rd, Lucinda, Ph: 07 4777 8307 for cost) to/from Lucinda. Bus transfers (Ph: 07 4776 5666) allow travel between the two towns.

Around Ingham

Just a short drive south of Cardwell across the Cardwell Range — with its lookout offering magnificent views over Hinchinbrook Island — is the township of Ingham. Boasting the largest sugar mill in the Southern Hemisphere, Ingham is easily explored via the **Hinchinbrook Heritage Walk**. Its friendly population, largely of Italian descent, celebrate their heritage during the **Australian Italian Festival** (May) and **Maraka Festival** (October). On the edge of town is **Tyto Wetlands** (Cooper St, Ingham), a 90 ha restored habitat, home to over 1000 species of birds, including the endangered Eastern Grass Owl. At nearby **Lucinda Port** is a 5.75 km bulk sugar conveyor jetty, the world's longest offshore loading facility. Other nearby seaside communities, **Forrest Beach**, **Taylors Beach** and **Halifax**, offer fishing, boating, camping and other outdoor adventures. **Broadwater State Forest Park**, some 45 km to the west of Ingham also offers outdoor pursuits.

Clockwise from top: **Herbert River, Ingham; Classic corrugation, Trebonne; Station Hotel, Ingham** For further information about the area's attractions, contact Hinchinbrook Visitor Centre (Cnr Bruce Highway & Lannercost St, Ingham, Ph: 07 4776 5211).

South of Cairns

Girringun (Lumholtz) National Park

Girringun (Lumholtz) National Park encompasses the traditional country of three Aboriginal tribal groups, the Warrgamay, Warungnu and Girramay people, who maintain a close spiritual connection to these ranges.

Several creeks and the Herbert River follow courses through a wide variety of terrain. The park protects different forest types, including various kinds of rainforest and open forest. Upland and gully areas abound with ferns, palms and cycads. She-oaks line the rivers. Kingfishers, Platypuses, water dragons, and even Freshwater and Estuarine Crocodiles can be seen around the creeks. Drier escarpments are dominated by eucalypts. These open forests are inhabited by kangaroos, wallabies, Emus, Laughing Kookaburras, Sulphur-crested Cockatoos and, in some places, the endangered Mahogany Glider. The Herbert River is home to freshwater turtles and a multitude of fish species, which provide ample food for sea-eagles and falcons, cormorants and shags.

The park is divided into two sections — the Wallaman Falls Section (accessed at two points from Trebonne and Abergowrie to the west of Ingham), and the Blencoe Falls Section (accessed in dry weather only via the Kirrama Range Road from Kennedy, north of Cardwell, and the Kennedy Development, Kirrama–Mt Garnet and Kirrama–Cashmere Roads from Mt Garnet, west of Ravenshoe). The recreation potential of the park is excellent and includes the Wet Tropics Great Walk, an 85 km trail linking Wallaman and Blencoe Falls.

Wallaman Falls Walks

Wallaman Falls (305 m), Australia's highest sheer drop waterfall is a truly spectacular sight to behold — particularly after rain, when clouds of rising mist envelope the raging torrent. The falls are most easily viewed from the Wallaman Falls Lookout, 300 m from the carpark, where picnic facilities are provided. More adventurous visitors may walk the Jinda (Falls) Track (2 km return) to the base of the falls. The Banggurru (Turtle) Walk is an easy stroll along the banks of Stony Creek, where Platypuses and water dragons may be encountered. Camping is permitted in the campground nearby (Ph: 131 304, or book online at www.qld.gov.au/camping).

From Wallaman Falls the Wet Tropics Great Walk is a marked trail with designated campsites to Henrietta Gate near Abergowrie (60 km, 3 days) or Yamanie Section pick-up (40 km, 2 days), which connects with the Dju:n Walk to Blencoe Falls (a further 45 km, 4–6 days).

Blencoe Falls Section

The stunning Blencoe Falls drops 91 m before flowing into the Herbert River Gorge a few kilometres downstream. Created by aeons of erosion, the Herbert River Gorge is a natural wildlife corridor between the Wet Tropics World Heritage Area and the drier Einasleigh Uplands.

The Dju:n (Herbert River Gorge) Walk is one of the most challenging walking adventures in Australia. Commencing at the Blencoe Falls campground, this Aboriginal pathway traverses 45 km (4–6 days) of breathtaking terrain. With no facilities, this walk should only be undertaken by extremely fit and well-prepared hikers.

Top to bottom: Blencoe Falls; Platypus; Wallaman Falls; Northern Brown Bandicoot.

Index

A

Abbott, Henry 15
Alexandra Bay 72
Alexandra Range 66, 72
Altonmoui Range 80
Anzac Memorial Park 92
Arthur, Bruce 116
Atherton 3, 4, 6, 8, 9, 10, 11, 13, 82, 86, 87, 88, 89, 90, 91, 92, 93, 94, 95
Atherton, John 90
Atherton Bat Hospital 91
Atherton Court House 90
Atherton Information Centre 90
Atherton Tableland 6, 10, 13, 30, 82, 86, 87, 88, 89, 90, 91, 92, 93, 94, 95
Atherton War Cemetery 90
Atherton War Memorial 90
Australian Butterfly Sanctuary 9, 37
Australian Institute of Marine Science 44
Australian Lurcher Butterfly 69
Australian Sugar Industry Museum 111
Australian Venom Zoo 37
Aviary, The 37

B

Babinda 10, 38, 39, 104, 106, 107, 108, 118
Babinda Boulders 106, 107
Babinda Central Mill 106
Babinda State Hotel 106
Balancing Rock 85
Baldy Hill 107
Bandjin 116, 117
Banfield, E J 116
Banks, Joseph 79
Barretts Lagoon 79
Barron Falls 28, 35
Barron Gorge 34, 35, 36
Barron Gorge Hydro Power Station 34
Barron Valley Hotel 90
Bartle Frere 109
Bat House Environment Centre 75
Bathurst Bay 80
BATReach Wildlife Rescue and Rehab Centre 37
Beaches
  Bramston Beach 105, 107, 109
  Cape Tribulation Beach 75
  Cardwell Beach 120
  Clifton Beach 32
  Cowley Beach 113
  Douglas Beach 33
  Ellis Beach 32, 33
  Four Mile Beach 58, 59
  Holloways Beach 32
  Kewarra Beach 32
  Kurrimine Beach 113
  Machans Beach 32
  Muggy Muggy Beach 102, 116
  Nudey Beach 46, 47
  Oak Beach 33
  Pebbly Beach 33
  Trinity Beach 32
  Turtle Beach 33
  Wangetti Beach 33
  White Cliffs 33
  Wonga Beach 61
Bedarra Island 11, 117
Behana Gorge 105
Bellenden Ker 105
Bellenden Ker Range 104, 105
Bicton Hill 115
Big Barramundi Barbeque Garden 62
Biggs Recreation Area 109
Bingil Bay 114, 115
Birkett, Pam 66
Birkett, Ron 66
Blencoe Falls 101, 119, 123
Bloomfield Falls 76
Bloomfield Track 74, 76
Bluff, The 61
Bowden Island 117
Buchan Point 33

Burra Inn Restaurant 87

C

Cairns
  Buildings
    Barrier Reef Hotel 16
    Bolands Centre 4, 16
    Cairns City Council Library 20
    Cairns International 23
    Cairns Post Office 16
    Central Hotel 16, 21
    Hides Corner 23
    Matson Resort 23
    Palace Backpackers 21
    Pier Marketplace 22, 23, 26, 27
    School of Arts 16
    Shangri-La Hotel 23
  Entertainment Venues
    Barnacle Bills
    Botanic Gardens Licensed Café 25
    Boydy's Café Bar & Grill 23
    Cairns Convention Centre 20
    Cairns Markets 12, 27
    Cairns Night Markets 22
    Cairns Night Zoo 32
    Cairns Post 16
    Cairns Showgrounds 24
    Cairns Tropical Zoo 32
    Cannon Park Racecourse 24
    Centre of Contemporary Arts 20
    City Place Soundshell 24
    Johno's Blues Bar 23
    Reef Hotel Casino 14, 20, 23
    Rondo Theatre 20
    Stumbling Goat, The 23
    Sugarworld 31
    Tanks Art Centre 20, 22
    Tjapukai Aboriginal Cultural Park 12, 34
    Yanni's Greek Taverna 23
  Galleries & Museums
    Cairns Museum 16, 20, 23
    Cairns Regional Gallery 20, 23
    Menmuny Museum 38
    RSL Hall of Memories 24
  Parks & Gardens
    Aboriginal Plant Use Garden 25
    Endeavour Fun Ship 24
    Flecker Botanic Gardens 20, 23, 24, 25, 27, 31
    Fogarty Park 20, 24
    Genoma Park 30
    Gondwana Garden 25
    Goomboora Park 30
    Muddy's Playground 24
  Transport
    Adventure Duck 20
    BTS Tours 15
    Cairns Explorer 15
    Cairns International Airport 9
    City Place Transit Mall 15
    Coral Reef Coaches 15
    Kuranda Bus 34
    Kuranda Railway Station 35, 36
    Reef Fleet Terminal 26
    Sun Palm Transport 15
    Sunbus 15
    Whitecar Coaches 34
Cairns Birdwing Butterfly 35, 37, 69
Cairns Cruise Port 26
Cairns Range Railway 36
Cairns Seaport 26
Cairns, Sir William Wellington 8, 14
Cairns War Memorial 16
Cairns Wildlife Dome 21
Canecutters Memorial 111
Canecutter Way 111, 113
Cane Toad World 38
Canopy Tower 66, 67
Cape Kimberley 62
Cape Melville 80
Cape Richards 121
Cape Sandwich 121
Cape Tribulation 4, 7, 13, 56, 60, 69, 71–78
Cape Tribulation Tourist Information Centre 74

Cape York 10, 11, 80, 81
Cardstone Weir 119
Cardwell 95, 100, 102, 114, 117, 118, 119, 120, 121, 122, 123
Cardwell Bush Telegraph Heritage Centre 120
Cardwell Carnivale 120
Cardwell Jetty 120
Cardwell Lookout 121
Cardwell Range 121, 122
Cassowary Coast 4, 6, 12, 102, 110, 113
Cedars Coffee Shop 86
Cedrella 87
Cenotaph, The 9, 16
Chillagoe 7, 11, 13, 85
Chillagoe Hub 85
Chillagoe Observatory & Eco Lodge 85
Chillagoe Smelter 85
Chinese Shrine 78
Clump Point 114, 115
Clump Point Jetty 114, 115
Cod Hole 49
Common Eggfly Butterfly 69
Cook, Captain James 8, 9, 12, 14, 26, 43, 46, 56, 74, 76, 78, 79, 81, 104, 116
Cooktown 4, 7, 11, 12, 13, 56, 76–81
Coombe Island 117
Copperlode Dam 30
Copperlode Falls 30
Court House Hotel 58
Cow Bay 66, 69, 72, 74
Cruiser Butterfly 37
Crystal Cascades 30

D

Daintree 4, 6, 7, 10, 13
Daintree Croc Spot Tours 63
Daintree Discovery Centre 7, 19, 66, 67, 71
Daintree Eco Lodge and Spa 62
Daintree Entomological Museum 75
Daintree Mangroves Wildlife Sanctuary 63
Daintree, Richard 62
Daintree River Ferry 62, 66
Daintree Timber Museum & Gallery 62, 63
Daintree Village 56, 60, 62, 63, 74
Dalrymple, Sir George Elphinstone 8, 62
Deeral 104, 105
Devil's Pool 106
Dicksons Inlet 58, 59
Dimbulah 84
Dinner Falls 93
Djabugay 14, 32, 34, 35, 36
Djabugay Country Tours 35, 36
Djiru 114, 115, 116
Donovan Point Lookout 76
Doongal Aboriginal Art 36
Double Island 32
Dunk Island 11, 102, 114, 115, 116, 117
Dunk Island Resort 116

E

Echo Creek 118
El Arish 115
Elinjaa Falls 10, 96
Ella Bay 109, 110, 111
Ellis Beach Surf Life Saving Club 33
Endeavour Falls 79
Esplanade, the 14, 15, 16, 20, 22, 23, 24, 26, 27
Esplanade Lagoon 14, 27
Etty Bay 110, 111
Evelyn Tableland 11, 82, 94, 95, 100
Exchange Hotel, Mossman 60

F

Family Islands 115, 116, 117
Fauna
  Amphibians
    Australian Lace-lid 68

124

Index

Cane Toad 38
Common Green Tree-frog 36, 68
Graceful Tree-frog 68
Lesieur's Frog 68
Marbled Frog 68
Mountain-top Nursery-frog 68
Northern Barred Frog 68
Northern Dwarf Tree-frog 68
Northern Tinker Frog 68
Orange-eyed Tree-frog 35, 68, 97
Ornate Burrowing Frog 68
Rattling Nursery-frog 68
Red Tree-frog 68
Rocket Frog 68
Roth's Tree-frog 68
Sharp-snouted Day-frog 68
Spotted Grass Frog 68
Striped Burrowing Frog 68
Tapping Nursery-frog 68
White-browed Whistle-frog 68
White-lipped Tree-frog 68
Birds
　Australian Brush-turkey 31, 35, 70, 89, 93, 97, 108, 117
　Australian Pelican 14
　Barking Owl 70
　Black-naped Tern 113
　Black-necked Stork 91, 107
　Black Bittern 63
　Black Butcherbird 63, 70
　Black Swan 84
　Bridled Honeyeater 89
　Bridled Tern 113
　Brolga 84, 91
　Brown Booby 44
　Brown Cuckoo-Dove 70
　Buff-breasted Paradise-Kingfisher 31, 47, 70
　Chowchilla 93
　Comb-crested Jacana 107
　Common Noddy 44
　Crested Tern 44, 113
　Crimson Rosella 71
　Double-eyed Fig Parrot 63
　Eastern Reef Egret 59
　Eastern Yellow Robin 97
　Eclectus Parrot 56, 70
　Egret 42
　Emerald Dove 35, 42, 47, 70, 113
　Emu 110, 123
　Figbird 71
　Forest Kingfisher 71
　Golden Bowerbird 70, 93, 97, 109
　Gouldian Finch 84
　Great-billed Heron 63
　Greater Egret 107
　Green Pygmy Geese 107
　Grey-headed Robin 89
　Helmeted Friarbird 63
　King-Parrot 70
　Large-tailed Nightjar 70
　Laughing Kookaburra 70, 123
　Lesser Crested Tern 44, 113
　Lesser Sooty Owl 70
　Lewin's Honeyeater 93, 97
　Little Kingfisher 70
　Macaw 37
　Magpie Goose 84, 91
　Masked Booby 44
　Metallic Starling 63, 105
　Nankeen Kestrel 81
　Nankeen Night Heron 63, 82
　Noisy Pitta 60, 70
　Orange-footed Scrubfowl 31, 35, 47, 70, 97, 113, 117
　Osprey 42, 47, 63
　Papuan Frogmouth 63, 70, 97
　Pied Imperial-Pigeon 37, 42, 47, 70
　Pied Oystercatcher 44
　Plumed Whistling-Duck 91
　Radjah Sellduck 91
　Rainbow Lorikeet 35, 71
　Red-winged Parrot 70
　Rose-crowned Fruit-Dove 42, 70, 93
　Roseate Tern 44
　Royal Spoonbill 14, 63
　Ruddy Turnpike 44
　Rufous Owl 70
　Satin Bowerbird 71
　Scaly-breasted Lorikeet 35
　Shining Flycatcher 63
　Silver Gull 44
　Sooty Tern 44
　Southern Cassowary 33, 35, 36, 66, 67, 70, 73, 97, 102, 109, 110, 114, 115
　Spotted Catbird 70, 71, 93, 97
　Striated Heron 117
　Sulphur-crested Cockatoo 47, 63, 123
　Tooth-billed Bowerbird 89, 93
　Variegated Fairy-wren 14, 28
　Victoria's Riflebird 70, 93
　Whistling Kite 64
　White-bellied Sea-Eagle 47, 64
　White-faced Heron 117
　Wompoo Pigeon 35, 60
　Yellow-bellied Sunbird 8, 70, 117
　Yellow-spotted Honeyeater 70
Mammals
　Common Bandicoot 69
　Common Brushtail Possum 94
　Common Ringtail Possum 95
　Coppery Brushtail Possum 95
　Daintree River Ringtail Possum 69, 94
　Dingo 64
　Fawn-footed Melomys 117
　Feather-tailed Glider 95
　Greater Glider 95
　Green Ringtail Possum 94, 97
　Herbert River Ringtail Possum 94, 97
　Koala 37, 59
　Lemuroid Ringtail Possum 94, 97
　Long-nosed Bandicoot 69
　Long-tailed Pygmy-possum 35, 69, 94, 95
　Mahogany Glider 95, 123
　Musky Rat-kangaroo 35, 69, 97, 99, 108, 109
　Northern Brown Bandicoot 123
　Northern Quoll 68
　Platypus 35, 36, 86, 91, 97, 123
　Red-legged Pademelon 69
　Rufous Hare Wallaby 82
　Spectacled Flying-fox 35, 42, 63, 69
　Spotted-tailed Quoll 69, 97
　Spotted Cuscus 94
　Squirrel Glider 95
　Striped Possum 35, 69, 72, 94, 95
　Sugar Glider 95
　Swamp Wallaby 69, 72, 107
　Thornton Peak Uromys 68
　Tree-kangaroo 59, 67
　　Bennett's 68, 69, 77, 95
　　Lumholtz's 69, 94, 95
　White-tailed Rat 69, 72
　Yellow-bellied Glider 95
Reptiles
　Amethystine Python 60, 63, 68, 72
　Boyd's Forest Dragon 60, 68, 72
　Brown Tree Snake 68
　Chameleon Gecko 68
　Estuarine Crocodile 33, 35, 63, 64, 65, 68, 72, 105, 109, 110, 123
　Freshwater Crocodile 33, 35, 36, 37, 64, 110, 123
　Freshwater turtle 35
　Krefft's Turtle 68
　Lace Monitor 35, 113
　Merten's Water Monitor 33
　Northern Crowned Snake 68
　Northern Leaf-tailed Gecko 68
　Prickly Forest Skink 68
　Saw-shelled Turtle 89, 117
　Thornton Peak Skink 68
　Water Python 64
　Yellow-spotted Monitor 64
Ferrari Estates 78
Festivals & Events
　Amateurs Racing Carnival 13, 23, 24
　Aussitaliano Carnivale 12
　Big Weekend, Chillagoe 13
　Cairns Show 24
　Carnival on Collins 23
　Cooktown Cup 13
　Discovery Festival 12
　Einasleigh Races 13
　Feast of the Senses 12, 111
　Festival Cairns 12, 13, 20, 23
　Festival of the Forest 12, 100
　Festival of the Three Saints 113
　Kulture Karnivale 12
　Kuranda Spring Fair 13
　Maize Festival 13, 90
　Mareeba Rodeo 13
　Mission Beach Aquatic Festival 12, 114
　Mt Garnet Races 13
　Opera in the Outback 13
　Parade of Lights 23
　Reef and Rainforest Festival 12
　Tinaroo Barra Bash 13
　Torimba Festival 12, 100
　Yungaburra Folk Festival 13
Fishery Falls 105
Fitzroy Island 11, 26, 38, 46, 47
Five Mile State Forest Park 121
Flagstaff Hill 58
Flames of the Forest 61
Flip Wilson Lookout 119
Flora
　Black Pine 100
　Brazilian Cloak 25
　Bromeliad 25
　Cassowary Plum 99
　Cluster Fig 99
　Crows Nest 67, 108
　Curtain Fig Tree 86
　Fan Palm 10, 56, 72, 74, 115
　Foxtail Palm 80
　Golden Orchid 74
　Green Dinosaur 73
　Hoop Pine 91
　Hybrid orchid 25
　Idiot Fruit 73
　Indian Almond 72
　Kauri Pine 100, 112
　King Fern 67, 107
　Lilly Pilly 98
　Mabi Forest 91
　Milky Pine 113, 117
　Pleomele 25
　Red Beech 74
　Rhododendron 4, 98
　Rock Orchid 99
　Satin Ash 117
　Silky Oak 100
　Strangler Fig 60, 99
　Zamia 67
Flower Beetle 69
Flying Fish Point 107, 109–111, 113
Frank Roberts Lookout 119

G

Garden Island 121
George Alley 38
Girramay 118, 119, 120, 123
Golden Gumboot 118, 119
Golden Hole 109
Goldsborough Valley State Forest 10, 39, 107
Goold Island 121
Gordonvale 10, 30, 38, 39, 102, 104, 105, 107
Graham Range 105
Grassy Hill 78, 79
Great Barrier Reef 4, 6, 8, 9, 10, 11, 14, 18, 26, 27, 40–55, 56, 59, 68, 72, 75, 77, 80, 81, 102, 104, 120
Great Dividing Range 10, 11, 30, 56, 85, 92
Great Pyramid Race 39

125

Index

Green, Charles 43
Green Island 11, 18, 26, 38, 42, 43, 44
Gribble, Reverend Ernest 38
Gulf Savannah 4, 11
Gungarde Aboriginal Community 79
Guugu Yimithirr 78, 79

H

Half Moon Bay Marina 28
Hallorans Hill 91
Hambledon House Community Centre 31
Hann Tableland 11, 82
Hartley's Crocodile Adventures 28, 33
Haycock Island 33
Helenvale 76
Henry Ross Lookout 34
Herberton 4, 84, 90, 91, 92, 100
Herberton Camera & Photography Museum and Gallery 92
Herberton Mining and Information Centre 92
Herberton Post Office 92
Herbert River Gorge 119, 123
High Island 104
Highlander Hotel 84
Hinchinbrook Channel 120, 121
Hinchinbrook Island 6, 11, 102, 121, 122
HM Bark *Endeavour* 26, 43, 56, 74, 76, 78, 79
Hogdkinson goldfields 14, 15, 58
Hopevale Aboriginal Community **79**
Hop Wah Plantation 31
Hotel Tully 118
Hotel Tully Falls 100
Hou Wang Temple & Chinese Museum 82, 90
Hudson Island 117
Hull Heads 115, 118

I

Ingham 4, 7, 12, 95, 122, 123
Innisfail 12, 92, 98, 100, 102, 107, 109, 110, 111, 113, 119
Innisfail Clock Tower 111
Innisfail Court House 111
Innisfail Festival 12, 111
Interpretive Display Centre 67
Irvinebank 92
Isabella Falls 79

J

Jacaranda Arts and Crafts Festival 92
James Cook Historical Museum 78
Japoonvale 111, 112
Jirrbal 100, 101, 118, 119
Johnson, Vera-Scarth 78
Johnstone River Crocodile Farm 110
Josephine Falls 102, 108, 109

K

Kalpower Station 80
Keatings Lagoon (Mulbabidgee) Conservation Park 79
Kennedy, Edmund 115
Kennedy Bay 115
King Reef 113
Kirrama Range 119, 123
Koombooloomba Dam 101, 119
Kuku Djungan 84, 85
Kuku Yalanji 56, 61, 62, 74, 76, 77, 80
Kuku Yalanji Dreamtime Walks 61
Kumboola Island 117
Kunggandji 14, 26, 38, 42, 44, 46
Kuranda 4, 9, 13, 28, 30, 32, 34, 35, 36, 37
Kuranda Arts Co-op 36
Kuranda Koala Gardens 37
Kuranda Markets 12, 36
Kuranda Range 28, 30, 34, 35, 36
Kuranda Railway Station 36
Kuranda Riverboat and Rainforest Tours 37

Kuranda Scenic Railway 9, 28, 30, 34
Kurrimine Beach Conservation Park 113

L

Lacey Creek Recreation Area 115
Lake Echam Hotel 86
Lakes
 Centenary Lakes 25, 27
 Lake Barrine 82, 88, 89
 Lake Eacham 86, 88, 89
 Lake Morris 30
 Lake Placid 34, 35
 Lake Tinaroo 87
Licuala Recreation Area 115
Lit Sing Gung Chinese Temple 111
Little Fitzroy Island 46
Little Millstream Falls 101
Lizard Island 11
Loudon House Museum 92
Lucinda 122
Lync-Haven Rainforest Retreat 74, 75
Lynch, Red 30

M

Ma:Mu 96, 97, 100, 111, 113, 119
Ma:Mu Bush Tucker Garden 111
Mabel Island 104
Main Range 62
Malanbarra Yidindji 39
Malanda 86, 87, 89, 96, 100
Malanda Dairy Heritage Centre 89
Malanda Hotel 89
Malanda Falls 89
Malanda Falls Conservation Park and Scenic Reserve 89
Malanda Falls Visitor Centre 89
Malanda Mosaic Trail 89
Maraka Festival 122
Mareeba 82, 84, 85
Mareeba Heritage Museum 84
Mareeba Multicultural Festival 84
Mareeba Wetland Reserve 84
Marina Mirage, Port Douglas 59
Marineland Melanesia Crocodile Habitat 43
Marine Life
 Anemonefish 42, 50
 Banded Goatfish 53
 Banded Sea Krait 45
 Barramundi Cod 53
 Black-tipped Fusilier 51
 Blacksaddle Filefish 50
 Blacksaddle Toby 50
 Black-tip Reef Shark 51
 Blotched Fairy Basslet 51
 Blue-ringed Octopus 55
 Blue Sea Star 55
 Bluebottle 55
 Bluethroat Wrasse 52
 Box Jellyfish 55
 Butterflyfish 52
 Chinamanfish 52
 Christmas Tree Worm 54
 Common Cleanerfish 50, 53
 Common Lionfish 48, 49, 51
 Cone shell 55
 Coral Cod 49, 51
 Coral Trout 50, 51
 Cowfish 51
 Cowry 55
 Crayfish 46, 49, 54
 Crown-of-Thorns 54, 55
 Damselfish 51, 52
  Dick's 53
 Diana's Hogfish 53
 Dolphin 40
 Dugong 40, 42, 117, 120
 Emperor Angelfish 51, 52
 Eyestripe Surgeonfish 53
 Feather star 49, 54, 55
 Fire coral 55
 Flatback Turtle 45
 Flatworm 48, 55
 Giant Clam 46, 55
 Giant Trevally 42

 Gorgonian sea fan 49, 54, 55
 Green Turtle 45, 80, 120
 Hard coral 40, 46, 54
 Harlequin Tuskfish 53
 Hawksbill Turtle 45
 Humpback Whale 46
 Humphead Maori Wrasse 48
 Irukandji 55
 Leaf Scorpionfish 53
 Lionfish 51
 Loggerhead Turtle 45
 Longfin Bannerfish 40
 Longnosed Butterflyfish 40
 Manta Ray 42, 46
 Masked Bannerfish 40
 Moon Wrasse 51
 Moorish Idol 52
 Moray eel 49, 51
 Moses Perch 50, 52
 Nudibranch 54, 55
 Oblique-banded Sweetlip 43
 Olive Sea Snake 45
 Pacific Man-o-War 55
 Painted Spiny Lobster 55
 Parrotfish 42, 51
  Humphead 53
 Pink Anemonefish 48
 Pink Tube Sponge 54
 Porcelain Crab 55
 Portuguese Man-o-War 55
 Potato Cod 49, 51, 81
 Pufferfish 51
 Queensland Groper 51
 Red Emperor 52
 Reef Stonefish 51
 Ringtail Cardinalfish 53
 Rose Sea Star 55
 Sea anemone 42, 49, 50
 Sea cucumber 42, 54
 Sea star 40
 Sea urchin 42, 54
 Seawhip Coral 50
 Seawhip Goby 50
 Shrimp goby 50
 Soft Coral 40, 49
 Spotted Blue Ray 75
 Spotted Sea Bream 53
 Spotted Sweetlip 52
 Stingray 50, 51
 Stripey Snapper 52
 Sunfish 51
 Sunshine Coral 54
 Toby 51
 Triggerfish 42, 52
 Trumpetfish 50, 51
 Wobbegong Shark 50
 Zooxanthellae 40, 54
Marlin Marina 26, 27
Melville Range 80
Mena Creek 111
Mena Creek Environmental Park 112
Mena Creek Falls 112
Michaelmas Cay 44
Milbi Wall 79
Millaa Millaa 89, 96, 100, 119
Millaa Millaa Falls 10, 82, 96
Millstream Express 100
Millstream Falls 10, 101
Miriwinni 107
Mission Beach 6, 12, 13, 19, 72, 113, 114, 115, 116, 117
Missionary Bay 121
Moffat, John 85, 92
Mossman 4, 56, 58, 60, 61, 62, 63, 69, 75
Mossman Gorge 19, 56, 60, 61, 98
Mossman Sugar Mill 58
Mountains
 Black Mountain 77
 Mt Baldy 91
 Mt Bartle Frere 10, 39, 70, 89, 96, 98, 102, 104, 106, 107, 108, 109, 110
 Mt Bellenden Ker 39, 98, 102, 104, 106, 107
 Mt Bowen 121
 Mt Carbine 61, 94
 Mt Cook 78
 Mt Demi 61

126

Index

Mt Diamantina 121
Mt Garnet 119
Mt Kootaloo 116
Mt Lumley 31
Mt Mackay 118
Mt Misery 76
Mt Sorrow 76
Mt Tyson 118, 119
Mt Whitfield 31
Mt Windsor 94
Thornton Peak 68, 69, 72, 94
Walshs Pyramid 10, 39, 104, 105
Mount Mulligan 85
Mount Surprise 101
Mount Windsor Tablelands 61
Mourilyan 111, 113
Mourilyan Harbour 111, 113
Mt Garnet 101
Mt Mulligan Station 85
Mt Whitfield Conservation Park 31
Mugana Caves 85
Mulgrave Central Mill 38
Mulgrave Settlers Museum 39
Mulgrave Valley 38
Mundoo 111
Mung-Um-Gnackum Island 117
Mungalli Falls 96
Murray Falls 118, 119
Murray Falls State Forest 119
Murray Valley 119

N

Nandroya Falls 96, 97
National Parks
  Barnard Islands National Park 113
  Barron Gorge National Park 34, 35
  Black Mountain (Kalkajaka) National Park 77
  Cape Melville National Park 80
  Cedar Bay National Park 76, 77
  Chillagoe–Mungana National Park 85
  Clump Mountain National Park 115
  Crater Lakes National Park 88
  Daintree National Park 56, 58, 60, 61, 62, 63, 66, 67, 68, 69, 70, 71, 72, 73, 74, 75, 76, 77
  Davies Creek National Park 84
  Ella Bay National Park 109, 110, 111
  Endeavour River National Park 79
  Eubenangee Swamp National Park 107
  Frankland Islands National Park 11, 26, 38, 104, 107
  Girringun (Lumholtz) National Park 123
  Grey Peaks National Park 105
  Hasties Swamp National Park 91
  Lakefield National Park 80
  Lizard Island National Park 11, 81
  Millstream Falls National Park 101
  Moresby Range National Park 111
  Mt Hypipamee National Park 93, 94
  Russell River National Park 105
  Undara Volcanic National Park 85, 101
  Wooroonooran National Park 96–98, 102, 104, 105, 107, 108
Nature's PowerHouse 78
Ngadjon 88, 89, 91, 108, 109
Noah Creek 73
Normanby Island 104
Norman Park 38, 39
North Barnard Island 113
North Johnstone River Gorge 97
North Mission Beach 114, 115
Nyleta Wetlands 91

O

Oliver Creek 73
Opal Factory, The 32
Outback Opal Mine 32

P

Palm Cove 28, 32, 33
Palmer River goldfields 56, 58, 76
Papina Falls 96
Paronella, José 112
Paronella, Margarita 112
Paronella Park 111, 112, 113
Peppermint Stick Insect 69
Pioneer Mill 31
Platypus Park 91
Porcelain Crab 55
Port Douglas 4, 6, 11, 12, 33, 56, 58, 59, 60, 75, 81
Port Hinchinbrook 120, 122
Purtaboi Island 116, 117
Pyramid Mill 38

Q

Queensland Heritage Trail Network 19
Quinkan Aboriginal Reserve 4, 80

R

RAAF Catalina Squadron's WWII Memorial 24
Rainforestation Nature Park 37
Rainforest Habitat Wildlife Sanctuary 59
Ramsay Bay 121
Ravenshoe 11, 91, 93, 96, 100, 101, 119, 123
Red Cliff Point 33
Rex Creek Suspension Bridge 19, 61
Rex Lookout 33
Rivers
  Annan River 76
  Archer River 80
  Barron River 10, 14, 30, 36, 37, 93
  Bloomfield River 60, 76
  Daintree River 56, 60, 62, 63, 66, 69, 72, 74, 77, 107
  East Mulgrave River 107
  Endeavour River 78, 79
  Herbert River 92, 119, 122, 123
  Hodgkinson River 82, 84, 90
  Hull River 114, 118
  Millstream River 100
  Mossman River 60, 61
  Mulgrave River 10, 39, 104, 105, 107
  North Johnstone River 97, 102, 110
  Palmer River 8, 56, 58, 76, 78, 81, 90
  Russell River 102, 104, 105, 109
  South Johnstone River 110
  Tully River 102, 118, 119
  Walsh River 84
  Wild River 92
Rockingham Bay 120, 121
Rocky Creek 9
Rocky Creek War Memorial Park 90
Rossville 76, 77
Round Island 104
Royal Flying Doctor Service Visitors Centre 20
Royal Hotel, Herberton 92
Russell Heads 104, 105
Russell Island 104

S

Seven Sisters, The 91
Sharkfin Bay 47
Shepherd Bay 121
Sheraton Mirage, Port Douglas 59
Silkwood 111, 113
Silkwood Hotel 113
Simpson Point 33
Skyrail Rainforest Cableway 28, 34
Smith Island 117
Snapper Island 62
Solander, Daniel 79
Souita Falls 96
South Barnard Island 113
South Johnstone 111
South Mission Beach 114, 115

Split Rock 80
Station Hotel, Ingham 122
St Mark's Anglican Church 87
St Mary's by the Sea 58
St Michael's Catholic Church 39
Stoney Creek Falls 34
St Patrick's Catholic Church 87
St Rita's Convent 106
Sugarama Gallery 111
Sugarcane 8, 9, 16, 31, 111

T

Tam O'Shanter Point 115
Tam O'Shanter State Forest 115
Tanner, Charles 78
Taste of the Tropics Food Trail 19
Tchupala Falls 96, 97
Thompson Range 104
Thornborough 84, 85
Thorpe Island 117
Thorsborne, Arthur 122
Thorsborne, Margaret 122
Tinaroo Dam 87
Tolga 89, 90, 91
Tolga Railway Museum 90
Tolga Scrub 91
Tolga Woodworks Gallery and Café 118
Trebonne 122, 123
Trevethan Falls 79
Trinity Bay 14, 15, 26, 27, 28, 30
Trinity Inlet 8, 18, 26, 27, 30, 31, 38
Trinity Wharf 26
Tully 102, 107, 115, 117, 118, 119, 120
Tully Gorge 119
Tully Gorge Lookout 101
Tully Gorge National Park 101
Tully Gorge State Forest Park 119
Tully Gumboot Festival 118
Tully Heads 118
Tully, William Alcock 118

U

Ulysses Butterfly 35, 36, 47, 60, 69, 114, 117
Umbrella Festival 106
Upolu Cay 44
Upper Grace St Lookout 92

V

Valley of the Palms 10

W

Walking Tracks
  Aerial Walkway 71
  Banfield's Grave 116
  Banggurru (Turtle) Walk 123
  Bartle Frere Summit Track 109
  Bicton Hill Track 115
  Blue Arrow Circuit 31
  Bush Tucker Trail 66
  Cannabullen Creek Track 119
  Cardwell Range Track 100
  Cassowary Circuit 66
  Circuit Trail, Lake Barrine 88
  Circuit Walk, Lake Eacham 88
  Circuit Walk, Fitzroy Island 46
  Coconut Beach 116
  Cooktown Scenic Rim Walking Trail 78
  Copper Mines Walk 92
  Crawford's Lookout–North Johnstone River 97
  Cutten Brothers Walking Track 115
  Dalrymple Gap Walking Track 121
  Devil's Pool Walk 106
  Douglas Track 37
  Dubuji Boardwalk 73
  East Town Walk 78
  Edmund Kennedy Memorial Walking Track 115
  Goldfield Trail 39, 107
  Goolagan's Tchupala Falls Entrance 97
  Gorrell Trailhead 113

127

Index

Great Northern Mines Walk 92
Great Northern Walking Trails 92
Henrietta Creek–Goolagan's Picnic Area 97
Heritage Smelter Walk 85
Heritage Walk Way 39
Hinchinbrook Heritage Walk 122
Historical Town Walk 85
Home Rule Falls 76
Island Circuit, Dunk Island 116
Island Circuit Walk, Green Island 43
Jack Barnes Bicentennial Mangrove Walk 27
Jinda (Falls) Track 123
Jindalba Boardwalk 67, 73
Jumrun Creek Walk 37
Jungle Walk 37
Koolmoon Creek Track 119
Kulki Boardwalk 73
Kuranda Rainforest Story 37
Licuala Children's Walk 115
Licuala Rainforest Circuit and Boardwalk 115
Lighthouse Road 46
Link Trail 115
Marrdja Boardwalk 73
Misty Mountains Trail 96, 100, 111, 113, 119
Mount Tyson, Scouts Rock & Summit Walk 118
Mt Kootaloo 116
Muggy Muggy Beach 116
Nandroya Falls Circuit 97
Old Town Loop Walk 87

Paddy Illich Track 113
Peterson Creek Wildlife and Botanical Walk 86
Photopost Walk 92
Rainforest Boardwalk 25
Rainforest Butterfly Walk 119
Rainforest Circuit Track 61
Rainforest Walk 115
Red Arrow Circuit 31
River Boardwalk 119
River of Life Path 78
River Walk 37
Secret Garden Walk 46
Specimen Hill Lookout Walk 92
Summit Trail 46
Tchupala Falls Walk 97
Thorsborne Trail 121, 122
Ulysses Link 115
Vision Falls Walk 88
Wabunga–Wayemba (Charmilla Creek) Rainforest Walk 101
Wet Tropics Great Walk 123
Wet Tropics Great Walk Yamanie Section 123
Wild River Walk 92
Wongabel Botanical Walk 91
Wongabel Heritage Trail 91
Wonga Track Rainforest Circuit 106
Wallaman Falls 123
Wallicher Falls 96
Walshs Pyramid 39
Warrgamay 123
Warrina Lakes 111
Warungnu 123
Weary Bay 76

Welcome Bay 47
Wet Tropics World Heritage Area 4, 6, 7, 8, 9, 10, 11, 25, 56, 60, 61, 67, 68, 69, 70, 72, 76, 77, 91–101
Wheelbarrow Race 85
Wheelbarrow Way 85
Wheeler Island 117
White Cliff Point 33
Wild River Lions Park 92
Wild Watch Australia 37
Win's Gallery 100
Windy Hill Wind Farm 101
Wondecla Sports Grounds 92
Wongabel State Forest 91
Wongaling Beach 114
Wrights Lookout 35
Wujal Wujal 76

Y

Yarrabah 38
Yarrabah Aboriginal Reserve 46
Ye Olde Gordonvale Pub 38
Yidindji 14, 26, 38, 39, 88, 91, 106
Yirrganydji 14, 26, 31
Yorkeys Knob 28, 32
Yungaburra 86, 87
Yungaburra Community Centre 87

Z

Zillie Falls 10, 96
Zoe Bay 121

Acknowledgements

Photography: Steve Parish

Additional photography: p. 12, Tjapukai Aboriginal Cultural Park, courtesy of Tjapukai Aboriginal Cultural Park; p. 13, Opening night & Parade, Festival Cairns, courtesy of Festival Cairns; p. 15, Abbott St, Cairns circa 1900, courtesy of Historic Photographs www.historicphotographs.com.au; p. 34, Tjapukai Aboriginal Cultural Park, courtesy of Tjapukai Aboriginal Cultural Park; p. 45, Banded Sea Krait, Ian Morris; p. 65, Crocodile submerged in mud & Crocodile's nest, Ian Morris; p. 68, Brown Tree Snake, Stanley Breeden; p. 69, Spotlighting in Daintree National Park, Steven Nowakowski; p. 76, Bloomfield Falls, Steven Nowakowski; p. 94, Lemuroid Ringtail Possum, Stanley Breeden; p. 109, Musky Rat-kangaroo, Stanley Breeden & Golden Bowerbird, Martin Willis; p. 120, Dugongs, Bob Halstead/OceanwideImages.com; p. 123 Blencoe Falls, Michael Cermak.

Front cover, clockwise from top right: Cairns Lagoon; Daintree Discovery Centre; Cairns City and Trinity Inlet; Snorkelling the reef; Millaa Millaa Falls; Green Island. *Title:* Port Douglas. *Back cover, left to right:* Cairns Lagoon; Mossman Gorge. *Inside front flap:* Driving in the Daintree. *Inside back flap:* Southern Cassowary.

Text: Lynne Adcock; Ted Lewis, SPP
Series design: Leanne Nobilio, SPP
Finished art: Leanne Nobilio, SPP
Editorial: Michele Perry, Ted Lewis & Karin Cox, SPP
Production: Tiffany Johnson, SPP
Maps supplied by MAPgraphics, Brisbane, Australia
Prepress by Colour Chiefs Digital Imaging, Brisbane, Australia
Printed in China by PrintPlus Ltd

Published by Steve Parish Publishing Pty Ltd
PO Box 1058, Archerfield, Queensland 4108 Australia
www.steveparish.com.au
© copyright Steve Parish Publishing Pty Ltd
ISBN: 978174021747 7
10 9 8 7 6 5 4 3 2 1

ALL RIGHTS RESERVED. No part of this publication may be reproduced, stored in a retrieval system, or transmitted in any form or by any means, electronic, mechanical, photocopying, recording or otherwise, without the prior permission in writing of the publisher.

The publishers are grateful for permission to reproduce copyright material. While every effort has been made to trace copyright holders, the publishers would be pleased to hear from any not here acknowledged.

FOR PRODUCTS
www.steveparish.com.au
FOR LIMITED EDITION PRINTS
www.steveparishexhibits.com.au
FOR PHOTOGRAPHY EZINE
www.photographaustralia.com.au